THE
BIBLE
FRAUD

THE
BIBLE
FRAUD

*An Untold Story
of Jesus Christ*

TONY BUSHBY

**THE PACIFIC
BLUE GROUP INC**

ISBN
0-9579007-1-6 PB
0-9579007-0-8 HB

Publisher
The Pacific Blue Group Inc
Hong Kong

Marketing and Distribution
Joshua Books
GPO Box 2115
Brisbane, QLD 4001
Australia
Tel: 1300 888 221
Email: joshuabooks@bigpond.com

Web site
www.thebiblefraud.com

Design
Layout and typesetting by Egan Reid NZ
Cover by Efex Graphic Design and Kean Design

Printing in Australia
Griffin Press

All enquiries should be made to the
Publisher at the following address
C/- GPO Box 2115
Brisbane, QLD 4001
Australia

First Printing August 2001

Truth is such a rare quality, a stranger so seldom met in this civilization of fraud, that it is never received freely, but must fight its way into the world.

Professor Hilton Hotema
Historian and author of *The Lost Wisdom of the Ancient Masters*

Contents

Medallion of Pope Leo X (1513–1521).
In the coin collection of the Vatican Library.
© Photo Archives

It was Pope Leo X who said:

How well we know what a profitable superstition this fable of
Christ has been for us.

(See Chapter Three)

Was this book foreseen by Nostradamus?

NOSTRADAMUS (MICHEL DE NOSTREDAME) WAS A CHARISMATIC 16th Century Provencal physician turned seer. He was the author of a book of prophecies written in unusual rhymed quatrains (four-lined verses) called 'Centuries'. His successful prophecies included the Great Fire of London in 1666, the French Revolution, Napoleon's defeat at Waterloo, Hitler's rise to power and its consequences, the atom bomb attacks on Hiroshima and Nagasaki, and much more. One of Nostradamus' predictions concerned the church of Rome and is yet to be fulfilled. This prophecy has been adopted and applied directly to the new information presented in this book. Nostradamus wrote:

> O vast Rome, your ruin draws near,
> Not of your walls, but of your blood and substance.
> One sharp in letters makes so horrible a mark,
> His sharp point goes all the way to the quick.[1]

It remains for the reader to ultimately decide whether or not this publication was foretold in prophecy.

No arguments

WITHOUT PREJUDICE.
Many people may find themselves at odds with certain conclusions reached within this book. Therefore, the author, publisher and associates of this publication will not engage in written religious argument with readers who hold a different opinion from those expressed here.

The history carried in this book is obtained from information found in official Christian texts, in the records of the early church, and in ancient biblical texts obscured from the public domain. Recorded facts have also been called from Celtic annals and British Chronicles, along with information from the sovereign, saintly and chivalric archives of Europe. Much of the documentation referenced is preserved in rare archival manuscripts and difficult-to-find ancient reference books. Many of these works are priceless historical documents.

This literary exposition therefore rests on supportable or specific historic information that demonstrates the point being made and pursues avenues of much hitherto suppressed knowledge for the benefit of all.

Two confused stories in the Gospels

JESUS CHRIST HAS CAPTURED THE IMAGINATION OF MILLIONS OF PEOPLE around the world for almost 2000 years. Few people know that he represents something far different and the following chapters unravel an entirely new story about the circumstances surrounding the birth and emergence of the Christian religion.

In order to cover this ground it is necessary to consider the *New Testament* stories from a different perspective. By stripping away their supernatural elements, the earliest church writings relay a confused skeletal outline of the lives of two separate men. This work unravels those stories and shows how the *New Testament* came into being and what it really is. Until now, this aspect of the Gospel story has never been fully developed and by coordinating new information with surviving records, a reconstruction of the probable course of events that resulted in Christianity today is presented.

Nabatean Arab/Indumean/Hasmodean Line

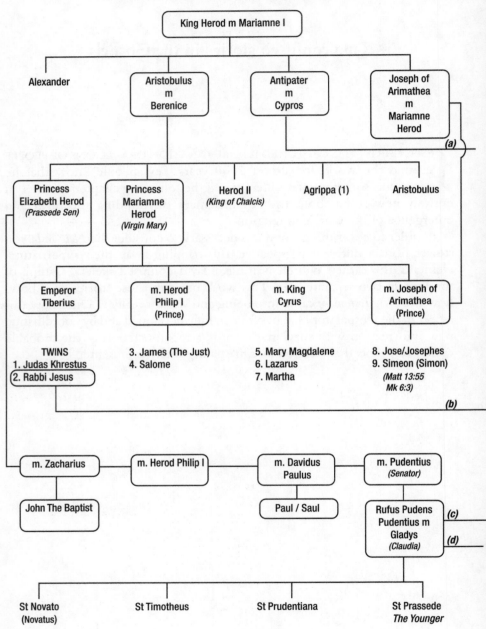

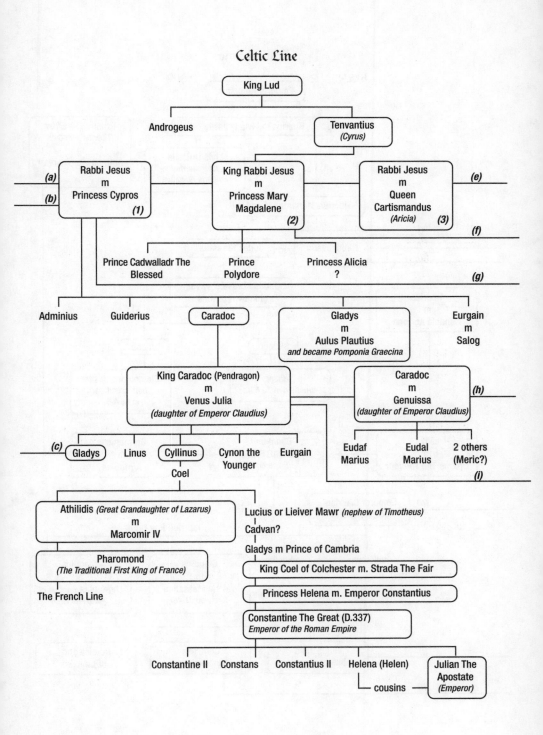

Celtic Line

King Lud

Androgeus

Tenvantius
(Cyrus)

(a)
(b)
Rabbi Jesus
m
Princess Cypros
(1)

King Rabbi Jesus
m
Princess Mary
Magdalene
(2)

Rabbi Jesus
m
Queen
Cartismandus
(Aricia) (3)
(e)
(f)

Prince Cadwalladr The
Blessed

Prince
Polydore

Princess Alicia
?
(g)

Adminius   Guiderius   Caradoc

Gladys
m
Aulus Plautius
and became Pomponia Graecina

Eurgain
m
Salog

King Caradoc (Pendragon)
m
Venus Julia
(daughter of Emperor Claudius)

Caradoc
m
Genuissa
(daughter of Emperor Claudius)
(h)

(c)
Gladys   Linus   Cyllinus   Cynon the
Younger   Eurgain

Eudaf
Marius

Eudal
Marius

2 others
(Meric?)
(i)

Coel

Athilidis (Great Grandaughter of Lazarus)
m
Marcomir IV

Lucius or Lieiver Mawr (nephew of Timotheus)

Cadvan?

Gladys m Prince of Cambria

Pharomond
(The Traditional First King of France)

King Coel of Colchester m. Strada The Fair

Princess Helena m. Emperor Constantius

The French Line

Constantine The Great (D.337)
Emperor of the Roman Empire

Constantine II   Constans   Constantius II   Helena (Helen)

Julian The
Apostate
(Emperor)

└── cousins ──┘

Roman Line

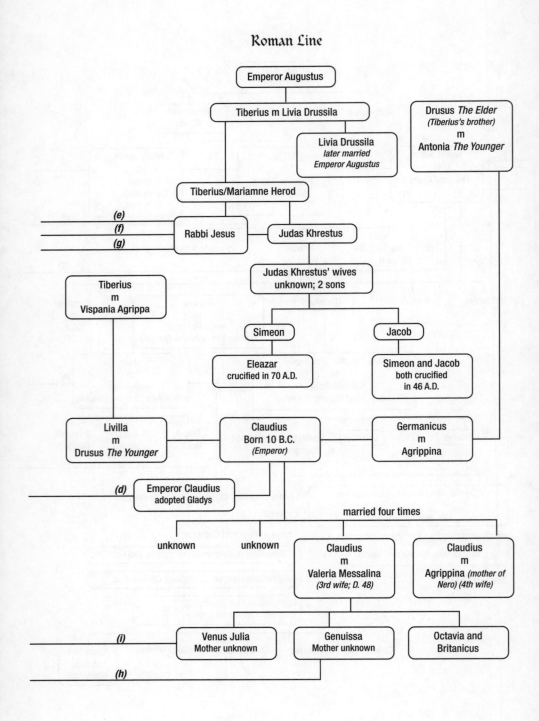

CHAPTER ONE

What was the church trying to hide?

IN 1415, THE CHURCH OF ROME TOOK AN EXTRAORDINARY STEP TO destroy all knowledge of two Second Century Jewish books that it said contained 'the true name of Jesus Christ.' The Antipope Benedict XIII firstly singled out for condemnation a secret Latin treatise called 'Mar Yesu' and then issued instructions to destroy all copies of the Book of Elxai. No editions of these writings now publicly exist, but church archives recorded that they were once in popular circulation and known to the early presbyters. Knowledge of these writings survived from quotations made by Bishop Hippolytus of Rome (176–236) and St Epiphanius of Salamis (315–403) along with references in some early editions of the *Talmud* of Palestine and Babylonia. The Rabbinic fraternity once held the destroyed manuscripts with great reverence for they were comprehensive original records reporting the 'Life of Rabbi Jesus'.

Later, in a similar manner, Pope Alexander VI (1492–1503) ordered all copies of the *Talmud* destroyed. The Council of the Inquisition required as many Jewish writings as possible to burn with the Spanish Grand Inquisitor, Tomas de Torquemada (1420–98), responsible for the elimination of 6000 volumes at Salamanca. In 1550, Cardinal Caraffa, the Inquisitor-General procured a Bull from the Pope repealing all previous permission for priests to read the *Talmud* which he said contained 'hostile stories about Jesus Christ'. Bursting forth with fury at the head of his minions, he seized every copy he could find in Rome and burnt them. Solomon Romano (1554) also burnt many thousands of Hebrew scrolls and in 1559 every Hebrew book in the city of Prague was confiscated. The mass destruction of Jewish books included hundreds of copies of the *Old Testament* and caused the irretrievable loss of many original hand-written documents. The oldest text of the *Old Testament* that survived, before the discovery of the *Dead Sea Scrolls*, was said to be the Bodleian Codex (Oxford), which was dated to circa 1100AD. In an attempt by the church to remove damaging Rabbinic information about Jesus Christ from the face of the earth, the Inquisition burnt 12,000 volumes of the *Talmud*. However, many copies survived and today provide opposing traditions about the person called Jesus Christ.

Burning Talmuds, Bibles and other Jewish books shown in a 17th Century etching.
© Copyright. A.C. Bushby 2001

In the mass destruction of Jewish writings, the church overlooked two particular British documents that also recorded 'the true name of Jesus Christ'. They survive to this day in the British Museum and are called the *Chronicles* and the *Myvyean Manuscript*, treasured ancient documents with a very early origin. Supporting evidence was also found on early First Century gold, silver and bronze coins discovered at the site of an ancient mint at Camulodunum (Colchester) in Britain. 'Thus the testimony of the Briton coins establishes clearly and positively the historicity of the traditional ancient 'Chronicles' as authentic historical records.'[1]

The evidence is compelling, and additional supporting clues are found on a mysterious headstone in Germany, in Vatican art treasures, and in a series of coded sentences in the Shakespearean Plays. Further concealed information was left in the form of specially created statues commissioned by a Catholic priest and positioned in a small hilltop church in Southern France. Coded ciphers were also secreted into the first English-language printings of the Bible and a combination of all clues provides interlocking information and presents a new insight into the origin of Christianity.

Secret ciphers in the New Testament

It was the 'wisest fool in Christendom',[2] who 'authorised' the translation and publication of the first Protestant version of the Bible into English. He came to the English throne in 1603 and quickly became unpopular because of 'his disgusting personal habits and his unsavoury character'.[3] He pretended to be a scholar in theology and philosophy, but his learning was shallow and superficial. He wallowed in filth, moral and physical, but was endowed with a share of cunning that his associates called, 'a kind of crooked wisdom'.[4]

For his new edition of the Bible he issued a set of personal 'Rules' the translators were to follow and ordered revisions to proceed, although he never contributed a farthing to its cost. Work began early in 1607 and took a committee of forty-seven men (some records say fifty-four, others say fifty) two years and nine months to rewrite the Bible and make ready for the press. Each man received thirty shillings per week for his contribution. Upon its completion in 1609, a remarkable event occurred—the translators handed over the reviser's manuscripts of what is now called the *King James Bible* to King James for his final personal approval. 'It was self-evident that James was not competent to check their work and edit it, so he passed the manuscripts on to the greatest genius of all time . . . Sir Francis Bacon.'[5]

Sir Francis Bacon (1561–1626) was a man of many talents, a lawyer, linguist and composer. He mastered every subject he undertook; mathematics, geometry, music, poetry, painting, astronomy, classical drama and poetry, philosophy, history, theology and architecture. He was a man of many aims and purposes, the father of modern science, remodeler of modern law, patron of modern democracy, and possibly the reviver of Freemasonry. His life and works are extensively documented, and his intellectual accomplishments widely recognized, particularly in academic circles. At the age of sixteen, he was sent to Paris 'direct from the Queens Hand' and there studied Egyptian, Arabian, Indian and Greek philosophy with particular attention given to the Ancient Mysteries and their Ritual Rites. He personally recorded that, while in Paris, he created a secret cipher system that could be inserted into a document without arousing suspicion. While living in Europe, Francis Bacon was initiated into the mysterious Order of the Knights Templar and learnt a very special secret. Before he returned to London, he travelled to France, Italy, Germany and Spain and at the age of twenty completely devoted himself to the study of law. From his understanding of the secret information he had learned during his initiation into the Knights Templar, he conceived the idea of reactivating various Secret Societies and in 1580 founded the secret Rosicrosse Literary Society in Gray's Inn. Later in the same year, he founded the Lodge of Free and Accepted or Speculative Masons, also at Gray's Inn.

On 25 June 1607 Sir Francis Bacon was appointed Solicitor-General and Chief Advisor to the Crown. He had presented new ideas to the Government for the Reformation of the church and was officially instructed to commence restructuring the Bible. Research in the Records Office of the British Museum revealed that original documents still exist which refer to important proceedings associated with Sir Francis Bacon's involvement with the editing of both the *Old* and *New Testaments*. They revealed that he personally selected and paid the revisers of the *New Testament* who completed their task under the instructions of Bacon's long-time friend, Dr Andrews.

Statue of the editor of the Bible, Sir Francis Bacon.
© Photography: Thomas L. Lithgow, Esq.

The first English language manuscripts of the Bible remained in Bacon's possession for nearly a year. During that time:

> . . . he hammered the various styles of the translators into the unity, rhythm, and music of Shakespearean prose, wrote the Prefaces and created the whole scheme of the Authorized Version.[6]

He also encoded secret information into both the *Old* and *New Testaments*. An ancient document recorded that the true history of early Christianity was known to the initiates of the Order of the Knights Templar, having originally been:

> . . . imparted to Hugh de Payens by the Grand-Pontiff of the Order of the Temple (of the Nazarene sect), one named Theocletes, after which it was learned by some Knights in Palestine.[7]

Regarding the months of editing work applied to the Bible by Bacon, his biographer, William T. Smedley, confirmed the extent of the editing:

> It will eventually be proved that the whole structure of the Authorised Bible was Francis Bacon's. He was an ardent student not only of the Bible, but also of early manuscripts. St Augustine, St Jerome, and writers of theological works, were studied by him with industry.[8]

At the completion of the editing, Sir Francis Bacon and King James I had a series of meetings to finalise editorial matters associated with the new Bible. It was at this time that King James ordered a 'Dedication to the King' to be drawn up and included in the opening pages. He also wanted the phrase 'Appointed to be read in the Churches' to appear on the title page. This was an announcement clarifying that King James had personally given the church 'Special Command' for this particular version of the *Bible* to be used in preference to the vast array of Greek and Latin Vulgate Bibles current at the time. His reason was personal, as King James had previously instructed the revisers to 'defend the position of the king' in their restructuring of the texts. This was seen as an attempt to distance the Protestant *Bible* from the Catholic version. The Protestant versions of the *Bible* are thinner by seven books than the Catholic version and the variant churches have never agreed on a uniform Bible. In their translation of 1 Peter 2:13 the revisors changed the phrase 'the emperor, as supreme' to 'the king, as supreme'. Because King James' *Bible* was written to support the authority of a king, the later church often referred to it as the one from 'authority', and it later came to be presented as if officially 'authorised'. In subsequent revisions, the word 'authorised' found its way onto the title page and later still came to be printed on the cover, giving King James' new Bible a false sense of authenticity.

The *King James Bible* is considered by many today to be the 'original' Bible and therefore 'genuine' and all later revisions simply counterfeits forged by 'higher critics'. Others think the *King James Bible* is 'authentic' and 'authorised' and presents the original words of the authors as translated into English from the 'original' Greek text. However, the 'original' Greek text was not written until around the mid-Fourth Century and was a revised edition of writings compiled decades earlier in Aramaic and Hebrew. Those earlier documents no longer exist[9] and the Bibles we have today are five linguistic removes from the first Bibles written. What was written in the 'original originals' is quite unknown. It is important to remember that the words 'authorised' and 'original', as applied to the Bible, do not mean 'genuine', 'authentic' or 'true'.

The clue to hidden messages

Sir Francis Bacon was a master of concealing secret information in his writings and his methods can be found in the Bible. Bacon took delight to hide his works, to the end they might be found out. It was a time of severe repression and of harsh government, and free speech was impossible. Able men could only dissemble and speak in allegory. 'If they had expressed their opinions openly they would have been sent to the Tower and the Block.'[10] The most famous of all literal cryptograms was the famous bilateral cipher described by Bacon in his De Augmentis Scientiarum. Sir Francis originated the system while still a young man residing in Paris and this particular cipher required the use of two styles of typeface, one an ordinary face and the other especially designed. The differences between the two fonts are in many cases so minute that it requires a powerful magnifying glass to detect them. Originally, the cipher messages were concealed only in italicised words, sentences or paragraphs, because the italic letters, being more ornate than the Roman letters, offered greater opportunity for concealing the slight but necessary variations. Sometimes the letters vary a little in size, at other times in thickness or in their ornamental flourishes.

Alphabets secretly adjusted were not entirely satisfactory, however, for although they rendered unintelligible the true nature of the writings, their very presence disclosed the fact of concealed information. Through patience or persecution, the keys to those alphabets were eventually acquired and the contents of the documents revealed to the unworthy. This was not good enough and necessitated employment of more subtle methods of concealing divine truths. The result was the appearance of cryptic systems of writing designed to conceal the presence of both the message and the cryptogram. Thus having devised a method of transmitting their secrets to posterity, Sir Francis Bacon and others like him encouraged the circulation of certain documents specially prepared by incorporating ciphers containing the deepest secrets of religion, mysticism and philosophy. Thus, medieval Masons and Rosicrucians disseminated their secrets throughout the World without evoking suspicion, since volumes containing these cryptograms could be subject to scrutiny without revealing the presence of the hidden message.

During the Middle Ages scores of members of secret political or religious organizations published books containing ciphers. Secret writings became a fad—every European court had its own diplomatic cipher, and the intelligentsia vied with one another in devising curious and complicated cryptograms. The literature of the 15th, 16th and 17th Centuries was permeated with ciphers, few of which have ever been decoded. Many liberal churchmen, it was interesting to note, used cryptograms, fearing excommunication or a worse fate should their research be suspected. Had they failed to conceal their discoveries under complicated cipher, they faced the possibility of persecution as heretics. Some of the ciphers are so intricate that they may forever baffle attempts at their decipherment. In those susceptible of a solution, sometimes the 'a's and 'b's have to be exchanged, at other times the concealed message was written backwards; or only every other letter is counted, and so on.

Any picture or drawing with other than its obvious meaning may be considered a pictorial cryptogram. Instances of strange pictorial ciphers abound in Masonic and Rosicrucian art. In addition to the simple pictorial cipher, there is the more technical form in which, for example, words or letters are concealed by the number of stones in a wall, by ripples on the surface of water, or by the length and order of lines used in shading. The shape, height or proportion of a building, the folds on a person's garment, were all used to conceal definite figures or characters which could be exchanged for letters or words by a person acquainted with the code. The key necessary for their decipherment sometimes accompanies pictorial cryptograms. A figure may point towards the starting point of the cipher or carry in its hand some implement disclosing the system of measurement used. There are also frequent instances in which the cryptographer purposely distorted or improperly clothed some figure in his drawing by placing the hat on backwards, the sword on the wrong side, the shield on the wrong arm, or by employing some similar artifice. The much-discussed sixth finger on the Pope's hand in Raphael's 'Sistine Madonna' and the sixth toe on Joseph's foot in the 'Marriage of the Virgin' by the same artist are cunningly concealed cryptograms.

A particular pictorial design with dogs, rabbits and archers is found over the address, 'To The Christian Reader', in the 1612 edition of the *Authorized Version of the King James Bible*. This identical design was also found in the folio edition of Shakespeare. However, it was the 1612 quarto edition of the *Authorized Version of the King James Bible* that was of most interest, for on the title-page of the Genealogies are two complex head-piece designs both of which were used by Sir Francis Bacon in previous books he wrote and published in 1593 and 1594. The selection of these designs was not made by chance but was deliberately chosen to create similitude between certain books and mark their connections with each other. Most noticeable was the light and dark capital A's (A.A) in the lower design which was also used on several Shakespeare quartos and elsewhere. This direct connection between the Bible and the Shakespearean plays has been long overlooked and the knowledge that hidden ciphers appear in both the *King James Bible* and the Shakespearean plays arrests attention. Those writings contain crypto-graphically concealed information that was purposely encoded into the actual text and is still there today.

What the Mystery Schools knew about Jesus

Scores of volumes were written to establish that Sir Francis Bacon was the real author of the plays and sonnets popularly ascribed to William Shakespeare. An impartial consideration of these documents cannot but convince the open-minded of the verisimilitude of the theory of Bacon being the author of the Shakespearean plays. Those enthusiasts who for years struggled to identify Sir Francis Bacon as the true 'Bard of Avon' might long since have won their case had they emphasized the most important angle—that Sir Francis Bacon, the Knights Templar, Masonic and Rosicrucian initiate, wrote into the Shakespearean plays the secret teachings of the Fraternity of the Rose Cross, the 'Lost Word' of the Freemason Order, and major clues to unlock the hidden story in the Gospels. A sentimental world, however, dis-likes giving up a traditional hero, either to solve a controversy or to right a wrong. Nevertheless, the Bacon/Shakespeare controversy, as its most able advocates realize, involves the most profound aspects of science, religion and ethics; he or she who solves its mystery may yet find therein the key to the supposedly Lost Wisdom of Antiquity.

Abundant proof exists that Sir Francis Bacon was concerned in one way or another in the production or editing of the Shakespearean plays. Sir Francis Bacon's personal cipher number was 33, indicating that he was a fully initiated Mason. In *The First Part of King Henry the Fourth*, the word 'Francis' appeared 33 times on one page. To attain this end, obviously awkward sentences were required, such as, 'ANON FRANCIS? No Francis, but tomorrow Francis; or Francis; on Thursday; or indeed Francis when then will; but Francis'. Here we see one example of the concealed use of the mystical number 33 in the Shakespearean Plays.

The Masonic order of degrees was divided into 33 symbolic sections (33°). The number 33 is often used in the Secret Mystery Schools and a variety of opinions exist as to why. The *Torah* employed the divine name 32 times in the Creation story at the beginning of the *Old Testament* book of Genesis. Of this, the Cabalists say that through these 32 paths, the soul descends to be clothed in the physical body and the 33rd path is the ultimate return to stand before God's presence at the end of life on Earth.

Sir Francis became heavily involved in the redevelopment of both Freemason and Rosicrucian Mystery Schools. It was suggested that he created his own secret Society, by the agency of which he carried through his works, but it was difficult to find any concrete evidence that such a

Society existed. Books came from his pen at a rate which, when the truth is revealed, will literally 'stagger humanity'.[11] He made translations of ancient classics and histories and his 'Good Pens' (other writers) wrote books under his direction. He saw them through to the press, and every book published under his direction carried his favourite secret cipher, stylised light and dark capital A's, side-by-side (A.A).

The double 'A.A' was Sir Francis Bacon's hidden signature cipher for 'AthenA', known in Mythology as Pallas Minerva, Athene or Athena, which meant Virgin. The letters making up PALLAS MINERVA, ATHENE OR ATHENA, VIRGIN numbered 33, and she was the esteemed Goddess of Sir Francis Bacon's Mystery Schools. The initiates dedicated themselves in her honour and vowed to uphold her ideals.

Athena, the Goddess of Wisdom, holding her spear.
© Cambridge Photo Archives.

Athena was the Goddess of Wisdom and usually depicted in art wearing a helmet and holding a spear in her right hand in readiness to strike at a serpent near her feet. She was known as the 'Spear-shaker' among the ancient Greeks because when the morning rays of the sun glinted on the spear, the common people were in the habit of saying smilingly, 'Athena is shaking her spear again', hence her name, 'Spear-shaker'. She was the Goddess to whom the Rosicrosse Brethren swore allegiance when they were initiated in the Secret Literary Order, the Knights of the Order, and Francis Bacon was the head of the Spear-shakers. Side by side with the Rosicrosse arose the Lodge of the Freemasons and the College of the Rosicrucian Fraternity, which persist to this day. Both Orders threateningly 'shake spears' at the candidate during the trials of his initiation. 'It was Francis Bacon's secret symbol to represent that he was 'The Spear-shaker's' representative known by the name of Shakespeare. Thus the "Spear-shaker" wrote under the name of Shake-speare and was Sir Francis Bacon.'[12]

Sir Francis Bacon used the first and last letters of Athena's name—A.A— as headpieces to subtly mark particular books connected with the Secret Orders of the Rosicrucians and Masons. 'In these books Francis Bacon had the opportunity to secrete his personal secrets which he dare not write openly about.'[13] There were many different designs of the 'A.A' cipher and numerous books that bear the coded signal are connected, including the Authorised Edition of the King James Bible and the Shakespearean Plays.

One 'A' was printed light and the other 'A' dark to indicate that while there was much open and straightforward in the designated book, there was also much in the shadow which could only be discovered by searching.[14]

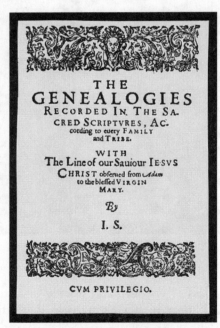

The title page of the 1612 edition of the New Testament. The design at the head of the page was used on the title-page of the first edition of Venus and Adonis, 1593, and the first edition of Lucrece, 1594. Note the use in the lower panel of the light and dark 'A.A' secret cipher that indicated hidden knowledge. The same design was used on several of the Shakespearean quartos and elsewhere.

Jesus in the Shakespearean Plays

The full name that Francis Bacon constructed to appear on the title pages of his writings was 'William Shakespeare', and was created (maybe) without reference to him of Stratford, who possibly bore, or had assigned to him, a somewhat similar name, (it seems his real name was originally Shakspur). There was good reason to suspect this was exactly what happened, for Sir Francis Bacon created a superstructure of numbers built up on the exact spelling of the words 'William Shakespeare'. Anybody looking closely at Bacon's clues will see also the year 1623 was specially selected for the issue of the complete volume of the plays, because of the extraordinary relations which the numbers composing it bear to the combined names William Shakespeare and Sir Francis Bacon. Simply put, the total number of the letters of the two names adds up to 33, the Masonic cipher number: WILLIAM SHAKESPEARE, SIR FRANCIS BACON = 33 letters. It was not surprising then, to note that the letters of the year 1623, when written in words, also added up to 33: SIXTEEN HUNDRED AND TWENTY-THREE YEARS = 33 letters. The chances of this letter/word/number combination happening by chance, according to mathematical experts, are 4.8 million to one. The intriguing relationship of numbers was also carried through to the year 1561, in which the birth of Francis Bacon was registered and, curiously enough, to 1564 and 1616, the reputed dates of the birth and death of the Stratford man.

The Shakespearean plays and the 'authorised' *Bible* of 1611 contained hidden messages about Jesus, Mary Magdalene and the substance of the Gospel story. Sir Francis knew the secret of Christian origins and concealed his knowledge in both the *Shakespeare Folio of 1623* and the *New Testament*. His secrets are encoded in a system of letters and numbers that reveal to the initiated the presence of concealed information. The secret of the Knights Templar, the Masons and the Rosicrucians was purposely encoded into the texts by Sir Francis, and several of his complex ciphers are decoded in upcoming chapters. With the availability of concealed records, a new interpretation of the Gospels is revealed, and the history of mankind has no counterpart to the strange story that unfolds.

CHAPTER TWO

Just who were the parents of Jesus Christ?

N THE OPENING SENTENCE OF A *NEW TESTAMENT* PARABLE, JESUS STATED:

> A man of noble birth was on a long journey abroad, to have himself
> appointed king, and return. (Luke 19:12)

Herein lies part of a profound Gospel truth revealing the substance of
historical information that the church has strived for 2000 years to conceal.
In this tale of long ago misconceptions and mistaken identities must be
clarified so that the original story may be seen to rest upon a true and sure
foundation. For this purpose we begin with the examination of church
writings purporting to record the birth of Jesus Christ.

The Gospels of Matthew and Luke stated that Jesus Christ was the first
born of Mary and Joseph and he had four younger brothers and at least two
sisters (Mark 6:3). Roman Catholics are obliged to hold the opinion that
the brothers and sisters of Jesus Christ were the children of Joseph by a
former marriage. This conclusion originally stemmed from the Gospel of
James (the Protevanglium) that related to the age of Joseph at the birth of
Jesus. However, it was clearly recorded that Joseph had sex with Mary after
the birth of Jesus. The statement in the Gospel of Matthew that Joseph
'knew her not until she had born a son' (Matt. 1:25) eliminated the church's
claim that Mary was a perpetual virgin. From the statements in the Gospels
of Mark and Matthew it was clear that the brothers and sisters of Jesus were
subsequent children of Mary in the fullest sense.

Joseph returned to Galilee with the intention of marrying Mary. The

Gospels according to Matthew and Luke clearly explained that they were 'betrothed' before Joseph's departure. This was the equivalent of being 'engaged' in modern-day terminology. However, upon his return some months later, it was plainly apparent that Mary 'was with child' (Luke 2:5) and it 'could not be hid from Joseph'. The Gospel of Matthew elaborated extensively upon the feelings of Joseph when he saw the violated condition of his bride-to-be. He was uneasy and being unwilling to defame her, he privately discussed ending their engagement (Matt. 1:19). From the description in the Gospels, it was clear that Joseph was not the biological father of Mary's child. So, who was?

The evidence of the Rabbis

The Jewish records of the Rabbis are of extreme importance in determining Gospel origins and the value of the church presentation of the virgin birth story of Jesus Christ. A common appellation for Jesus in the *Talmud* was Yeshu'a ben Panthera, an allusion to the widespread Jewish belief during the earliest centuries of the Christian era that Jesus was the result of an illegitimate union between his mother and a Roman soldier named Tiberius Julius Abdes Panthera.

The *Talmud* enshrines within its pages Jewish oral law. It is divided into two parts, the Mishna and the Gemara. The first discusses such subjects as festivals and sacred things. The Gemara, is basically a commentary on these subjects. When the *Talmud* was written is not known. Some authorities suggest a date of 150–160, around the same time the Christian Gospels began to emerge, while others say 450.

The *Talmud* writers mentioned Jesus' name twenty times and quite specifically documented that he was born an illegitimate son of a Roman soldier called Panthera, nicknamed the 'Panther'. Panthera's existence was confirmed by the discovery of a mysterious tombstone at Bingerbrück in Germany. The engraving etched in the headstone read:

> Tiberius Julius Abdes Panthera, an archer, native of Sidon, Phoenicia, who in 9AD was transferred to service in Rhineland (Germany).[1]

This inscription added fuel to the theory that Jesus was the illegitimate son of Mary and the soldier Panthera. Classical scholar Professor Morton Smith of the Columbia University, USA, described the tombstone as possibly 'our only genuine relic of the holy family.'[2] In many Jewish references, Jesus was often referred to as 'ben Panthera', 'ben' meaning, 'son of'. However cautious one ought to be in accepting anything about Jesus from Jewish sources, in the matter of Jesus 'ben Panthera', the writers seem more consistent than the men we now call the church fathers.

Scholars, for centuries, have discussed at length why Jesus was so regularly called ben Panthera. Adamantius Origen, an early Christian historian and church father (185–251), recorded the following verses about Mary from the research records of a highly regarded Second Century historian and author named Celsus (c. 178):

> Mary was turned out by her husband, a carpenter by profession, after she had been convicted of unfaithfulness. Cut off by her spouse, she gave birth to Jesus, a bastard; that Jesus, on account of his poverty was hired out to go to Egypt; that while there he acquired certain (magical) powers which Egyptians pride themselves on possessing.[3]

Later, in passage 1:32, Origen supported the Jewish records and confirmed that the paramour of the mother of Jesus was a Roman soldier called Panthera, a name he repeated in verse 1:69. Sometime during the 17th Century, those sentences were erased from the oldest Vatican manuscripts and other codices under church control.[4]

The traditional church writings of St Epiphanius, the Bishop of Salamis (315–403) again confirmed the ben Panthera story and his information was of a startling nature. This champion of Christian orthodoxy and saint of Roman Catholicism frankly stated:

> Jesus was the son of a certain Julius whose surname was Panthera.[5]

This was an extraordinary declaration simply recorded in ancient records as accepted church history. The ben Panthera legend was so widespread that two early stalwarts of the Christian church inserted the name in the genealogies of Jesus and Mary as a matter of fact.

Enlarging on that statement, this passage from the *Talmud*:

> Rabbi Shiemon ben Azzai has said: I found in Jerusalem a book of genealogies; therein was written that Such-an-one (Jesus) is the bastard son of an adulteress.[6]

'Such-an-one' was one of the well-known substitutes for Jesus in the *Talmud*, as has been proved and admitted on either side. Shiemon ben Azzai flourished at the end of the First and beginning of the Second Century. He was one of four famous Rabbis, who according to Talmudic tradition 'entered Paradise'. He was a Chassid (the pious Jews of Palestine), most probably an Essene and remained a celibate and rigid ascetic until his death.

The story of Mary's pregnancy by a Roman soldier also appeared in the sacred book of the Moslems, the Koran. It stated that 'a full-grown man' forced his attentions on Mary, and in her fear of the disgrace that would follow she left the area and bore Jesus in secret. This story was supported in the Gospel of Luke, with the description of the departure of Joseph and Mary from their home prior to the birth. Rape was a common event in

Palestine during the Roman occupation and soldiers were notorious for their treatment of young women. It would be unthinkable for Mary to admit such an event had occurred for, under the Law of Moses, a betrothed virgin who had sex with any man during the period of her betrothal, was to be stoned to death by the men of the city (Deut. 22:21). Simply put, Mary faced the death penalty unless she could prove her innocence.[7]

The mother's name

There was another, lesser-known name Jesus was called during those early years and that was 'Yeshu'a ben Stada' (Son of Stada). This name was recorded in the records of the Sanhedrin and also in the *Talmud*. What can also be found in the Gemara, and has embarrassed Christian authorities for centuries, was this:

> Ben Stada was Ben Panthera, Rabbi Chisda said; The husband was Stada, the lover Panthera. Another said; the husband was Paphos ben Jehuda; Stada was his mother . . . and she was unfaithful to her husband.[8]

These apparently contradictory assertions can be ironed out when read in context. In summary, Stada was Yeshu'a (Jesus) ben Panthera's mother.

The Gemera goes on to record that Yeshu'a ben Panthera 'was hanged on the day before the Passover'. That is to say, apparently, that after stoning, ben Panthera's body was hung or exposed on a vertical stake. Crucifixion was an unused mode of execution amongst the Jews who favoured stoning as the main form of capital punishment. To shorten the cruelty of death by stoning, the victim was first rendered unconscious by a soporific drink, and subsequently the stoned body was exposed on a vertical stake as a warning to others.

They found an old book

The name 'ben Stada' given to Jesus in the *Talmud*, was found paralleled in the ancient Mehgheehlla Scroll that was discovered by Russian physician D.B. de Waltoff near Lake Tiberius in 1882 and is now called simply the Safed Scroll. In this old text, there were two brothers called Yeshai and Judas ben Halachmee who were the illegitimate twin sons born of a fifteen year old girl called Stadea. The closeness of the name Stada in the *Talmud* to the Stadea in the Safed Scroll is extraordinary and the slight difference in spelling can be explained by variations in translations. The interesting point here is that the name ben Halachmee was the name of Stadea's later husband, not the biological father of her sons. Unfortunately, no mention was made of the real father's name but ben Halachmee was the name given to Stadea's illegitimate twin boys. According to the Safed Scroll, Yeshai and his brother Judas ben Halachmee were taken in, raised and educated by the religious order of Essene monks. The Essenes were a perennial Jewish colony that particularly flourished in Judea for some centuries previous to the time ascribed to the *New Testament* stories. Subsequently one of the boys became a student of Rabbi Hillel's school of philosophy and the other became the leader of the Essenes. An older Essene named Joseph was assigned as Yeshai's 'religious father' and guardian.

The Safed Scroll suggested that eventually, Yeshai ben Halachmee's outspoken religious views angered the Jewish priests. He was tried by a Roman court on a charge of inciting the people to rebel against the Roman Government. He was found guilty and sentenced to death, but escaped, left the area and traveled to India.

The Mehgheehlla Scroll mirrored aspects of the hidden story in the Gospels and provided external evidence that the conclusion reached in this volume was known in ancient tradition.

Who was Stada/Stadea

One of the most popular aspects of etymology is the history of names—those words or phrases which uniquely identify persons, animals, places, concepts or things. The earlier forms of a name are often uncertain and different dialect pronunciations have led to divergent spellings of the same name. The social pressure to use a standard spelling did not emerge until the 18th Century and earlier writers saw no problem presenting a person's name in a variety of ways. In one study, for example, over 130 variants of the name 'Mainwaring' were found among the parchments belonging to that family.

Many Hebrew names in the *Old Testament* were believed to bear a special significance, as originally individual subjects were called by a name expressive of some characteristic, e.g. Edom, red; Esau, hairy; Jacob, supplanter and Sarai (Sara) from the base word, 'Sharat'. A similar concept applied in Jewish writings and for a long time confused researchers.[9] Like Roman and Hebrew tradition, the names of the characters 'often appear in distorted form in Rabbinic literature' and were sometimes an attempt to disguise their true personality.[10] This type of understanding provided the key to researchers that enabled them to unlock the true essence of what was really being relayed in ancient writings.

'Names research' is an open-ended and complex domain, and one which is particularly greedy of the researcher's time. In any study on the *New Testament*, however, it must be remembered that the first Gospels were written in Hebrew[11] and this was a vital point in determining who Stadea really was. 'The name (Stadea) has various forms and may have been borrowed from a fanciful name that meant a scholar; or had a regional identity like Stabiae or Statila, or a woman of good family.'[12] According to Jewish writings,

Stadea was 'the descendent of princes and rulers'[13] and her royal heritage provided a clue to her real name. The *Talmud* further stated that Yeshu'a (Jesus) ben Panthera's mother 'was also called Miriam, yes but she was nicknamed Stada . . . Stat-da, this one has turned away, being unfaithful [Stat-da] to her husband'.[14]

St Jerome explained the difficulty that he had in translating the earliest Gospels into Latin[15] and added that the 'original Hebrew' versions of Matthew's Gospel and the earliest Luke Gospels were written in the Chaldaic language but with Hebrew letters. The 'original Hebrew' version of the name 'Mary' was 'Mariamne'.[16] Therefore, 'Mary' in the English-language Gospels of today was originally written 'Mariamne' in the Hebrew versions and was sometimes translated 'Miriam'.[17]

Mary unknown in early church history

What was actually recorded of Mary/Mariamne in the only accepted Christian writings provided scant information indeed about the woman the church now call the mother-of-God. In the Gospels she was rarely mentioned. In fact, she was not mentioned by name in the oldest version of the Mark Gospel in the oldest Bibles. Nor was she mentioned in the oldest version of the John Gospel. The church said, 'the reader of the Gospels is at first surprised to find so little about Mary . . . this obscurity has been studied at length'.[18] Both the Gospels of Mark and John first introduced Jesus as an adult. Only in contrived narratives does Mary play an important role in the biblical texts and, excluding these, she was mentioned only briefly on three occasions. The church presbyters were also silent on Mary. There was nothing recorded of her external to the church for more than four centuries after the time she was said to have lived. She had no ancestry or background except in spurious apocrypha.

The earliest documented reference to Mary was found in the Mark Gospel of the Sinai Bible (Mark 3:32). This narrative referred to her as simply the earthly mother of several sons and daughters. The reference was actually about a group of people who addressed Jesus and said, 'Your mother and your brothers and your sisters are outside asking for you'. Here was a profound truth. Modern Bibles show the three words 'and your sisters', to have been removed or indexed to a footnote. From here onwards, Mary almost vanished from the church texts, and apart from an obscure final reference to her in the Acts of the Apostles (1:14) she disappeared forever from the *New Testament*.

However, when the name 'Mary' in the Gospels was replaced with the original Hebrew version, 'Mariamne', an historic aspect arose. Combining the evidence available, the position advanced in this book is that Mary, the mother of Jesus in the Gospels, Stadea of the Jewish writings, and Mariamne of the House of Herod were one and the same person.

At the time of the development of the Gospels, Mariamne was the younger sister of Herodias and the two girls were an integral part of the vast 'family of Herodes' (Herod today). They were the much loved granddaughters of King Herod and he 'cared for them with great devotion'.[19] Their mother, Berenice, later remarried and moved with her teenage daughters to live in Rome, where she gained the friendship of Emperor Augustus.[20]

Mariamne and Herodias Herod were of noble birth through King Herod (c. 73–74BC) and his wife, Mariamne I. Mariamne Herod's father was Aristobulus, the son of Herod the Great, and her mother Berenice was the daughter of Herod's sister, Salome. Mariamne also had two brothers named Herod II, king of Chalcis, and Agrippa, who became Agrippa I. King Herod himself descended from a noble line of kings through his Nabatean mother, Cypros of Petra. The Nabateans were a Semitic people and the earliest sources regarded them as Arabs. Today they are generally referred to as Nabatean Arabs. Owing to its secure location, Petra was adopted by the Nabatean kings as their capital city which became incorporated into the Roman Empire in 106. The Nabatean Arabs passed out of history with the advent of Islam.[21] The House of Herod was founded by the marriage of Cypros of Petra to Antipater (Antipas), the Idumean, to whom Cypros bore four sons, Herod being one.

The name Herod subsequently became the title of seven rulers mentioned in the *New Testament* and in Roman history. King Herod was known to the Romans as 'The Great' but in the eyes of the people over whom he ruled however, he was always known as 'The Impious', despite his costly restoration of the Temple in Jerusalem. In 7BC he strangled to death two of his sons, Aristobulus and Alexander, drawing a comment from Roman Emperor Augustus (27BC–14AD) that it was safer to be one of Herod's pigs than one of his sons. Another son was later born to Herod and, for his safety, his mother dispatched him to the care of her family in Ariminum, a city near Ravenna in Northern Italy.[22] He was Prince Joseph, the Joseph of Arimathea in the Gospels, and he later became the unseen power behind his father's throne. Herod the Great was a Roman citizen, governor of Galilee by 47BC and then King of Judea from 37 to 4BC. He was one of the major figures in politics of Palestine in the early years of the Roman Empire.

Mariamne Herod's ancestors can be traced back on her grandmother's (Mariamne I) side to the Hasmonean 'priest-kings' and 'hereditary priests' from the tribe of Benjamin. She, her sister, and her brothers were descendants of the legitimate Hasmonean dynasty and 'carried the Hasmonean blood'.[23] They also carried the blood of the Nabatean Arabs, so much so that King Aretas IV, who was legally confirmed a Nabatean Arab king by Emperor Augustus[24] divorced his wife to marry Herodias (who died after 41AD) to maintain the Nabatean bloodline, but she declined him. It was Herodias who was involved in the Gospel story of the beheading of John the Baptist, for which she received a level of notoriety and defamation similar to that of Mary Magdalene.

The available records reflect an intricate tangle of marriages, intermarriages and divorces between the Herods and the Romans. In the account of the Gospel of Mark (6:17), for example, Herodias later married Herod Philip I, her own uncle, by whom she had a daughter, Salome. Salome was named after her Hasmodean ancestor Salome Alexandra, herself a priestess-king.[25] Later in time, Herod 'Without-land' Antipas apparently fell in love with Herodias and proposed to her. Seeing that his fortunes were rising faster than her husband's, Herodias accepted his hand. She longed for social distinction, and accordingly left her husband and initially entered into an adulteress union with Herod Antipas, who was also her uncle.[26] She was not married to Antipas at this time but married him at a much later stage (c. 38).

When Herodias saw how well her brother Agrippa I had fared in Rome, whence he returned a king, she urged her husband Herod Antipas to go to Caesar and obtain the royal title, for she believed his claim to it was far greater than that of her brother. Antipas was not king, but only Tetrarch of Galilee.[27] Contrary to his better judgment he went, and soon learned that Agrippa I by messengers had accused him before Emperor Caligula of conspiracy against the Romans. The Emperor banished Herod Antipas to Lyons, Gaul (France) in 41 and although he permitted Herodias to return to her home in Rome, she chose to accompany her husband into exile.

It was recorded that the male offspring of the House of Herod were forced to become circumcised Jews in the reign of John Hyrcanus, a Hasmonean of the earlier Maccabean period. In other words, the Herod family adopted the religion of Judaism. The religious movement of the Essenes was also connected to the Hasmonean bloodline through the High Priest, Mattathias—the father of the military king, Judas Maccabeus.

We know that Herod the Great was favorable towards the Essenes, maybe because they made it their invariable practice to refrain from disobedience to the political authority. The Jewish historical writer, Philo, recorded that they had never clashed with any ruler of Palestine, however tyrannical, until his lifetime in the mid first century. This was a passive attitude which could not fail to commend itself to King Herod, and it was reported he even went so far as to exempt the Essenes, like the Pharisees, from the oath of loyalty to himself.

In the reconstruction of the story, and drawing upon the concept of the Safed Scroll, the pregnant Stadea (Mariamne Herod, née Mary) secretly went to one of the Essene communities until the time of the birth, and bore twin boys. Numerous groups of Essenes existed 'all over, as they were a very numerous sect'[28] and were found in secluded country areas as well as cities. Upon the birth of the twins, she then moved into the palace of Emperor Augustus and there she lived until the boys were old enough to receive schooling. It was due to their solidarity and the family affinity that the young Mariamne Herod had her illegitimate twin boys educated within the Essene community. The Essene hierarchy were her blood relatives and expounded similar principles and traditions to the Herodian philosophy. 'They perpetuated their sect by adopting children . . . above all, the Essenes were the educators of the nobility, their instruction being varied and extensive.'[29] To avoid confusion in developing the premise provided in this work, Mary, the mother of Jesus in the *New Testament*, shall be called Mariamne Herod except when quoting from the Gospels.

The Roman father of the twins

As with ancient Hebrew, Christian and Jewish names, it is also difficult to be exactly sure of the real names of many of the Roman characters with which we are dealing and many irregularities arise. The allocation of names was unlike today's Western procedure and a great many were purposely compounded with the names of Caesars, deities, and hybrid variations such as Caracalla, Emperor of Rome 211–217. Caracalla was a name derived from a long tunic worn by the Gauls, which he adopted as his favourite dress after he became emperor. His proper name was M. Aurelius Antoninus. The name Caesar developed from Caesarian, being the nature of the birth of Julius Caesar. Sometimes a new name was afterwards substituted for the original one, just as Plato was originally called Aristocles. The Jewish name of the First Century historian Joseph ben Matthias became Titus Flavius Josephus when he took Roman citizenship late in life.

A popular loan-name among Roman men was Silvanius[30] that developed from the Roman god 'of uncultivated land beyond the boundaries of tillage'. A man with the name of Silvanius was depicted as 'uncanny and dangerous'. In many cases, the name was not given until the person was grown up and was then adapted from personal qualities such as Modestus, for example, and from servile condition Servus, or the name of an historical celebrity, Cornelia being one instance. In another Roman tradition, the name was sometimes a reference to peculiar circumstances at birth: e.g. Lucius—born by day; Manius—born in the morning; Alphus—the first born; Quintus— the fifth born and Decimus—the tenth born. As a rule, the eldest received the 'proenomen' (Christian name) of his father, and this helps to determine exactly who Tiberius Julius Abdes Panthera, as it appears on the headstone at Bingerbrück in Germany, really was.

The name Tiberius Julius is the first part of the full name of Tiberius,

Emperor of Rome,[31] the adopted son and heir of Emperor Augustus. Whether Tiberius was a native of Sidon in Phoenicia as recorded on the headstone, is difficult to establish, for there are conflicting references to his birthplace. From a very early age Tiberius' parents were in fear of their lives through the uncertainty of the civil war, where wrong political allegiances could result in an early death.

> His childhood and youth were beset with hardships and difficulties, because Claudius Nero and Livia [his parents] took him wherever they went in their flight from Octavius . . . He was next hurried all over Sicily . . . His parents finally fled to Greece but were still in pursuit . . . escaping with him from Sparta at night.[32]

The Monumentum Ancrya[33] reported that at one stage the family sailed from Phoenicia to Egypt to avoid persecution. With such persistent pursuers it was probable that the family lived at Sidon in Phoenicia and left when they were found, but this information was not publicly recorded.

The words that are important in establishing whether or not the headstone actually referred to Emperor Tiberius are 'Panthera' and 'Abdes'. In order to understand this inscription, it shall be shown that the headstone was composed well after the time of the events in question and therefore benefited from the hindsight of history. There appeared to be a very deliberate plan in place in the manufacture of this headstone, and whoever was responsible for its construction knew the essence of what is revealed in this book. Its unknown creator encoded vital information in the form of a cipher and anagram, which when decoded revealed the identity of the father of Mariamne Herods' twin boys.

In many cases a name was a reflection of that person's character and that view of ancient understanding can be used to trace an individual's life and illuminate that person's intimate character peculiarities. That was the case with Tiberius Julius' nickname, Panther. Variations were Panter-Panetier-Panterer (Roman) which all meant 'adulterer'[34] and Tiberius was a man noted for his sexual excesses. This was an indication of how historical characters received their confusing multiplicity of names, for their names came to reflect their nature and the events that surrounded their lives.

Not even Tiberius' friends would deny that he often committed adultery, but said in justification that he did so for reasons of state, not simple passion— he wanted to discover what his enemies were doing by becoming intimate with their wives or daughters.[35] The reputation of being a womanizer stuck to Tiberius, and as an elderly man he was said to have still harboured 'a passion for deflowering young girls, indulging in his sensual propensities on the island of Capri'. The name of 'Panther' may have originally developed from a little-known ancient Roman city of debauchery called Pantherin or

Pantherine. 'Panther' may have also been attached to Tiberius Julius because of his beastly nature for the cat-like tactics he used in stalking and pouncing on his opponents in wars against the Dalmatians and Pannonians. 'In the old *Physiologus* [an anonymous Second Century book of fifty allegories], the panther was the type of Christ, but later, when the savage nature of the beast became more widely known, it became symbolical of evil and hypocritical flattery.'[36]

From the year of his adoption by Augustus, circa 4AD, to the death of that emperor, Tiberius was in command of the Roman armies and because of his wicked nature, his troops named him 'the savage beast'.[37] Modern historians described him as a bloody tyrant.

There may be another clue in the name 'Panther' associated with the lusty, untamed, horned Greek god Pan, who amused himself with the chase of nymphs. He was forever in love with one nymph or another, but always rejected because of his foul nature. Pan dwelt in forests and was dreaded by those whose occupations caused them to pass through the woods by day or night. Hence sudden fright without any visible cause was ascribed to Pan, and called a 'Panic' terror. This blackened his image so that he was seen to correspond to the Devil himself. The name 'Pan' may have originally developed from the earlier Greek myth of Pan-darus, the term meaning 'to shoot an arrow'. Pan was the bowman (archer) of the Zodiac which is also the sign of Sagittarius, encompassing parts of the months of November and December, and it was no surprise to find that Tiberius, an archer in his youth,[38] was born in November. There does seem to be some historical doubt as to accuracy of the time and place of his birth and this may account for the modern birth date given to him—16 November[39]—falling slightly outside the prescribed range of the current Sagittarius dates, 26 November– 23 December. It should be recognized, however, that the calendar has been adjusted over the course of 2000 years. Sometime shortly before the 17th Century, the Latin Sacred College quietly restored fifteen years to the Roman calendar. The net result of that, and earlier alterations, shows a present difference between Oriental and Western chronologies of sixty-three years, when both are compared from any certainly known astronomical date— for example, Halley's Comet.

The Roman leaders were renowned for their personification of earlier gods and the story of Julius Caesar acting out the role as Zeus was well recorded. 'Then there was Augustus' private banquet, known as "The Feast of the Divine Twelve", which caused a public scandal. The guests came dressed as gods or goddesses, Augustus himself representing Apollo.'[40] Apollo was the son of Zeus, who was the equivalent to Jupiter in the Roman pantheon, with the 'Divine Twelve' representing the gods of the zodiac. Zeus was also the father of Hermes and Pan was Hermes' son. The great importance of the gods in Roman history at the time was seen when Emperor Augustus enlarged the temple of Apollo near Nicopolis, built in recognition of the victory at Actium.[41] This was the victory over Mark Antony that cleared the way for his Imperial Dictatorship.

'Abdes' was the third name found on the tombstone and applied to Tiberius Julius Panthera. The origin of 'Abdes' may be connected with Emperor Augustus' liking for ciphers and this may be what the originator of the tombstone was alluding to when he applied it to Tiberius. It was said of Emperor Augustus that:

> Instead of paying strict regard to orthography, as formulated by the grammarians, he inclined towards phonetic spelling . . . When Augustus wrote in cipher he simply substituted the next letter of the alphabet for the one required, except that he wrote AA for X.[42]

By applying both of these rules to the word Abdes on the German headstone, a hidden code is thus revealed:

$$Abdes = Ab\text{-}des = Bc\text{-}des = \underline{BC\ days}$$

> Note: The extra twist for the reader is to apply the cipher rule forward as the person creating it, not backwards as would have been the case to decipher.

The person or persons who created the headstone cipher could have only done so after the Sixth Century when the Julian calendar was first instituted. The proposed suggestion is that the cipher was designed to draw attention to the fact that circumstances surrounding the fathering and birth of Mariamne Herod's twin boys occurred BC rather than AD. Presumably the inscription on the tombstone was placed there to convey a special message, for it is unlikely to have been put there 600 years or more after the actual event to honour the site of an actual body, if there ever was a body buried at the site.

The inscription stated that Tiberius Julius Abdes Panthera was transferred to service in Rhineland (Germany) in the year 9AD. The young Tiberius was indeed in that area at that time:

> Tiberius was given another three years of tribunicial power, with the task of pacifying Germany . . . There followed the Ilyrian revolt, which he was sent to suppress . . . Tiberius conducted it for three years . . . but, though often called back to Rome . . . Tiberius was well paid for his stubbornness, by finally reducing the whole of Illyricum—an enormous stretch of country enclosed by Northern Italy, Noricum, the Danube, Thrace, Macedonia, and the Adriatic sea—to complete submission.[43]

This timely victory prevented the victorious Germans, who had defeated three legions of Rome under Varus in 9AD, from linking up with the Pannonians. 'Proposals were made for decreeing him (Tiberius) the surname Pannonicus, or the "Unconquered", or "the Devoted"; but Emperor Augustus vetoed all these in turn, promising on each occasion that Tiberius would be satisfied with that of "Augustus", which he intended to bequeath him'.[44] The evidence is compelling in locating Tiberius for service in the area of the Rhineland in 9AD.

However, to switch the era from AD to BC as the 'Abdes' cipher suggested, the person named on the headstone was in the Rhineland in 9BC, not 9AD, and Tiberius was located there on active duty at that time also. Suetonius recorded that 'in the third [instance] he took some 40,000 German prisoners, whom he brought across the Rhine and settled in new homes on the Gallic bank',[45] the years verified as 7 and 9BC. Although Tiberius was in active duty in that area at that time, 'he visited Rome several times'.[46] The date, nevertheless, was curious for locating the tombstone at Bingerbrück at all, because it did not say that Tiberius Julius Abdes Panthera died and was buried there, only that he was on service in the Rhineland. The evidence of the assertion was supposed that this time of 9BC was a coded message revealing the year the twin boys were born to Mariamne Herod. At that time she would have been fifteen years of age.

The territory known as Germany today was never identified with this title until at least the time of Napoleon, when the 'Confederation of the Rhine' was formed in July 1806. From that time on, the area began to be called Rhineland. This knowledge brings the placing of the tombstone forward some 1200 additional years from the First Century designation and nearly 1800 years after the death of Tiberius. On further examination, a remarkable materialization of information appeared, for on a modern map of Germany we find that Bingerbrück is located on the Rhine River in the Rhineland Palatinate, a district of southwest Germany west of the Rhine, which belonged to Bavaria until 1945. Formerly, portions of the neighbouring territory (Upper Palatinate) constituted an *electorate* of the Holy Roman Empire, now part of Rhineland Palatinate State. The Latin word Palatinate was a different sense of the word *Palatine*, whereas Palatinus meant 'of the *Imperial House*' and the electorate indicated the state contained one of the German princes entitled to elect the *Emperor* of the Holy Roman Empire.[47] Palatine is one of the Seven Hills of Rome where the Emperor of the Roman Empire resided in the Imperial House, whom, according to the above, the Emperor of the Holy Roman Empire succeeded and now resides in the Vatican. The interesting matter is that in earlier times, there was built on the Palatine hill the shrine to 'The Heavenly Twins' and it still remains there to this day.

Conclusion

The cipher on the Bingerbrück headstone connected the ancient Panthera tradition of the Rabbinic writings with the First Century Roman emperor, Tiberius. The conclusion drawn is that by reason of her mother's friendship with Emperor Augustus, the teenage Mariamne Herod met Tiberius when he returned to Rome to see his emperor father early in 9BC, and her twin sons were conceived by rape or adultery by him at that time. It was possible Mariamne Herod was then married, for the traditions of the time accepted the early marriage of young girls. The oldest daughter of Agrippa I, for example, was married at the age of thirteen.[48] Mariamne Herod named her sons Judas and Yeshu'a and the populous subsequently nicknamed them 'ben Panthera' (son of Panthera) after their 'adulterer' father. The name Yeshu'a came to be pronounced and spoken as Jesus in English language translations and, to avoid confusion, shall be used as such throughout this work.

Unraveling the headstone cipher has now completed a full circle, beginning with the illegitimate birth of twin boys to Mariamne Herod, the Virgin Mary of the Gospels, and ending with their father being the 33 year old Tiberius who was to later become Emperor of Rome in 14AD. The two boys, although illegitimate by birth, were the legitimate kingly heirs to the throne—the next in line to the imperial purple toga—and that is exactly what the Gospels of the *New Testament* recorded. This leads to an underlying truth hidden below the surface level of the Gospel story and one that the church has suppressed for seventeen hundred years.

The Gospel of Mark suggested Judas and Jesus were commonly regarded as illegitimate by the people of their time. The fact that they were each identified as a 'son of Mary' (Mark 6:3), not 'son of Joseph', was interpreted by scholars to mean Judas and Jesus were regarded at the time as Mary's illegitimate sons. In the Gospel of John (8:41) the scribes and Pharisees challenged Jesus about his birth, '*we* are not born of fornication', again revealing that the general populous knew that Jesus' birth, and thus Judas', was illegitimate. Related, in Luke (4:22) was Jesus' irritated reaction to the words, 'Is not this Joseph's son?' Why would Jesus (or maybe it was Judas speaking) react to this seemingly harmless question? The answer was documented in the oldest Greek texts of the *New Testament*, which read, 'not son of Joseph, this one'.

The scriptural and historical data being presented in this work shows that the *New Testament* was never an authentic record, but was, in its entirety, a corpus of corrupted documents specifically constructed to induce a particular belief (John 20:30–31). This conclusion rests firmly on known facts and the ensuing chapters analyse ancient Roman, British and church reports that support this assertion.

CHAPTER THREE

The hidden twin

*T*HE PREMISE FOR THE CONCLUSION IN THIS WORK IS THAT THE 'BEN Panthera' twins were of royal birthright and legitimate contenders to the throne of Palestine and the Emperorship of Rome. The Gospel appellations, 'king of the Jews' and 'son of God', were correct titles because of the tradition of the times and the identity of both the mother and father. The boys were 'brought up by Augustus Caesar',[1] their grandfather, and at least one of the boys publicly called himself the 'son of God' and 'Son of the archangel'.[2] This he could legally do for he truly was the 'son of God' in the Caesar family tradition.[3]

The adopted process for the deification of humans into a god had for centuries remained within the reserve powers of the Roman Emperor. Roman writer, Ovidius (43BC–18AD), recorded the deification of Julius Caesar (*Divus Julius*) after his death in 44BC. Augustus and others styled themselves '*Divine Filius*' or '*son of a god*' and were hailed as 'divine emperors' after their deaths.[4] Their offspring were all 'sons of a god', and Mariamne Herod's twins were no exception. Her sons actually had an additional advantage, for a similar tradition existed in the Herod family lineage. The *New Testament* writers stated King Herod was 'a god and not a man' (Acts 12:22) merely because all kings of Judea were called 'God' by the people.[5] There is a solid basis for such an image in the wording of the Gospels, and a wealth of narratives exists with which to work. There are over forty direct references in the *New Testament* to the twins each being a 'son of God' and 'born a king' (Matt. 2:2). Nathanael said to Jesus, for example,

'You are the King of Israel' (John 1:49), but there was no record in world history of Jesus ever being a king. Surely King Jesus' existence would have been of immense significance to Israelite history, so why then a blank page? There is an answer.

Thomas the Twin

The life of Mariamne Herod's twin sons provided the essence of the entire Gospel story. To unravel the 'King' story of Jesus ben Panthera, it is first important to clarify the Gospel identity of his twin brother, who was called Judas Thomas or 'Thomas the Twin' in the *New Testament*.

The name Thomas as applied to Judas is a Graecized form of the Aramaic name Toma. In the Gospel of John,[6] Thomas was also called Didymus, a translation of Toma meaning 'twin'. The Hebrew form of the name, Teom[7] corresponds almost exactly to the English colloquial abbreviation, Tom. In an ancient version of the Syrian *New Testament*, Thomas was actually called Tommy Didymus (twin twin). In 1945, the Acts of Thomas was discovered in a collection of thirteen old writings now called the Nag Hammadi Scrolls and presented Thomas as Judas Thomas, that is, Judas the Twin. 'The eleventh act introduces Thomas' twin, the other Didymus, as an identical twin who is the lord himself'.[8]

The Acts of Thomas was preserved with some variations in Greek and in Syriac and bearing the unmistakable signs of its Gnostic origin. The general church belief was that it was written by a Syrian named Bardesanes (154–222).[9] If the place of its origin was really Edessa, as others for sound reasons supposed,[10] this would lend considerable probability to the statement explicitly made in the Acts that the relics of the apostle Thomas had come from the East. In more than one place[11] the Acts of Thomas clearly represented Judas Thomas as the twin brother of the one now called Jesus Christ. In the reconstruction of the two stories provided in this work, the names of the main Gospel players have been reinstated to what was understood to be their original state of being.

The Acts of Thomas recorded an incident where Jesus appeared to a young man who 'saw the Lord Jesus in the likeness of the apostle Judas Thomas'. Jesus then called: 'I am not Judas the Twin who is also Thomas, I am his brother . . .'

Another narrative from the Acts of Thomas included the phrase: 'the one who art mother of twin young ones; come, hidden mother'.

During the Second and Third Centuries, the church writings recorded that Judas Thomas was not only Jesus' blood brother, but also his identical twin brother with the identity of their mother suppressed. In another ancient writing in the Thomas tradition called the Book of Thomas, Judas Thomas is again explicitly called Jesus' 'brother' and 'double'.[12]

What a suppressed Gospel said

The Acts of Thomas recorded that the populous 'saw as two beings, one single Royal token consisting of two halves' (112:80) and 'united their adoration of the two persons of Christ'. Not surprisingly, this Gospel along with others was suppressed after the first Christian council at Nicaea in 325. Again in the Acts of Thomas, the issue of 'Judas the Twin' was further clarified by a remarkable statement that referred to the '. . . twin brother of Christ, apostle to the most high and fellow initiate into the hidden word of Christ who does receive his secret sayings . . .'

The church claimed that the 'secret sayings' in the Gospel of Thomas were collected and recorded by Judas the Twin from words recited to him by Jesus.[13] When referring to the Acts of Thomas (Acta Thomae) and the Gospel of Thomas the *Catholic Encyclopedia* commented:

> His name [Judas the Twin] is the starting point of a considerable apocryphal literature, and there are also certain historical data which suggest that some of this apocryphal material may contain germs of truth.[14]

The Acts of Thomas 'recounts the wanderings and adventures of Didymus Jude Thomas . . . and his twin brother Jesus'[15] and made several references to the twin boys being raised in a Palace. The church attributed these words directly to Judas Thomas:

> When I was an infant too young to talk, in my father's Palace reposing in the wealth and luxury of those who nourished me.[16]

In a section of the Acts of Thomas sometimes called 'In the Country of the Indians', the following words of Judas Thomas appeared:

> I remembered that I was a son of Royal parents, and my noble birth asserted its nature.[17]

A fragment of parchment believed to also be from the Acts of Thomas, had Jesus saying to Judas Thomas, 'Greetings Twin, my second messiah'. This statement supported the reference to two messiahs documented in one of the *Dead Sea Scrolls* called the 'Book of the Community Rule'.

A crucial fact to be remembered when discussing those 'lost' works is that the texts in which Judas Thomas appeared as Jesus' twin brother were once accepted works of scripture and widely used by the early presbyters in all Western congregations.[18] Also to be borne in mind is the fact that the Gospel of Thomas and the Acts of Thomas are from the same era as the four canonical Gospels of the *New Testament* today. This can only mean that during the establishment years of the Christian texts, the idea of a twin was perfectly acceptable, and with the naivety of the times, the birth of identical twins was seen as a miraculous and fascinating event.[19]

Twins in Roman tradition

The birth of twins was seen by the people of the times as a supernatural occurrence, one of divine origin. 'Once upon a time, in Myth, twins signified whatever dualisms a culture entertained: mortal/immortal; good/evil; creation/destruction, what they had.'[20] A highly respected ancient tradition of the Roman people held that divine twin boys were born to the god Mars and an earthly virgin woman called Ilia. They were Romulus and Remus, the mythical founders of Rome, believed by the people to have been sent to earth as beautiful human beings and reared as infants in the wild by a she-wolf. They were especially honored in Rome, where they were worshipped as 'The Great Twin Brethren to whom all pray'. Romulus slew Remus and subsequently ascended into heaven and joined the gods. Later, a certain Julius Proculus announced that he had seen Romulus alive, who told him that he had become the god Quirinus. Romulus was then deified as Quirinus. The story of Romulus and Remus became essentially the myth of Rome in the sense that it embodied the high ideals and values to which they referred over the centuries when they wanted to explain to themselves what it was to be Roman. In this way, the stories of Romulus and Remus may have been deliberate creations, but they could be said to have assumed mythical status over years of repetition and reference.

Because of their Roman father and the royal blood of their mother, it shall be shown that the stories of the lives of Mariamne Herod's twin boys later became a rationalization of the Romulus and Remus story of the twin founders of Rome. That Emperor Tiberius carried the genes of twins was noted in the writings of the First Century Roman historian, Tacitus who recorded the birth of twins to Livilla (d. 31AD) and Drusus (d. 23AD), the son of Emperor Tiberius, as 'a rare event [that] so delighted the Emperor that he did not refrain from boasting before the senators'.[21]

That Jesus had a twin brother has been debated for centuries. The great Italian painter, Leonardo da Vinci (1452–1519), in his famous interpretation of the 'Last Supper', appeared to subscribe to this ancient belief with his depiction of one of the disciples (fifth from Jesus' right). He bore an uncanny resemblance to Jesus, not only in physical appearance but also in the matching design and colour of his clothing, complete to the fine detail of the width and shading of the narrow neck band on his costume.

Michelangelo reveals a papal secret

The supreme sculptor and painter, Michelangelo Buonarroti (1475–1564), also avidly preserved the 'twin boys' theme in dozens of his famous works of Mary. A Catholic theologian, John Eck (1486–1543) argued against persistent rumours which alleged a secret had been confided to both Leonardo da Vinci and Michelangelo by the Borgia pope[22] and later the de

Leonardo da Vinci's Last Supper. The person fifth from Jesus' right has a remarkable similarity to Jesus, particularly in coloured versions. The Last Supper was painted in the dining room of the Cloister of the Dominican monks of Santa Maria delle Grazie. Leonardo's painting is still there, or at least the ruins of it. Restored firstly in 1746 and eight times since, a door was at one time, cut through the middle of the lower part of the painting.

© Photography; Thomas L. Lithgow, Esq.

Medici pope, Leo.[23] Pope Leo X was a 'pleasure loving',[24] self-confessed homosexual and one of his partners was Michelangelo.

At some period in their lives, both Michelangelo and Leonardo da Vinci lived in luxurious quarters at the Belvedere[25] on the Vatican Hill and worked on private commissions for both popes. But it was a statement made by Pope Leo X to the Latin church that strengthened the suspicion that both Leonardo da Vinci and Michelangelo were privy to secret information. Pope Leo X frankly declared, 'How well we know what a profitable superstition this fable of Christ has been for us'.[26] Truly remarkable words and if Pope Leo X did pass this 'fable' on to Leonardo da Vinci and Michelangelo, they may well have preserved the information in their sculptures and paintings.

It seemed strange that both Leonardo da Vinci and Michelangelo constantly portrayed twin boys. The church reasoned that one of the boys was Jesus Christ and the other John the Baptist. However, these artists clearly created identical twins, and in some cases one appeared slightly unfinished as if implying something was being held back. Maybe these men left clues for later generations to unravel.

Pope Leo X. A Portrait by Raphael.
© From 'The Collection of the Masters'. Milan.

Here are two of Michelangelo's depictions of Mary with twin boys. Left: Madonna Pitti; About 1505; Florence; Museo Nazionale del Bargello. Right: Madonna Taddei; About 1504. London Royal Academy. See a painting by Raphael, 'La Belle Jardiniere', Musée du Louvre. It also shows Mary with twin boys.
© Film Library of Renaissance Art. Italy.

An intriguing little mystery

The suggestion that Jesus of the Gospels was one of two identical twins was again supported by the discovery of four antique parchments in an old church in the hilltop village of Rennes-le-Chateau, in Southern France. There, around 1886, the parish priest Berenger Saunière, uncovered the concealed scrolls while removing the altar stone during restoration. Another discovery of immense importance was also made. While repairing the floor in front of the altar, a flat stone was removed and its underside bore a well-preserved relief of knights on horseback. It was believed to have dated from the time of the building of the church and is known as the 'Dalle des Chevaliers'. Saunière used this stone as a step in the garden and it can still be seen in the little museum today.

The scrolls were written in Latin and the first text was a combination of *New Testament* excerpts from the Gospels of Matthew (12:1–8), Mark (2:23–28) and Luke (6:1–5). All three recorded almost identical information about what was lawful or not lawful to do on the Sabbath. The second scroll provided narratives from the Gospel of John (12:1–11) about the anointing of Jesus Christ. Both writings were said to contain secret, coded messages. The two most valuable parchments were believed to consist of genealogies of Jesus Christ recorded within a lineage of descent listing the Counts of Rhedae until 1244.[27]

It was said that these parchments were of immense importance and contained 'incontrovertible proof' that the crucifixion was a fraud and Jesus was alive as late as 45AD. The church showed immense interest in the Scrolls, and it was said Saunière later traveled to Paris and revealed their contents to an unknown party. At the same time, he seemed to have been introduced into esoteric circles and returned to his church with a painting of a medieval pope, suspected to have been the aforementioned Pope Leo X.

Shortly thereafter, Saunière began to receive a supply of funds that lasted until his death. He spent huge sums of money, much more than his income as a priest allowed.[28] Some of it he used to continue the renovation work. Around this time Saunière and his housekeeper, Marie Denarnaud, started to dig in a nearby cemetery at night. The local villagers were so concerned they lodged an official complaint in writing with their mayor. Saunière destroyed an ancient tomb and defaced its headstone. It was, for nearly one hundred years, the last resting place of a certain Marie Nègre Dables Dame de Hautpoul. He was searching for something. Some say he was looking for the mortal remains of Jesus Christ, others say he was searching for one of the many gold hoards said to be hidden in the region and maybe once belonging to the Knights Templar, the Cathars or the Visigoths who all once occupied the area.[29]

Whatever secret he knew, he seems to have left behind an intricate and elaborate system of clues including veiled references to Mary Magdalene. He built a luxurious villa named Bethanie and in 1902 started a four year construction project to build a tower he called Magdala (named after Mary of Magdala?). He also had carved an enigmatic bas-relief of Mary of Magdala and an outsized statue of a horned Devil supporting the holy-water font

(Pan?). These items are in the church today. For some reason, he chiseled a cross into a stone pillar and then erected it upside down.[30]

For the restored interior of the church, Saunière commissioned the creation of a series of special decorative wall plaques and some painted statues. Each was characterised by some odd, but subtle contradiction of the church presentation of the birth and death of Jesus Christ. One decoration portrayed a body being carried from a tomb in a nighttime scene with a full moon in the background. The fourteen stations of 'The Way of the Cross' were shown in the opposite direction to other churches and one illustration showed the Magdala Tower in the background. Two statues, one each side of the altar, depicted Mary and Joseph each holding an identical baby Jesus (twin boys in the church, as the suppressed Acts of Thomas recorded). All statues in the church look sadly at the ground and one of Mary Magdalene has a skull resting at her feet. A curious painting showed a Scotsman in a kilt watching the crucifixion.

In 1916 Saunière commenced negotiations over a construction contract worth FF8,000,000 but ill health intervened. Upon his deathbed, Saunière summoned a neighbouring priest and long time friend to his side. After a brief discussion with Saunière, the priest left the room ashen-faced, 'never to smile again'. On 22 January 1917 Saunière, at his own request, died unshriven, taking with him the secret of the Scrolls that made him rich.[31]

Because a number of priests were involved in the suppression of Saunière's scrolls, conspiracy theorists considered a great church secret had been concealed. But whatever the secret, what was not secret was the Gospel information on this matter. Judas Thomas was somebody's twin for the Gospel writers' recorded, 'Thomas, one of the twelve called the Twin'[32] and that Jesus Christ had a brother called Judas Thomas.[33] Put two and two together and just what other Gospel evidence does the church need to supply?

Postscript. For those who wish to research this topic further, check out the writings of a close priesthood friend of Saunière, Henri Boudet, edited in 1886. He was an initiate into the Secret Mysteries and left clues to the Rennes-le-Chateau secret in the page numbers of a strange book he wrote towards the end of the 19th Century. It was called *La vraie langue Celtique et le Cromleck de Rennes-les-Bains*, (The True Language of the Celts and the Cromlech of Rennes-les-Bains).

CHAPTER FOUR

The anointed leader of the Essenes

Just who were the Essenes?

IN AN ATTEMPT TO CLARIFY THE STORY OF THE JUDAS AND JESUS TWINS, A link must be made between narratives in the *Dead Sea Scrolls* and the Gospels of the *New Testament*. In the presentation of this evidence, *The Bible Fraud* confines its hypothesis to a framework of known historical documents and the probabilities and possibilities of information contained in them. The adopted and general ancient beliefs are the chief sources and have been applied to the broad facts of what is currently accepted, and the minor day-to-day details are a lesser consideration. What must be remembered in correlating this evidence, Gospel information is the primary source on Judas and Jesus, but once 'the true name of Jesus Christ' is known, other documentation can be accessed. Much of the Gospel material shall be shown to be riddled with uncertainty, but some narratives contain elements of a well-known tradition.

The *Dead Sea Scrolls* made no mention of Jesus Christ or the early Christian church. At the time of their discovery, the Professor of Archaeology at the Hebrew University of Jerusalem, Dr Yigel Yadin, said the omission was 'strange'. It has long been known there was information in the *Dead Sea Scrolls* damning to Christian beliefs and the church's high-level involvement with interpreting the Scrolls fostered a grave element of suspicion. Since the Scrolls were found some six decades ago, close associates of the Vatican were placed in dominant positions in every phase of the investigation and translation of the Scrolls. The priests regulated the flow of information and controlled its release. Michael Baigent and Richard Leigh discovered during research for their work *The Dead Sea Scroll Deception* (Corgi 1992) just 'how fiercely the world of orthodox biblical scholarship was prepared to fight to retain its monopoly of available information'. J. Edgar Hoover, of the American Central Intelligence Agency (CIA) and FBI summed up the church attitude when he once said, 'it can be held certain that information that is withheld or suppressed contains truths that are detrimental to the persons involved in the suppression'.

To provide conclusions on the lives of Judas and Jesus ben Panthera, the highly regarded and comprehensive work of Professor Robert Eisenman,[1] was drawn upon. Professor Eisenman has devoted his life to the specific study of Palestinian history and has analysed and lectured extensively upon the *Dead Sea Scrolls* and various aspects of Christian origins at the Hebrew University in Jerusalem. It was Professor Eisenman who provided the now-accepted and spectacular connection between the *Dead Sea Scrolls* and James, the Gospel brother of Judas and Jesus. This connection established crucial information had been painstakingly concealed from the public by a small enclave of Catholic priests who controlled the release of the material. Unlike a number of personalities in the *New Testament*, James was an historical person, one who played a more prominent role in the affairs of his time than generally acknowledged.

At the time of the lives of the ben Panthera twins, the now-called Essenes were one of three religious sects in the Roman provences, the other two being the Pharisees and Sadducees. The Sadducees were a Jewish sect of the time, opposed to the Pharisees. They denied the resurrection of the dead and the validity of oral tradition.[2] Old records said that Pharez, who developed a school of Predestination, founded the Pharisees. It seemed that the Sadducees were founded by Sadoc, a disciple of Antigonus Scohaeus, the person said to have been associated with the development of an institute called the School of Infidels. Sadducees were mentioned fourteen times in the *New Testament*, the Pharisees ninety-eight times, mostly in the Gospels.

The weight of scholarship heavily supports that the *Dead Sea Scrolls* found in the caves at Qumran being the products of the Essenes, although this is debated by Christian apologists. It was possible these writings were compiled (or stored) in various settlements and moved to the Dead Sea caves from other areas for protection and preservation. It is not improbable to suggest the manuscripts were deposited in the Dead Sea area as late as 132 by the Jewish leader Simeon bar Cochba, but the general opinion is the oldest and largest of the three separate discoveries was hidden for safe keeping when the destruction of the Qumran settlement seemed imminent sometime shortly before the beginning of the Jewish War in 66AD.

Nowhere in the *Dead Sea Scrolls* collection was the term 'Essene' found. The Qumran community never referred to itself as Essenes, but they did use a number of other Aramaic terms. From these terms, it was clear the Community did not have a single definite name for themselves although the term 'Ebronites' (Ebionites in some translations) was used within the later-dated scroll discoveries.[3] These particular writings were found in the ruins of a Byzantine monastery further up the hills from the oldest and largest collection of Qumran. In academic circles, it is generally believed a high priest of the early Essene community wrote the Book of Enoch in order to fulfill an *Old Testament* 'prophecy' in Jeremiah (31:31–34): 'the days are coming when I (the Lord) will make a New Covenant'. The authors of the *Dead Sea Scrolls* constantly referred to a New Covenant and regularly called themselves the 'Keepers of the New Covenant' and the 'Community of the New Covenant'.

The First Century classical writers, Josephus, Philo and Pliny indicated that in their time these people were known as the Essenoi or Essaioi in Greek, but a variety of opinion exists among scholars and researchers as to the origin of the name. Some explain the Greek name Essenes as meaning 'Silent Ones' and others as signifying 'Healers' and assert the term means 'Pious'. Some called them Seers, Performers of the Law, Retired Ones, Stout Ones, Mysterious Ones, Daily Baptists or Apron-Wearers. In the latter respect, echoes of the Essene beliefs can be found in the rituals of the Masons. Josephus recorded that they 'don a white apron' before their ceremonies after which they 'then take off their white aprons, which they consider sacred clothes'.

The writings of the early church extended another opinion about the identity of the body of monks now called the Essenes. St Epiphanius of Salamis (315–403) left behind some extraordinary records about Jesus, Mary and the Gospel stories. The modern-day church claimed these records 'exhibit a marvelous mixture of valuable traditions', but many of those ancient traditions oppose the canonical writings of today. Lipsius, in his article[4] on this interesting early churchman said he was:

> . . . honest, but credulous, a narrow-minded zealot for church orthodoxy. . . His frequent journeys and exhaustive readings enabled him to collect a large but ill-arranged store of historical information, and this he used with much ingenuity in defending the church orthodoxy, of his time, and opposing every kind of heresy . . . The accounts he gives of the Jewish, Christian and Gnostic sects . . . exhibit a marvelous mixture of valuable traditions . . . and [he] collects a rich abundance of genuine traditions from what seemed a worthless mass.

Some of his 'genuine traditions' are recorded throughout this book. When

St Epiphanius wrote of allegedly 'heretical' sects once existing in occupied Roman territories, he called them the 'Men of Yesu'. The term 'Yesu' was taught in Druidism as one of the three aspects of the Druidic trinity, the other two being Beli and Taran.

St Epiphanius went on to say the 'Men of Yesu' were sometimes called Yesseans after Jesus of the Gospels. Epiphanius sought to justify this startling connection with the Yesseans and Jesus by asserting that in Hebrew, the name Jesus meant 'physician', and the 'Men of Yesa' were highly regarded herbal healers supporting the same doctrines as those applied to Jesus in the *New Testament*. The assertion that Jesus and the 'Men of Yesa' were in some way connected was a documented church fact during the very earliest years of recorded Christian history.

The First Century historian, Josephus, believed that the Essenes were formed shortly after the Maccabean period (168BC) by an exiled High Priest named Mattathias, the father of the military king, Judas Maccabeus.[5] A very obscure tradition held that Mattathias, in search of truth and true righteousness, traveled to India and having studied there for many years, returned to his brethren, and founded the first body of monks. In Dead Sea Scroll tradition, this man was afterwards called by his disciples the Master, or, in some translations, the Orthodox Teacher. He was never portrayed as a divinity so he cannot in any way be equated with the Gospel Jesus as some recent authors have tried to do. In fact, it was said in one of the *Dead Sea Scrolls* (Zadokite) that he was 'gathered in'—an expression used in the *Old Testament* to describe natural death.

Some modern researchers give the Essenes a much earlier origin and again connect them with Druids of Gaul, circa 250BC. Druidism was a mystical profession, and in the earliest of times, mystery and magic were always confounded. The association between the Essenes and Druids developed from the similarities between the two groups that both formed a class apart and kept the people who were culturally inferior to them in subjection. Both the Essenic and Druidic high priests were regarded as the most just of men, of a priestly class with secret writings, sacred songs, special clothing, strict rules of divination, hidden instruction and a human skull displayed in certain initiatory ceremonies. Both fraternities taught esoterically the existence of a Supreme Being, a future state of rewards and punishment and immortality of the soul. It was not lawful to commit their doctrines to writing and 'secret ciphers' were used to conceal their innermost mysteries.[6] Julius Caesar (d. 44BC), who came into contact with the Druids, was probably the oldest authority on the mysterious ways of the Gaulish clergy.[7]

The remarkable coincidence between the chief features of the Druidic and Essenic fraternities can be accounted for only by referring them to the same origin. The truth appeared to be that the Druids and Essenes derived their similarity from the spirit of brotherhood which had prevailed in all ages of the civilized world. The inherent principles they adopted seemed to be that all members were engaged in the same pursuit and assenting to the similar religious creed, that being a belief in life after death, and it was their secrecy in that knowledge that gave them their exclusiveness.

Archival records indicated that the Essenes may have been of very early origin. Theophilus Gale, who wrote a work called *The Court of the Gentiles*[8] said:

> Now the origination or rise of these Essenes I conceive by the best conjectures I can make from antiquity, to be in or immediately after the Babylonian captivity [circa 397BC] though some make them later.

John Yarker, author of the book, *The Arcane Schools*,[9] linked the common ancient brotherhoods together and also associated the Essenes with the ending of the Babylonian exile. 'It is possible . . . that Chaldean, whence Culdeean, was as appropriate to the Druids as to the Babylonian, and that as the Essenes were Babylonians, the Culdees were Essenes, as held by Bede (English church historian; 673–735) and thus the Essenes were Culdees and the Culdees were Druids.' With what was known about the Essenes, any of the names given to them could be successfully applied. The oldest research papers variously called them Therapeutes, Ascetics, Monks or Ecclesiastics, which are but different names for one and the self-same sect. The best qualified researchers explain the word Essene is nothing more than the Egyptian word for the Greek Therapeute, signifying the character of the Ascetic sect of Ecclesiastic Monks as professing to the practice of healing.[10]

The 'Ascetic' aspect of their existence indicated severe discipline, long fasting and the willingness of many of them to become eunuchs. The name 'Monks' indicated their contemplative life and their abstraction from the world. 'Ecclesiastics' was of the same sense and indicated their being called out, elected and set apart to the more immediate services and honour of God.

> They had a flourishing university, or corporate body, established on these principles, at Alexandria in Egypt, long before the period assigned for the birth of Jesus Christ. From this body they sent out missionaries, and had established colonies, auxiliary branches, and affiliated communities, in various cities of Asia Minor, which colonies were in a flourishing condition before the preaching of Paul. They also resided in monasteries on the lake of Parembole [or Maria] also in Egypt.[11]

The Fourth Century writings of the church confirmed that the Essenes abounded in Egypt, especially about Alexandria.[12] Their missionaries established stations or colonies in Rome, Corinth, Galatia, Phillippi, Colosse and Thessalonica. At Ephesus they had a well established 'College of Essenes'.[13] They also established and maintained at least one settlement in the Qumran area by the Dead Sea and others in Jerusalem, Antioch, Bethlehem, Damascus and Mount Carmel.

They gained their recruits in two ways. They adopted children and reared them into the way of the principals and practices of their Order,[14] and they took in people in trouble or homeless, wandering ascetics. They were generally celibates, although Josephus indicated the Essenes were quite divided within themselves and there was one particular sect that accepted a kind of marriage between men and women.

The central aspect of Essenic literature was its pre-occupation with prophecy and it was recorded that they had an uncanny ability to successfully predict future events. Philo, a First Century writer, compared them not only with the Persian Magi but also with the Indian Yogis. Later researchers also connected the Druids with 'the Magi of the old Persians'.[15]

The etymology of the word 'Essenoi' or 'Essaioi' has not been settled. In the 16th Century, the name 'Essene' was generally applied retrospectively to every ascetic religious sect living throughout Europe during the last two centuries BC and the First Century or so of the Christian era. Among the contending opinions today, the preferable title seems still to be 'Essenes', and to avoid confusion, that name has been adopted for this work. In using this title, however, it should be remembered that the early church called them the 'Men of Yesu', and the origin of that title shall become clear in later chapters.

The special name of John the Baptist

The Dead Sea is the saltiest body of water in the world and is located at the mouth of the River Jordan, the place where John the Baptist, according to the Gospels, baptised Jesus. The Gospels also recorded that John the Baptist's mother, Elizabeth, was the sister of Jesus' mother, Mariamne Herod.[16] This reference made John the Baptist the cousin of Jesus and thus Judas, and the Gospels said he was six months older than the twins. Aunt Elizabeth was married to a priest and this has been interpreted in some quarters as giving John the Baptist and his family Sadducee (far-right) connections.

The constant references in the *Dead Sea Scrolls* to a 'New Covenant' are directly linked to the *New Testament* letters (today called Epistles) that are attributed by the church to the apostle Paul. The Bible, however, recorded that there were many authors associated with the Epistles and they are named in a later chapter. The two authors of the second letter to the Corinthians (2 Cor.; 3:6) stated that they were 'ministers of a New Covenant' which connected them with the 'Keepers of the New Covenant' or the 'Community of the New Covenant'. In other words, they were members of one of the various Essene communities of the time. The 'New Covenant' basically entailed a belief in certain of the Essene Master's religious writings and included a formal oath of obedience, totally and eternally to the Law of Moses.[17] As part of this understanding, candidates for Essene leadership had to pass through a strenuous training program for three years before being granted permission for entry into the higher ranks. 'The ceremonies were numerous, the physical proofs painful, and the mental trials appalling.'[18] The Essene elders would then impart special secret teachings, special titles, and knowledge given under strict vows of secrecy. Josephus recorded that the Essenes 'considered it a grave sin to reveal their secret knowledge to outsiders, with death preferable by comparison'.

To further establish that much of what the *New Testament* contained was directly related to the doctrines of the Essenes, Paul, for example, mentioned his Essene community in Hebrews (8:7), where he said, 'For if that first Covenant had been faultless, there would be no occasion for a second'.

This narrative indicated new religious documents had been written. Paul also quoted from the *Old Testament* book of Jeremiah (31:31–34) relating to the 'prophecy' of the creation of a 'New Covenant'. From this, and other *New Testament* verses can be ascertained the now-called Christian authors were firm supporters of the Essene New Covenant idea and this can be confirmed in many other places throughout the writings attributed to Paul.[19] The church agreed, for the Introductory Page of the Revised Standard Version of the King James Bible (1971) described the Christian writings of today as 'The New Covenant, commonly called the *New Testament*'.

The publication and subsequent interpretation of most of the *Dead Sea Scrolls* has established direct and close relationships between the sect of the scrolls, the Epistles and the entire substance of the Gospels. A close study of those documents has resulted in a growing consensus that Judas and Jesus' cousin, John the Baptist, was also directly associated with the sect of the *Dead Sea Scrolls*. The Gospels said John was of priestly stock and lived in the Judean wilderness facing the Dead Sea 'until the day of his manifestation' (Luke 1:80). From this Gospel information, John the Baptist is now generally recognised, like Paul, as an Essene. Dr Franz Hartmann added further information saying in his book *The Life of Jehoshua*,[20] that John the Baptist 'was of a noble family and had many influential friends'. The discovery in 1929 by Hugh J. Schonfield of the lost *Book of the Nativity of John* (the Baptist) revealed that originally:

> John the Baptist [as a baby] was considered by the early church as the infant messiah. Its loss [of this document] at a very early date is not to be wondered at, as the church had the best possible reasons for suppressing it.

The fact that John the Baptist was regarded as the messiah by a numerous following may be a new one to many people.[21]

Mr Schonfield then set out a chapter outlining the features of the Baptist's messianic mission and traced the fortunes of the sect which accepted him as their leader.

The *Dead Sea Scrolls* recorded that the 'Community of the New Covenant' possessed a hierarchy, an inner circle of initiated members, and their leader was known as 'the anointed one'. The practice of greasing or smearing with oil is supposed by many to be an exclusive Christian ceremony but was actually in vogue by pre-Christian oriental nations. A statement in the *New American Cyclopedia*[22] confirmed that 'anointing with perfumed oil was in common use among the Greeks and the Romans as a mark of hospitality to guests. Anointing was an ancient custom throughout the East, by pouring aromatic oils on persons as a token of honor . . . it was also employed in consecrating priests, prophets and kings, and the places and instruments appointed for worship'. Obelisks, images and statues had long been consecrated by the devotees of the earlier oriental systems. The *Old Testament* recorded the anointing of ten stones set up by Joshua and also the stone upon which Jacob slept at the time of his vision. Aaron, Saul, David and Solomon were anointed with oil in the same way as the sick were anointed on the Sabbath.[23] In ancient Palestinian tradition it would seem kings, political and military chiefs, village heads and, in fact, any claimants to high office, were anointed and hence called the 'anointed ones', leaders, or messiahs in the true sense of the word. Interestingly enough, some leaders and village heads, after anointing, then became called 'lord', as in landlord, or 'lord mayor'.

Origen (185–251), one of the shining lights of the early church, said on the matter, 'There are some who said of John (the Baptist) that he was anointed'.[24] St Epiphanius also said John the Baptist was 'one of the anointed', confirming there was more than just one 'anointed' man in the Gospel story. Roman Emperor Julian (361–363) in his book *The Arguments of the Emperor Julian* supported the opinion and introduced an extraordinary word by stating:

> At any rate neither Paul nor Matthew nor Mark dared to say that Jesus is God, but only the Krist John, they adventured to assert this.

The Krist John. Origen, Epiphanius and Julian the Emperor all clearly recorded that John the Baptist, Judas and Jesus' cousin, was a 'Krist' figure, but made no reference to Jesus himself attaining that status. Bishop Theodoret, writing in the Fifth Century, provided further confirmation that Jesus was not one of the 'Krist' personalities although many others of his time were.[25]

But what was a 'Krist' figure?

It seemed the word 'Krist' had its origin in ancient Egypt and was the name of a highly regarded early god. This ancient name was found extensively inscribed into the Palermo Stone, the largest and best preserved of six basalt stones, originally uncovered in Egypt. The ancient hieroglyphic inscriptions helped archaeologists to date the early pharaohs up to the Fifth Dynasty. These original Egyptian records were carved into tablets of stone and deposited in the tomb of a pharaoh more than one thousand years before the *New Testament* was written. In these old records, now in the Palermo Museum, Horus, the Egyptian god of Light, was called Krist or Krst. His mother was the goddess Isis, who conceived him as a virgin.

'Krist', according to St Epiphanius,[26] was the spiritual Self in each and every living person. This explained why Epiphanius was baffled when he said he could find no writings to confirm his own later orthodox views concerning 'Jesus Christ' as an actual living person. He was naturally puzzled at the unhistorical nature of his Christian god. Bishop Epiphanius added to the concept of the Krist figures. He frankly recorded that Alexander of 100BC was 'one of the anointed',[27] a statement which clearly established a long history of Krist figures preceding the canonical date of Judas and Jesus. In fact, the 'anointed' or Krist figures actually preceded the writing of the *Old Testament* in the story of Krishna. The *Old Testament* priest and author, Ezra, subsequently made references to anointing (c. 397BC), providing two separate examples in just one narrative.[28]

From the Essenes many of their manuscripts referred to Kristo, Krst, or Krist, and was a divine internal figure in Essenic minds and set forth primarily in the Book of Enoch as One eternal with God. The Book of Enoch was written sometime around 150–120BC.[29] Krist was also established in the doctrine of the Gnostics who held Kristo to be the personal and immortal Spirit of man. The son of Poseidon and Meduse was called Khryst and the priests of Apollo were known as Khyrstes. In fact, the word Kristo and its derivations, Krst, Krist, Kristo, Khyst and Krish-na appeared in every ancient religious system and showed the original Kristo concept was believed to be the personal and invisible mediator and guide between God and everything spiritual in man. The Krist concept has been an ancient religious tradition continually suppressed by the Catholic church through the centuries.[30]

(Dany anointed ones

In a document called 'Dialogue with Trypho' written by St Justin Martyr sometime around 160, Trypho, a Jewish gentleman, claimed that the church 'invented a Kristo'. Trypho was intimating that a Kristo-type figure similar in concept to the Hindu Krishna, was purposely devised by Justin Martyr and his associates. Around 130 years after the canonical date of the death of

Jesus Christ, Trypho's comments clearly showed the Jesus Christ promoted today was actually 'unknown' among the general populace but the Krist concept from the Book of Enoch and Kristo, the Hindu name of the Sun, were.

Adding further depth to the story, Trypho, again in the writings of Justin Martyr, said the word Krist was really a substitute for a very ancient divine name, and its power was known to the 'Elect' alone of the fully initiated Rabbis. In other words, the most advanced Rabbis were initiates of secret knowledge and knew the substance of an ancient mystery.

Both Judas and Jesus said on several occasions in the canonical Gospels and on more occasions in the apocryphal Gospels, particularly the Gospel of Thomas, that they knew the 'secret of the Kingdom of God'. Jesus later learnt the ultimate Secret in Egypt, which exceeded the secrets of the Lesser Mysteries of the anointed Essenes. That great secret, as an inner circle of Rabbis know today, is still preserved in the Bible.

The Gospels do not record the anointing of Krist John, the Baptist, but they do record the anointing of Jesus.[31] Judas was also anointed, probably before Jesus, because he was the 'first born son' (Luke 2:7). Simon Peter called Judas 'a Krist' whereupon Judas commanded his followers to 'tell no man that secret thing'.[32] Though it is now impossible from the imperfect record to ascertain the exact state of the earliest Christian texts, the salient fact dwelt upon by the church today was that Jesus was the only person anointed in the Gospels and therefore, in their opinion, that made him *the* messiah, not just one of many, as there were.

Rabbi Jesus elected to be anointed

Christian tradition has preserved the 'Good Principle' of the Krist as the ideal of all their aspirations, and this was apparent in the writings of the early presbyters. Hippolytus (d. 236), for example, said the sect of Ebronites/ Ebionites felt Jesus had been justified by his perfected practice of the Law of Moses.[33] In other words, he had excelled in the preaching of the *Torah*, the first five books of the *Old Testament*, and had qualified as a Rabbi. Amazingly, St Justin Martyr in his *Dialogue with Trypho* put the following argument into the mouth of his learned Jewish opponent:

> Those who affirm him [Jesus] to have been a man, and to have been anointed by election, and then to have become a Krist [anointed] appear to me to speak more plausibly than you . . . [Trypho responding to Justin Martyr].[34]

Summarised, Justin Martyr, who maintained the virgin birth dogma, had in the previous chapter of his *Dialogue with Trypho* actually confessed:

> . . . even if I cannot demonstrate so much of this [namely evidence that Jesus was God incarnate in a virgin's womb], you will at least admit that Jesus is the anointed of God, in any case he can be shown to have been born as a man of a man, and proved to be raised by election to the dignity of messiah-ship [anointed]. For there are some of our persuasion [early presbyters] who think that he is a messiah but declare him to have been a man of a man.

St Justin again referred to 'anointed by election', but what exactly was 'election'? The academic opinion was that certain persons who had been initiated into the Lesser Mysteries were elected by a body of priests to be anointed, and then called Krists. This was an established 'Essene tradition'[35] and the 'election' was consummated at 'baptism' which, in Rabbi Jesus' case, was 'at about the age of thirty years'. This highly-valued ancient religious 'Krist' tradition had been relentlessly crushed by the Catholic church as 'heresy' throughout the centuries.[36]

The early Christian presbyters thought of and used the term 'Krist', with a significance at considerable variance with that of the later Nicene belief which actually personified this long and mysterious Krist concept going back as far as Horus.

The 'Star' figure

A key factor in determining the significance of the *Dead Sea Scrolls* in relation to the ben Panther twins related to the leader of the 'Community of the New Covenant'. *The Bible Fraud* proposes John the Baptist, being 'Krist, the anointed one', was the messianic leader of the Essenes. As such, he would have been called the 'Star'. In old writings available, four anointed (messiahs) leaders are recorded in association with the Essene community. In this regard, Josephus said some Essenes were 'involuntarily anointed'. Of extreme interest is the knowledge that a vial of oil was found in the Qumran caves with the *Dead Sea Scrolls*. It was wrapped and sealed in a protective manner, indicating it was very precious to those who preserved it. One could be excused for thinking it was safely stored for the anointing of their future Krists/messiahs. One of the *Dead Sea Scrolls* called 'The Book of the Community Rule' outlined the instructions for specific use of the 'Star', the head of the Order. It stated he shall:

> . . . admit into the Covenant of grace, all those who have freely devoted themselves to the observance of God's precepts that they may be joined to the Council of God. He will cleanse him of all wicked deeds with the spirit of holiness, like purifying waters he will shed upon him the spirit of truth, and when his flesh is sprinkled with water, it shall be made clean by the humble submission of his soul to all the precepts of God.

This verse shows that the head of the Essene community had the authority to admit new general members into the Order after baptising them. Baptism was most certainly *not* part of the orthodox Jewish tradition, so John the Baptist was at some time, the head of the Order. Most likely, he had been a leader excelling in his position and surpassed the other members by being proclaimed a prophet by a large number of people. He was declared to be 'more than a prophet' by Rabbi Jesus (Matt. 11:9).

The 'Star of Bethlehem' mystery solved

Nothing was recorded about the earlier life of Judas or Rabbi Jesus in the Essene community.[37] Being anointed seemed to indicate both Judas and Rabbi Jesus had previously undergone the required three years of strenuous training required for entry into the hierarchy of the Essene Order, and anointing was their 'token of honour'[38] before full admission into the 'inner circle of initiates'. That both Judas and Rabbi Jesus knew certain 'secrets' was manifest from the Gospel of Mark[39] and they knew too much of the secret rituals of the Essenes to have been outsiders.

As a result of his fanatical dedication to the Law of Moses, the Gospels narrated that the career of John the Baptist came to a sudden and dramatic end when he was supposedly beheaded for condemning the marriage of Herod Agrippa I to his sister-in-law (and niece), Herodias, because 'it is against the Law [The Law of Moses] for you to have your brother's wife' (Mark 6:18). 'There is no historical foundation' to the beheading of John the Baptist and the story 'has been doubted',[40] but it seems certain that he was executed by the Romans.

Comment. The execution of John the Baptist was not carried out under Herod the Great. Herod Antipas, son of Herod the Great (who went to live in Gaul in 39AD) married Herodias, the wife of his half-brother, Herod, who was the other son of Herod the Great. Herod Antipas was 'the tetrarch' of Galilee and Peraea.[41] He styled himself as 'Friend of the Romans'. It was Herod Antipas who ordered the death of John the Baptist.[42]

After the death of John the Baptist, Judas inherited the leadership of the Essenes because of family bloodline and the status of the tradition of the first born. Because he was now Judas the 'anointed' initiate, he was called Judas the Krist (or Krist Judas), which developed to Judas Khrestus in subsequent Latin translations. He became the 'Star', the head of the Essenes at their Bethlehem community, the town in which two of the Gospels later recorded that he and his twin brother Rabbi Jesus were born.[43] As Professor Eisenman stressed, this documentation linking the messiah-figure with the word 'Star' occurred elsewhere in the *Dead Sea Scrolls* and was of crucial importance. Significantly the 'Star' reference was cited by sources independent of both the *Dead Sea Scrolls* and the *New Testament*, including historians and chroniclers of the First Century Rome such as Josephus, Tacitus and Suetonius. According to Josephus, the arrival of a 'Star' character was a major factor in the revolt of 66AD.

Some 220 years or more after the church claimed that Jesus Christ died for our sins, the 'Star' of Bethlehem found its way into the second Gospel to be written, that of Matthew (Matt. 2:2). Here it was retrospectively made to herald the arrival of a messiah, 'a governor who shall rule the people' (Matt. 2:6) and was presented in the usual glamorized fashion of the early presbyter's writings. Just as important was the presence of Simeon bar Cochba and his troops in the Qumran area between 132 and 136AD. Simeon bar Cochba, a Jewish army leader, claimed to be, and was accepted as a very popular messiah.[44] Even more remarkable was that bar Cochba means 'son of a Star' in Aramaic[45] and was the name commonly used to describe him. Simeon bar Cochba was just another in the succession of the many Jewish messiahs who had come and gone but only those people who study Jewish history knew anything of them. That some of bar Cochba's own documents were found in the Qumran caves clearly suggested he was himself an Essene leader. It would be very interesting to know who Simeon bar Cochba's father and grandfather were, for it appears obvious the 'Star' figures were all successive (related) members of one family.

Two messiahs expected

The book of the Community Rule from the *Dead Sea Scrolls* collection introduced the Essene belief that they lived in expectation of two important messiahs. This was strikingly similar to the two messiahs recorded in the Acts of Thomas. One was to be of the priestly caste, and the other would be a warrior who would restore the kingdom of his people, a military commander. With the birth of the 'royal' ben Panthera twins, and their education in the Essene community, it was highly probable they were regarded as the two anticipated messiahs. In the context of the tradition of the time, 'messiah' did not signify what it later and incorrectly came to signify in Christian preaching. It simply meant a leader, 'an anointed one', and in Essenic belief, one was expected to deliver them from Roman bondage.

The Essenes were not the only community to believe in the coming of special leaders. Du Perron, in his *Life of Zoroaster*, gave an account of certain prophecies to be found in the sacred books of the Persians. One was to the effect that, at successive periods of time, there would appear on Earth certain 'Sons of Zoroaster' who would 'redeem mankind'. Among the Greeks the same prophecy was found. The *Oracle of Delphi* was the depository, according to Plato, of an ancient and secret prophecy of the birth of a 'Son of Apollo' who was to restore and reign justice on Earth.[46]

Among their then-secret doctrines, the Essene community believed that one of their messiahs would eventually lead them to victory over their Roman oppressors. This was to be the first born, Judas Khrestus, and the Essene hierarchy acclaimed him as the restorer of the Kingdom of God. One section of one of the *Dead Sea Scrolls* was written in readiness for the blessing to be extended before the (hopefully) successful outcome of the radical events expected to happen when their oppressors were challenged. This outline was carried in a scroll called 'The Messianic Rule':

> When they shall gather for the common table, the priest shall bless the first fruits of bread and wine thereafter the messiah of Israel shall extend his hand over the bread, and all the congregation of the community shall utter a blessing.

This was the blueprint of the Last Supper found recorded in the *New Testament* and established that Judas Khrestus was the messianic leader of the Essenes. The *New Testament* recorded in several places that he raised the 'cup of the New Covenant' in true Essenic fashion.[47] The word 'New' has now been dropped from modern Bibles, but appeared in all ancient Bibles.

From *Old Testament* times, Jewish meals included a blessing over bread and wine (Gen.14:18), and over the centuries assumed special importance as can be seen in many sections of the *Dead Sea Scrolls*. Josephus said of the Essenes, 'They consider it a grave sin to rest or touch food before praying'. The *Old Testament* changeover from simply reciting a short prayer over the bread and wine (Grace) into the symbolic ritual of eating the body and drinking the blood of a god had a long previous history and came to be introduced 'officially' into Christian practice during the latter part of the Fourth Century.

CHAPTER FIVE

The character of Judas Khrestus

TO DETERMINE THE SEPARATE CHARACTERS OF JUDAS KHRESTUS AND Rabbi Jesus from so little information, especially where much of it depends upon stray Gospel references, is problematical. Given the complex nature of the development and transmission of the *New Testament* it cannot be said with any degree of certainty what particular elements belonged to which of the twin brothers and, in many cases, there remain obscure points. However, some particular aspects are clear. From their different life styles it was possible to attribute to each of them various Gospel narratives and therefore determine who said or did what.

How to make a clergyman squirm

Probably the most damaging of the Gospel statements refuting the church assertion that Jesus Christ was God on Earth was carried in the Gospels of Matthew (11:19) and Luke (7:34). Here, Jesus frankly admitted he was 'a glutton and a drunkard', words used by him in describing how the people of the time perceived him to be.

During the research for this book, various members of the Christian ministry were asked to define the church's position relating to these two 'drunkard' statements. One honest answer suggested that the narratives created 'special difficulties'. Others angrily claimed they were nothing more than words 'written between the lines'. However, they were words written in the *Bible* and presented by the church as words of God.

The impression they created of Jesus Christ was embarrassing for the church in light of the divine nature in which it desires to present him to the public. Some clergymen refused to discuss the subject and questioned why the verses needed to be raised, because Jesus didn't really mean what he said. To be told by the church that Jesus Christ did not mean to say what it plainly said he did say in the official church texts, was the simplest way of getting out of the difficulty. This particular expedient was used often by the church in defending statements of Jesus that are impossible to defend.

Knowing the extent of editing undergone by the *New Testament*, it is quite remarkable that these two verses were not deleted centuries ago, but the tradition current at the time of the writing of the Gospels allowed those verses to be documented. There were some later attempts to 'water down' these statements and some newer Bibles now say Jesus Christ was 'a winebibber', meaning 'a person who drinks a great deal of wine' while others simply say he was 'a drinker'. However, Christians the world over must accept the church presentation of the *New Testament* and that made the Lord of their faith a self-confessed 'drunkard'.

In reconciling the two traditions in the Gospels, the 'drunkard' narratives are attributed to Judas Khrestus, not Rabbi Jesus. It is interesting to read from the *Old Testament* Book of Proverbs, 'for the drunkard and glutton will come to poverty' (23:20–21). Gluttony and drunkenness were obviously condemned in the *Old Testament* with the prevailing tradition under the Law of Moses clearly being 'a glutton and a drunkard shall be stoned to death'.[1] This belief may provide a reason why there are constant references in the Gospels to large crowds of people trying to stone Judas Khrestus. The Wicked Priest in the *Dead Sea Scrolls* was also considered a drunkard. He 'would drink his fill' when 'the Cup of the Wraith of God' came around to him. In Dead Sea Scroll research, this was generally interpreted to mean that he 'drank too much wine'. The parallels between the two Qumran messiahs and the story of Judas Khrestus and Rabbi Jesus in the Gospels are extraordinary. One character in both cases represented a military commander who wished to restore the earthly Kingdom of God, and the other character in both cases was of a priestly nature believing 'the Kingdom of God is within'.

Gluttonous revelries reached their peak in the First and Second Centuries and the excessive and obsessive enjoyment of food and wine was taken to extremes during this period, particularly in Roman society:

> Such dishes as peacock brains, flamingo tongues and elephant ears were served as part of a feast that could contain as many as a hundred courses. When one had eaten too much, a 'vomitorium' permitted seclusion to allow removal of the ingested food; a long feather was provided to induce the process. A guest could empty his stomach, rest for a time and then start dining again.[2]

Although Judas Khrestus clearly did not abstain from drinking wine, there may have been a very good reason for his indulgence and it was associated with the real meaning of the word 'Nazarene'. The *Old Testament* made reference to a body of pre-Christian people (male and female) called, Nazars. The word 'Nazar' signified a particular group of people who vowed or consecrated themselves to the devoted service of the Jehovah god of the *Old Testament*. There was more to the Nazar group than that recorded in the *Old* and *New Testaments*. By tracing the term 'Nazar' throughout the best-known works of ancient writers, they were connected with Pagan as well as Jewish adepts. Thus Alexander the Historian (c. 311) said of Pythagoras that he was a disciple of the Assyrian Nazarite whom some supposed to be Ezekiel of *Old Testament* fame. Famous biblical characters such as Samson and Samuel were described as Nazars. Singularly, they were called 'a Nazarite', in a group 'Nazarenes', and at the time of this story, the Nazarenes were the military arm of the Essenes.

The Nazarenes were known to have existed at least as early as 397BC and lived on the eastern shore of the Dead Sea, according to the records of Josephus.[3] Pliny confirmed Josephus' statements and said Nazars 'lived on the shores of the Dead Sea for thousands of ages', simply meaning a lengthy time. In the *Old Testament* they were directly mentioned on three separate occasions and in the Book of Numbers (6:20) it was recorded 'a Nazar (Nazarite) may drink wine'. In the Syric Version of the Gospel of Luke (4:34) there was a reference to, 'Iasoua, thou Nazar'. Dr Constantine Von Tischendorf (1815–1874), German biblical scholar and Professor of Theology, transcribed these words in his English translation to read 'Iesou (Yeshu'a) Nazarene', referring to Rabbi Jesus. To take the 'drunkard' references one step further another narrative in the *Old Testament* stated that Nazars were actually 'made to drink wine' (Amos 2:12), implying alcohol was forced upon them by scriptural law.

What are these verses doing in the Bible?

Judas Khrestus made this very straightforward statement when he commanded that he and his followers must 'hate our own father and mother, and wife and children and brothers and sisters and even our own life' (Luke 14:26). In the Gospel of Thomas (101/114), this concept was further supported while the Gospel of Luke (12:51) recorded this statement of aggression from the mouth of Judas Khrestus, 'Do you think that I have come to give peace on earth? No, I tell you, but rather division.' This extraordinary Gospel verse hardly supported the clerical claim that Jesus Christ loves you:

For I have come to set a man against his father, and a daughter against her mother, and a daughter-in-law against her mother-in-law, and a man's enemies will be those of his own household. (Matt. 10:35–36)

This was Judas Khrestus talking and there are many more such statements sprinkled throughout the *New Testament*. The Temple of Jerusalem used by livestock merchants and moneychangers for business enraged Judas Khrestus who 'making a whip of cords (a cat-o'-nine-tails), he drove them out, overturning the tables and seats' (John 2:15). Along the way he created a stampede of cattle and sheep. The 'whip of cords' phrase was edited out of most later editions of the Bible, but appeared in all the oldest manuscripts of the Matthew, Mark, Luke and John Gospels. In some Fourth Century manuscripts, the word 'scorpion' was used in lieu of 'a whip of cords'. This weapon was a whip with leather thongs set with sharp iron points or nails, called, in Latin, 'horribilia'.

After Judas Khrestus' violent performance, many of the local inhabitants considered him to be insane and said, 'he has a demon, and he is mad, why listen to him?' (John 10:20). Surprisingly enough, there were six references in the *New Testament* to Judas Khrestus being 'mad'.[4] Judas Khrestus' own family said, 'he was outside himself' and were in constant conflict with him. In the Gospel of John, Judas Khrestus was turned away when he 'came into his own home, and his own people received him not' (John 1:11).

Commentators have often questioned the mental stability of the Gospel Jesus Christ and refer to some bizarre dialogue between him and his disciples, both in the canonical *New Testament* and in texts of suppressed Christian writings. Just two such examples, both from the Gospel of Thomas, recorded Jesus Christ saying, 'every woman who makes herself male will enter the kingdom of heaven'. Later, when the disciples asked Jesus: 'When will you be revealed to us?', Jesus replied: 'When you take off your clothing, without shame, and like little children, put your clothes on the ground and tread on them'. In the Gospel of Mark, Jesus Christ made the curious claim that there were worms inhabiting hell that are fireproof and possessing eternal life (Mark 9:43–48).

The Gospels revealed that Judas Khrestus could be a little peeved when awakened from sleep[5] and he 'did not wash before dinner' (Luke 11:38). When his host commented upon this lack of hygiene, he received a full-scale verbal assault from his 'angry' guest as Judas Khrestus' uncontrollable temper flared again.

People could further question the mental stability of Judas Khrestus if they were to read a strange event recorded in the Gospel of Mark. Judas Khrestus was hungry and, seeing a fig tree in the distance, approached it with the intention of obtaining something to eat 'knowing it was not the season for figs'. This irrational act has intrigued biblical analysts for centuries.

Not surprisingly, the word 'knowing' has been quietly dropped from newer editions of the Bible and subtly replaced with the word 'for'. The passage was then made to read: 'for it was not the season for figs', which takes away the strange act of the Gospel Jesus Christ approaching a fig tree for a meal of figs out of season. However, the passage quoted was documented in the oldest texts of the Mark Gospel. When only leaves were found, Judas Khrestus placed a curse upon the tree; 'may no one ever eat fruit from you again.'[6] The next morning, Judas Khrestus and his followers again passed by the fig tree and saw that it was withered away to its roots. Simon Peter said, 'Look, the fig tree which you cursed has withered'.[7] The Gospel of Matthew, incidentally, carried a conflicting account of this verse: 'the fig tree withered at once'.

A Christian layman, when talking to author and translator of the *New Testament*, Mr Hugh Schonfield, made the following comment:

> If you can get around Jesus cursing the fig tree, you will have done us a great service.

It wasn't the singular Jesus Christ of today's Gospels who was talking, but Judas Khrestus. Schonfield would also have done the church a great service if he could have deleted the verse which described the peculiar act of Jesus Christ sticking 'his fingers into his ears, and he then spat, and touched his tongue' (Mark 7:33).

Judas Khrestus' attitude towards divorce and remarriage was made very clear indeed when he declared: 'If you divorce your wife and marry another, you commit adultery' (Matt: 19:9). In this Matthew narrative, however, there was a strange anomaly. In some Bibles of the Fourth, Fifth and Sixth Centuries, this passage was recorded: 'and he who marries a woman commits adultery and makes her commit adultery'. Here is a narrative full of tantalizing obscurities and uncertainties. It provides an apt example of what the researcher is really up against when comparing the presbyter's old texts and the surprises to be found in trying to determine the true nature of the customs of the times. Which particular version of the text is meant to be the original understanding is difficult to determine.

The apostle Jesus 'loved'

In 1960, the Anglican Bishop of Birmingham, Hugh Montefiore, suggested Jesus Christ might have been homosexual. Montefiore was motivated by Christ's unusual attitude towards male nudity in certain statements in the Gospels of Mark and John, and a reference in an Epistle to the Essenes at Colosse referring to an incident of 'complete stripping'. Montefiore suggested the 'closeness to men' in narratives associated with Jesus was firmly supported by the passage: '. . . the disciple who Jesus loved was leaning back on Jesus' breast' (John 13:23–25).

This was not Rabbi Jesus but Judas Khrestus.

The apostle John was traditionally identified as the unnamed disciple 'who Jesus loved' and who has been depicted as the one 'leaning back of Jesus' breast' at the Last Supper. This assumption was drawn from a Gospel statement applied to Jesus Christ during his last hours in which he entrusted his mother Mary to care for John as 'her son'.[8] The many medieval devotional images of John with his head resting in an effeminate Jesus' lap (in others, kissing Jesus' neck) gave rise to mystical texts in which John was said to 'have enjoyed the milk of the Lord' which verbally and pictorially implied an act of oral sex with Jesus Christ.[9]

Pietro Lorenzetti's Fresco of the Last Supper (1305–1348).
Lower church of San Francesco, Assisi, ©The Assisi Film Library.

Although a 'special relationship' between the Gospel Jesus Christ and the apostle John was clearly indicated, Bishop Montefiore's theory did not find widespread Christian acceptance. Assertions that Jesus Christ and some of the apostles were gay or bisexual was an issue dismissed by the church as purely speculative. However many homosexual elements in the New Testament are subtle and easily missed while many forms of early Christian rites involved male nudity.

In one of Professor Morton Smith's books, *The Secret Gospel of Mark* (1974), he recorded how he recognised the transcript of a hitherto unknown letter from the Second Century church presbyter, Bishop Clement of Alexandria

(160–215). The main purpose of Clement's letter (to Theodotus) was to attack the teachings of one of the most important Gnostic groups, the Carpocrations, who flourished at least as early as the Second Century. In the course of his writing, Bishop Clement revealed the original sequence concerning the 'raising of Lazarus'. Clement's correspondent had been taken back when confronted by 'heretics' who told him they had read another version of Mark's Gospel which appeared to be genuine, but of which Theodotus knew nothing. Bishop Clement frankly acknowledged the authenticity of the other Mark Gospel and said it was an enlarged version he called 'the secret Gospel of Mark'. More extraordinarily, Bishop Clement went on to record that 'the secret Gospel . . . is now carefully guarded', but denied that the phrase 'naked man to naked man' was recorded in association with Judas Khrestus' activities in the original 'secret Gospel' of Mark as the Carpocrations had apparently told Theodotus.

Professor Morton Smith also found a verse in the Secret Gospel of Mark that paralleled today's canonical Gospel of Mark. It said: 'going to where the youth was [Judas Khrestus], stretched forth his hand and raised him, seizing his hand. But the youth, looking upon him, loved him, and began to beseech him that he might be with him . . . in the evening the youth came to him wearing a linen cloth over his naked body and he remained with him all that night and Judas taught him the mystery of God.' From the Gospels, and also the apocryphal works comes knowledge that the instruction course for teaching the 'secret of the Kingdom of God' involved a private overnight ritual in which a young male pupil came to Judas Khrestus naked, apart from a loose linen cloth about his body. A confirming episode appeared in the canonical Gospel of Mark (14:52), where a young man who had been with Judas Khrestus 'ran away naked after a linen cloth about his body had fallen off'. This episode followed a scuffle during the arrest and removal of Judas Khrestus and raises this intriguing question: 'Just what did Judas Khrestus do with these young boys in the secret nocturnal rites?'

In both the *Old* and *New Testaments* there are constant references to 'a secret' known only to initiates, and one wonders whether it had some connection with nudity or homosexuality. Leonardo da Vinci showed John the Baptist naked[10] and there were numerous pictorial indications that exist to this day showing the baptismal candidate naked. In the earliest frescoes, the Ravenna mosaics and in a large number of later Greek Icons, the Gospel Jesus Christ was depicted naked when receiving baptism. Interestingly enough, there was no mention in the Gospels of Rabbi Jesus baptising anyone.

Baptism, or the supposed purification from past sins by sprinkling water upon the skin, was supposed by many to be an exclusive Christian ceremony. Rev. J. P. Lundy[11] provided evidence that the rite was introduced sometime after the Babylonian captivity (c. 397BC). Eusebius Pamphilius, Bishop of Caesarea, wrote that it was 'an ancient custom' in his time (260–339). When a Greek historian called Diogenes (c. 400) witnessed someone undergoing baptism, he said of the rite, 'Poor wretch! Do you not see that since these sprinklings cannot repair your grammatical errors, they cannot repair either, the faults of your life'.[12]

What the Gospels really recorded

The church depicted Jesus Christ as a bit of a softy, a real pushover, 'gentle Jesus, meek and mild', as recorded in Sunday school literature. But they had it wrong for the Gospels portray mainly the character of Judas Khrestus, not Jesus the Rabbi. In summation of this section, Judas Khrestus has been shown to be a man with a violent temper, an unwashed drunk carrying a sword and brandishing a whip. There are suggestions of homosexuality from a man who ate like a pig, was uncaring about family lives and was considered by many to be insane, as was also the apostle Paul (Acts 26:24). A narrative in the *Sinai Bible* said Judas Khrestus' followers were 'all thieves and robbers', confirmed by Ernest Renan of the French Academy who said they 'were the dregs of the nations, a poor dirty set, without manners, clad in filthy gabardines and smelling strongly of garlic'.[13] Judas Khrestus constantly defended himself against verbal and physical assaults, struggling to prove his royal identity. Did he not ask, 'Who do they say I am?' (Matt. 16:13–15). Also revealed was a man of courage, quite prepared to assert his right by force and, if necessary, to employ savage physical violence against his enemies. This was shown by the army he developed, and he was the anointed leader.

CHAPTER SIX

The Life of Judas Khrestus

THAT A MESSIAH WAS GENERALLY EXPECTED BY THE COMMON populace around the time of the lives of the ben Panthera twins may be inferred from the writings of the First Century Roman historian, Tacitus (c. 56–126), who said:

> The generality had a strong persuasion that it was contained in the ancient writings of the priests . . . that someone, who should come out of Judea, should attain the empire of the world; But the common people according to the influence of human wishes, appropriated to themselves, by their interpretation, this vast grandeur foretold by the fates [foretellings]; nor could be brought to change their opinion for the time, by all their adversities.

Suetonius (70–140), another Roman historian confirmed Tacitus' record:

> There had been for a long time all over the east a constant persuasion that it was recorded in the fates, that at that time some one who should come out of Judea should obtain universal dominion . . . It appears by the event, that this prediction referred to the Roman emperor, but the Jews, referring it to themselves, rebelled.

This was corrobated by Josephus, the First Century Jewish historian (c. 37–98), who said:

> That which chiefly exited them to war was an ambiguous prophecy which

was also found in the sacred books, that at that time someone, within their country, should arise, that should obtain the empire of the whole world. For this they had spoken of one of their nation; and many wise men were deceived with the interpretation.

As Reverend Dr Geikie remarked,[1] the central and dominant characteristic of the teaching of the Rabbis was the certain advent of a great national Deliverer—a messiah—but not a god from heaven. The national mind had become so inflammable by constant brooding on this one theme, that any bold spirit rising in revolt against the Roman power, could find an army of fierce disciples who trusted that it should be he who redeem Israel.

The first fifty messiahs

The death of King Herod in 4BC was followed by frightful social and political convulsions in Judea. For two or three years all elements of disorder were current and Judea was torn and devastated. Revolt assumed the wildest form and the celestial visions of a kingdom of heaven were completely banished by the smoke and flame of political hate. From that time until the death of Simeon bar Cochba in 132, no less than fifty enthusiasts applied the ancient 'ambiguous prophecy' to themselves, obtained a following, and set up as the messiah.[2]

After Herod's death, Galilee passed into the hands of his son, Herod Antipas, who almost immediately had to deal with a local rebellion led by probably the first messiah, a certain Jude, the son of Ezekias. This developed into a full-scale battle after Cyrenius, the Governor of Syria, heavily taxed the Jewish people circa 6AD. Jude bar Ezekias declared that 'this taxation was no better than an introduction to slavery' and exhorted the nation to assert their liberty. He prevailed upon his country men to revolt,[3] and this uprising compelled the Roman officer entrusted with its suppression to appeal to Rome for reinforcements. Subsequently two thousand insurgents were crucified and many others sold as slaves.[4] Around this same time, according to Josephus, a curious 'fourth school of philosophy' developed, and to determine what was meant by this statement was difficult. It seemed that the new 'philosophy' required a program of conversion to a particular cause or movement that opposed the Roman authorities and their tax, and any challenge was believed by the converts to indeed be just and worth fighting for. The firm conviction that 'God alone' was their 'leader and master'[5] was confirmation in the mind of the believer that any success would be evidence that God was on their side.

Claimant after claimant of the dangerous supremacy of the messiah then appeared, pitched a camp in the wilderness, raised the banner, gathered a force, was attacked, defeated, banished or crucified, but the frenzy did not abate. The 'taxing' that took place under Cyrenius excited the wildest uproar against the Roman power. A Samaritan named Menander, who was contemporary with Judas Khrestus and Rabbi Jesus, was one of those fanatics who believed himself to be a messiah, 'sent down from above for the salvation of man.'[6] Manes also proclaimed himself a messiah, and recruited twelve followers.[7] Simon the Magician of *New Testament* fame was believed to be 'He who should come' and was worshipped as a god. In Rome, in the reign of Emperor Claudius, a statue was erected in his honour.[8] The heart of the nation swelled big with the conviction that the hour of destiny was about to strike, that the Kingdom of Heaven was at hand. The crown was ready for any kingly head that might assume it.

When Rome annexed the regions south of Galilee as the province of Judea in the early decades of the first century (c. 30), another uprising broke out in the new provenance, led by a certain Judas from Gamala (in the Golan) who was known as 'the Galilean' (which virtually meant anarchist) and came to be celebrated by a series of subsequent revolutionaries as their forerunner. The body of evidence currently available validated the church opinion that Judas 'the Galilean'[9] and Judas Khrestus, the twin in the Gospels of the *New Testament*, were one and the same person.

Judas the Galilean's 'philosophy' was notable for the almost unconquerable 'passion for liberty' that distinguished him, and it seemed that he was also a follower of the 'fourth school of philosophy'. It was possible that the prophecy of the Cumaean Sibyl in Virgil's Fourth Eclogue that predicted 'the new Kingdom of God' was an influencing factor in the philosophy that Judas Khrestus seemed to adopt, for the Essenes held a great respect for the *Sibylline Books*. In the Gospels, Judas Khrestus constantly proclaimed the advent of the Kingdom of God and withdrawal into the wilderness was a transitional step toward that Kingdom. But why was he so convinced that the Kingdom was at hand?

'The field of Gospel history had its beginnings in remote Galilee,'[10] the most northerly of the three provinces of Palestine (Galilee, Samaria, Judea) and included the large eastern areas of Ituraea, Trachonitis and Lysanias (Eastern Upper Galilee). Measuring approximately fifty miles north to south and 120 miles east to west, it was bounded in the west by the coastal plain along which ran the road from Egypt to Phoenicia. The caravan routes from the coast to Damascus and the east crossed its Southern part through the valley of Esdraelon.[11] In *Old Testament* times, King Hiram was unimpressed with the twenty Galilean towns Solomon gave him as payment for services. He called the inhabitants 'Cabul' meaning 'good-for-nothing' (1 Kings 9:13) and their 'despised' reputation endured into *New Testament* times. Josephus described them as 'only representations of living things'. Galilee was known as 'the insurgent district of the country. They were a restless, excitable body of people, remote from the centre of power, ecclesiastical and secular. The Romans had more trouble with the Galileans than the natives of any other province. The messiahs all started out from Galilee and never failed to collect followers around the standard'.[12]

The origin of the Galileans

The Gospels clearly stated that Jesus Christ was a Galilean (Matt. 26:70) with twelve followers. This was in reality Judas Khrestus and, excluding Judas Iscariot, 'all the apostles were Galileans',[13] recruited from the inhabitants of the Gamala area of Galilee. But just who were the inhabitants of Galilee who became the apostles of the *New Testament*?

The Romans named the region of Northern Galilee, Gaulantius (originally Gaul-anti-us, today Golan Heights) and this word provided a clue to who was originally living there. Place names can provide a unique source of information about a society's history, structure, customs and values and often was the only record of a people's existence or of an historical event. The original form of a name was derived from various sources, for instance: agriculture—Agricia; flowers—Narcissus; jewels—Margarite and military life (or the sea)—Navigia. From months—Junia, and from countries—Gaul.[14] Gaul-anti-us therefore was a composite name commencing with a place called Gaul. The structure of this word implied that Northern Galilee was originally populated by Gauls. Who then were the Gauls?

In classical geography, Gaul was a country inhabited by people who became called Gauls—hence, in modern use, France. However, when Julius Caesar (d. 44BC) wrote of 'Celtae' he referred specifically to the people of middle Gaul (the Roman name was Gallia) only, which was the territory in Upper Italy and Southern France (Gallic). The French of this area were later called Gallican, which later pertained to the church of France. The plural of Gallia was Gallicans, which was linguistically related to Galileans. Celts was the name applied by ancient writers to a population group occupying mainly lands north of the Mediterranean region from Galicia and Ireland in the west to Galatia in the east. Fable accounted for the word 'Celt' by the story of Celtina, daughter of Britannus, who had a son by Hercules, named Celtus, who became the progenitor of the Celts. Celts or Celtae were representatives of the ancient Gauls. The ancients knew the Celts as fierce fighters and superb horsemen, and noted the fervor of their religious rites conducted by the priesthood, the Druids, who derived their doctrine from Britain. 'According to Caesar, it was a tradition in Gaul in his time that the Druids were of British origin.'[15]

'With the Roman conquest of Gaul the Druids lost all their jurisdiction, druidism suffered a great decay . . . and if some of them remained scattered here and there in Gaul, most of them were obliged to emigrate to Brytayne

(Britain)'.[16] But they didn't all go to Britain. Large groups traveled 'east along the Danube into Hungary, Greece, Turkey . . . and a splinter group established itself in Galatia, a country in Asia Minor that derived its name from its inhabitants, who were Gauls. Pomponius Mela (d. c. 37AD) of Tingentera (near Gibraltar) wrote a geographical survey in Latin of the inhabited world (*De Chorographia*) in three books. He recorded that some of those living in south Gaul had relocated as far as Palestine, and Upper Galilee was part of Palestine.

The church recorded that the highlanders of Upper Galilee were violently opposed to the Romans and this completed the structure of the name, Gaulantius. The inhabitants were Gauls and anti-Roman, hence the full structure of the name of the place the Romans called Gaul-anti-us (Gaulantius). But they weren't all Gauls—some were Nabatean Arabs, the founders of the 'Baptist sects'.

'Simon (called Peter) and his brother Andrew' were clearly Galileans (Luke 22:59) and the first recruited. St Jerome recorded that 'Simon was of mature age and Andrew was a youth'. They were both Nabatean Arabs and Simon received the appellation of Peter which theologians, both ancient and modern, expressed difficulty in explaining. The Gospel name of Simon Peter originated from:

> Simon, originally from the rock of Petra, a fortified rock city south of the
> Dead Sea, the dome upon which they hoarded their wealth.[17]

Traces of 'the Peter' or 'the rock' tradition can be found in all four Gospels and they recorded the prominent role he played as a 'pillar' in the circle of Judas Khrestus' disciples (Gal. 2:9). Roman Catholics today regard Simon Peter as the first pope and leader of the apostles. The tradition that made Simon Peter the founder of the church of Rome depended only on the writings of Bishop Irenaeus[18] who did not define in what circumstances Simon Peter went to Rome. Simon Peter was really Simon of Petra—his name being in the same biblical tradition as that of Mary of Bethany and Saul of Tarsus.

Mariamne Herod, the mother of Judas Khrestus and Rabbi Jesus, also had family links with the city of Petra, for her grandmother, Cypros, the mother of King Herod, was also a Nabatean Arab from Petra. Curiously enough, an Arabic tradition in Rabbi Jesus' family was further recorded in the suppressed 'Book of the Nativity of John' (the Baptist). John's mother, Elizabeth, 'hurried outside veil-less . . . and for this she received a bill of divorcement'.[19]

Since the term 'Galilean' was synonymous with aggression and the Zealots, it was revealing to read that Judas Khrestus was called 'one of them' three times in the Gospel of Luke.[20] The Gospel of Matthew (26:73) stated the

Galileans 'spoke with a peculiar accent' and warmly welcomed Judas Khrestus upon his return to Galilee from a journey to Jerusalem (John 4:45). Josephus called the Galilean followers of Judas Khrestus 'his disciples' and the Spanish-born, British-educated Governor of Judea, Pontius Pilate later asserted (Luke 23:5) that they were rabble-rousers who set about to 'stir up the people'. In the effort to build up large numbers for his army, Judas Khrestus publicly expressed the position that he would 'never turn away anyone who comes to me' (John 6:37). The church now call these men the 'apostles' of Jesus Christ, but they were, in reality, the militia of Judas Khrestus.

In itself, the mere suggestion of an association of 'gentle' Jesus Christ with the vicious, war-mongering Zealots (anti-Roman nationalists) was highly provocative in the church and promoted a violent reaction when raised with some of the more learned priests. This Gospel association immediately eliminated the meek and humble, lamb-like saviour image that Christian tradition has developed to portray Jesus Christ. But it was Judas Khrestus, not the Gospel Jesus Christ nor Rabbi Jesus, 'who began his ministry in Galilee and from whence he drew his apostles'.[21] Judas Khrestus was, in fact, more militantly inclined than was generally portrayed and he was also more politically committed than we have been given to understand in the presentation of the Gospels. The most able of Herod's sons, Antipas, became the Tetrarch of Galilee after the territory was given to him and he had the arduous task of controlling Judas Khrestus and his extremist Galilean entourage. Judas Khrestus described his opponent, Antipas, as 'a fox' (Luke 13:32).

The reality of the issue was that the now-called early Khrestian/Christian movement was actually a body of brutal Galilean militants and this may explain why modern day Christian encyclopedias and dictionaries fail to record an A–Z entry under the heading of 'Galilean'.[22] This is a particularly strange omission, for the church proudly stated that 'the early Christians were called Galileans and the apostles, except Judas Iscariot, were all Galileans'.[23] Yet the church seemed reticent to fully describe the history and nature of the Galileans.

The Galilean fortress

During the course of Judas Khrestus' leadership of the Bethlehem Essene Community, he and his odd assortment of troops moved to the imposing fortress in the rugged hills outside Gamala in Galilee because he had 'no honor in his own country' (John 4:44). 'He lived almost as an outlaw in the more mountainous and unpopulated regions of Upper Galilee,' said the church.[24] It was Josephus himself who, as the former governor general of Galilee, equipped the fortress with ramparts and tunnels. Josephus gave an extraordinarily precise description of the site and convinced his readers that it was to all intents and purposes impregnable. 'The houses were built against the steep mountain flank and astonishingly huddled together, one on top of the other, and this perpendicular site gave the city the appearance of being suspended in air and falling headlong upon itself.'[25] Here Judas Khrestus combined and developed his radical offshoot team of the Nazarenes and Zealots with the intention of advancing on Rome in a military action to free his people and claim his rightful title of Emperor. The people 'believed in him . . . and because of his words many more became followers' (John 4: 39–41).

From what can be established from the records available, it appeared certain the Nazarenes were more or less an independent Essene-derived military sect and in some way were definitely connected to the Zealots and the Zadokites. The possibility that a member of the Essene sect headed up a division of youthful aggressive fighting men did not seem to fit the pacific and peaceful nature of old monks depicted by Josephus, Pliny and Philo. The answer lies in one of the most important characteristics of the Essenes— their apocalyptic vision that was recorded as an 'end of the world prediction' in their prophetic writings.

In general, their apocalyptic vision foretold an end and a new beginning. Interpretations respecting the date of the fatal day exhibited a constant and wide divergence, and on numerous occasions men believed the end of the world was near. Both Rabbi Jesus and John the Baptist preached the end of the Age, which established their knowledge of the Essenes' prophecies. The Essenes certainly believed the end of the world was near for they continually documented their insistence that the 'Last Times' were at hand. They were paranoid about it and several of their texts deal specifically with the impending end of their particular world. The fact that they had a manuscript called the *War Scroll* among their writings attested to this and established the Essenes had readied themselves for some kind of war.

The Essenes prepare for battle

The *War Scroll* gave detailed directions for the conduct of combat, with the battlefield operations personally directed by priests who sound off the trumpet calls, 'Advance', 'Attack', 'Retreat', 'Re-assemble', 'Pursuit' and 'Ambush'. One specific section of the *War Scroll*—of which several copies were found in Caves One and Four—documented a definite plan of tactics and strategy to be used in the physical encounters of man-to-man combat against the anticipated attack from invading forces called the 'Kittim'. In the *Old Testament* book of Daniel (11:30) the Kittim were the Romans, named because they maintained a garrison on the island of Kittim in the Mediterranean Sea (today called Cyprus).

Later Jewish authors used the term cryptically of any victorious power.

However, the important point to be stressed here is that, as recorded in the *War Scroll*, the ultimate Essenic army leader to oppose the combatant forces of the 'Kittim' is called, quite unequivocally, the 'messiah'. The orthodox church translators of this Scroll sought to disguise or dismantle this nomenclature by referring to the commander as 'thine anointed' which obscured the import of this passage[26] in a Christian sense.

The vital point here is to establish the date of the composition of the *War Scroll*. If this could be determined, we would know better whether or not it referred in any way to the now-called messiah of the *New Testament*. And it is certainly possible to date this scroll to within certain time frame parameters. Within the *War Scroll* itself, a vital clue to its dating and chronology can be found. When speaking of the 'Kittim', the text referred explicitly to their 'king'. The 'Kittim' concerned cannot, therefore, be the soldiers of republican Rome, who invaded Palestine in 63BC and who had no monarchy. On the contrary, they would have to be, and could only be, the soldiers of Imperial Rome operating after the empire began under Emperor Augustus (27BC–14AD), and fell in the Fifth Century.[27] Those soldiers invaded in the wake of the revolt of 66 which eventually saw the sack of Jerusalem by the Romans in the year 70 involving an opposing 'Star' figure. His name was Simon bar Giora and he surrendered to the Romans in dramatic fashion—dressed in a white tunic with a purple mantle, presumably to indicate royalty.[28] He was taken to Rome, displayed in a victory procession and ceremonially executed as the leader of the defeated Jews.

Messiahs at work

Evidence of a messiah-type figure in known operation more than thirty years after the church claimed that Jesus Christ was crucified, was the sort of *Dead Sea Scroll* documentation that the church contrived to suppress or, in some cases, ignore. Militarism was always associated with the 'Star' (or messiah) figures and the *New Testament* accounts graphically indicated this to be so in the Gospel story of Jesus Christ. That person was actually Judas Khrestus, whose followers had been conspicuously involved in tumults and disturbances wherever they went. It was Judas Khrestus who said, 'I have come not to bring peace, but a sword' (Matt. 10:34) and instructed his followers to also equip themselves with swords and clubs (Luke 22:36). From these Gospel words and descriptions, the church's desire to present the singular Jesus Christ and his followers as placid and peaceable holy men was very different to the reality of the personality of Judas Khrestus overlaid in the *New Testament*. The most sensitive of all Gospel documentation for later Christian tradition was that of narratives in which Jesus (Judas Khrestus) was clearly made to have included Zealots, of all people, among his supporters. Simon the Zealot was one,[29] and he was recorded in the records of Bishop

Dorotheus of Tyre to have 'at last' been caught and slain in 'the east of Britain'.[30] The violent Zealots were members of an extreme Jewish sect (or political party) that resisted all aspects of Roman rule and aggression in Palestine in the First Century. They were, in today's terminology, a body of far-left militant revolutionists, fearless of death, in fact, ruthless assassins and they were directly associated with Judas Khrestus and his actions recorded in the confused narratives of the *New Testament*.

CHAPTER SEVEN

Khrestus goes to Rome

Origin of the Christian messiah

IN AN EXHAUSTIVE EXAMINATION OF ALL AVAILABLE EXISTING FIRST AND Second Century Roman documents, are found buried away two separate historical references to Khrestus. These two writings were purported to be written late in the First Century or early in the Second Century and the information they gave about him was sparse. The earliest was by Publius Cornelius Tacitus, a classical Roman historian who wrote three works during his lifetime: the first was *Agricola*, the second *Germania* and the last was called *Annals* (originally titled *After the Death of the Deified Augustus*). In *Annals* (15:44) Tacitus mentioned a man called Khrestus who suffered death by crucifixion at the hands of Pontius Pilate during the reign of Tiberius. That which is now known as the second Medicean manuscript of Tacitus was generally assigned to the latter half of the 11th Century and thought by some researchers to have been one of the many transcripts of works by ancient authors made at that time in the great monastery of Monte Cassino. Nothing appeared to be known of the history of this manuscript until the time of Poggio Bracciolini who received it in Rome in 1427 from Nicola Nicoli of Florence, one of the agents employed by him for collecting ancient manuscripts.

The later report came from another Roman historian called Suetonius (70–140). He served as secretary to Emperor Hadian (d. 117AD) and, it was said, had access to the Imperial Roman archives. His major historical work

The Lives of the Caesars, published about 120, gave accounts of the reigns of Julius Caesar and the eleven emperors who followed him. In a chapter of his writing called *The Life of Claudius* (25:4), Suetonius made reference to a man called Khrestus 'acting in Rome, the part of a leader of insurgents'. Claudius (10BC–54AD) was the Emperor of Rome during the years 41–54AD.

The document attributed to Suetonius said Emperor Claudius expelled all Jews from Rome because of disturbances instigated there by Khrestus. This expulsion was confirmed in the *New Testament* (Acts 18:2–3) in an undateable narrative that described Aquila, a Jew, and his wife Priscilla, being driven out of Rome by an edict of Claudius forcing them to travel to Corinth to start a building business. The Roman historians' statements provided conflicting information because Tacitus citied Tiberius as the Emperor at the time and Suetonius recorded that it was Claudius, thus providing a discrepancy of some eight years. The expulsion by Claudius may have been caused by Judas Khrestus' sons (Jacob and Simeon) whose combined messianic uprising was violently suppressed in 46 by Claudius' appointee, Fadus, and they were subsequently crucified.[1] Both historians were writing long after the events that they described, and many similar conflictions are found in their records. Suetonius, for example, said Tiberius 'was of fair complexion and wore his hair rather long at the back'. Tacitus, on the other hand, said that the emperor had a head 'without a trace of hair'. They sometimes disagree with one another so markedly that only one of them can be right, and both may be wrong.

Tacitus was writing around fifty years after the events he was recording and Suetonius some forty years after Tacitus. As Tacitus was living closest to the time of the event and 'he is always careful to ascertain and record the truth',[2] his report was adopted for this work. He placed Judas Khrestus in Rome under the reign of Emperor Tiberius. Tacitus described Rome at the time as a place 'where every horrible and shameful iniquity from every quarter of the world pours in and finds a welcome'. This may have been the reason why Emperor Tiberius stated that he 'hated the place' and spent much of his time a little further south on the island of Capri. There, in his 'pleasure palace', he trained little boys, whom he called his 'minnows' to lick and nibble his genitals while they all swam together in his pool. On occasion he even had unweaned babies suck his penis.[3]

Tbe Roman Imperial Secret Service
Judas Khrestus possessed an hereditary right to the Emperorship of Rome and the throne of Judea and, because of this, he rallied popular support among the Galileans, hoping maybe that he could regain for them the land the Romans had taken. Judas Khrestus and his rebels 'started in Galilee' and

came 'all the way here' (Luke 23:5) to Rome to challenge his father, Emperor Tiberius. They subsequently arrived at 'a farm called Gethsemane which belonged to a man called Joshua',[4] situated on the outskirts of the city. Some early English-language Bibles (c. 1611–1687) recorded the name Judas, not Jesus, in this Matthew passage (26:36), revealing the true nature of the original story and neatly accounting for the amalgamation of the two life stories. The later church deemed 'Judas' was a 'misprint' and *New Testament* versions recording Judas' name subsequently became valuable collector's items today called the *Judas Bible*.[5]

It was at Gethsemane that the Galileans readied themselves for battle with the Romans. Unbeknownst to leader Judas Khrestus, his father Emperor Tiberius had died during the long journey and Caligula (d. 41) had come into power on 16 March 37. A dangerous and unpleasant individual, he became the third emperor of Rome. The records of the Roman historians consistently paint him as a capricious and cruel young man, powerful and scheming. Suetonius, for example, said, 'So much for Caligula as emperor; we must now tell of his career as a monster'.[6]

There was now a dynastic problem which demanded immediate and urgent action by Emperor Caligula. Judas Khrestus was the son of Tiberius and Mariamne Herod and that constituted a serious problem for the Roman Emperor, for Khrestus was the illegitimate, but natural successor to the King of Judea and the Emperorship of Rome. However, the official Roman policy was now to 'rid Judea of the royal line and any other government of the sort and hand administration of the country over to the Roman legate in Syria', such was the dimensions of the hatred against Herod and his dynasty.[7]

It had been a long-standing policy of the Roman legion and armies of occupation to utilize informers and spies. They were called the Delatores (later, the Frumentarii), the Roman Imperial Secret Service, and were set up with the express purpose of spying on the citizens of Rome's far-flung domains.[8] They were common in the Tiberian principate and were usually Roman officials in positions, for example, of collectors of corn in a provenance that brought them into contact with locals and natives. Flavius Sabinus Titus,[9] for example, destroyer of the Second Temple in Jerusalem in the year 70, employed special messengers and killers to carry out executions and liquidations arising from information derived from the Secret Service.[10]

From the information in the Gospels, it can be argued that Judas Khrestus was preparing his attack but before he could get under way, Judas Iscariot, an informer to the Delatores, betrayed him. On a particular night, and under Emperor Caligula's orders, the *cohortes urbanae,* the city police force of Rome and a division of the Roman Army, was assembled and in place ready to nullify Judas Khrestus' imminent uprising. There were originally three *cohortes urbane* stationed in Rome, each with five hundred soldiers. This number was increased to one thousand each between the years 43 and 69. Little is known of the course of the ensuing battle but there is epigraphic evidence that a large Roman force was needed to suppress it, maybe requiring all three *cohortes*.

On that night, the Gospels stated that Judas Iscariot embraced and kissed Judas Khrestus in order to identify him to the Roman military leaders (Luke 22:47–48). Judas Khrestus was obviously unknown to them and upon the signal of Judas Iscariot identifying the leader of the Galileans, 'a great multitude with staves and swords' attacked, and a significant battle raged in which Simon of Petra used his sword and cut off Malchus' ear (John 18:10). Judas Khrestus was subsequently overpowered, arrested and removed from the scene. Strangely enough, a great variation was given in the Gospels as to the numbers of Judas Khrestus' followers. The amount in the Gospel of Luke was given as seventy-two.[11] However, he was attributed a figure of 'five hundred disciples' in the first book of Corinthians (15:5–8). In the *Talmud*, 'five disciples' were recorded.[12] They were the followers of Rabbi Jesus, not Judas Khrestus.

At that time large areas were under Roman occupation, and to fully understand the situation, we must compare it with the occupation of France by the Germans during World War II. There was a civil law administered by the French, and there was the law of the occupational forces, which only concerned itself with offences against the occupational authorities. The same sort of arrangement applied during the first decades of the First Century. The civil law of the Jews demanded death penalties be carried out by stoning, in accordance with the Law of Moses. Offences against the Roman state came under the Roman authorities whose method of execution was by crucifixion. To be sentenced to such an execution, Judas Khrestus would have had to commit an offence against the Roman Empire.

A crucifixion with a difference

Judas Khrestus was tried on a charge of treason against the Romans, found guilty of revolutionary activity and sentenced to die by crucifixion. In his defence in front of the Roman Council he argued that 'he was a king' but they replied: 'we say he is not a king, but he saith it of himself'. The whole multitude called out he was 'born of fornication',[13] expressing the local knowledge that Judas Khrestus was born out of wedlock. As a Roman citizen of noble heritage, Judas Khrestus then 'appealed to the Emperor', Caligula, as was his right, but to no avail. The death penalty stood. This was the year 37. Being aware of his royal blood, Judas Khrestus then exercised an age-old tradition that came with his birthright. This advantage allowed him to order the placement of a 'substitute' to take his allocated punishment. An ancient Babylonian clay tablet determined the actual origin of the tradition of a 'substitute'. The priests ordained a substitute should 'go to meet his destiny' and undergo, on somebody else's behalf, the afflictions in store for that person.

An echo of this ancient rite was found in the story of Barabbas, who was offered as a substitute to Judas Khrestus (Matt. 27:16–17). Barabbas 'had been put in prison for his part in a rising in the city and for murder' (Luke 23:19). It should be mentioned the name of Barabbas in all ancient Bibles was originally written Jacob Barabbas.[14] The word 'Barabbas', interestingly enough, means in Aramaic, 'son of the father' (or 'son of a father', in some translations) exactly as the Gospel Jesus Christ was made to be the son of the Father. By exercing this option, Judas Khrestus not only saved his own life but also the life of his son Jacob Barabbas. This was nevertheless at a cost. He had played the 'substitution' card at the expense of his 'birthright' which now passed to the second born, his twin brother, Rabbi Jesus.

In the 'substitute tradition', at first, it seemed, the unlucky victim had to suffer but not necessarily die. 'Therefore I have decreed that thou should first be scourged according to the law of the emperors' said the Emperor himself.[15] Judas Khrestus was then 'flogged' (John 19:1) and subsequently invested with the honours of a 'purple' toga (Mark 15:17), the distinctive mark of royalty.[16] A crown called the Corona Triumphalis, among the Romans the highest distinction awarded for service in war, was placed on his head. Tradition recorded that this crown was always made from grass growing at the scene of the battle. With the official Roman formalities now completed, Judas Khrestus was then led away.

The mystery man in the Gospels

The inside man in the story was a notable member of the Sanhedrin, Joseph of Arimathea—'a secret disciple' who had met with Judas Khrestus that night and expressed his concern about 'the new Kingdom of God.[17] Historians considered Joseph a man of little significance and the tradition of him subsequently settling in Glastonbury, England, will later be shown to be more than 'an old legend'. The *Talmud*, however, recorded that Joseph of Arimathea was the youngest uncle of Mariamne Herod and Herodias and therefore Judas Khrestus and Rabbi Jesus' great-uncle. Joseph was the youngest son of King Herod. He was, at the time of the uprising, married to Mariamne Herod with her earlier husband, Herod Philip, now deceased (c. 33–34), and Joseph was therefore the legal step-father of her twin sons, Judas Khrestus and Rabbi Jesus. At that stage, Joseph of Arimathea was at least sixty-seven years old, Mariamne Herod was around sixty-one, and the twins forty-six.

Joseph of Arimathea and Mariamne Herod were the 'Joseph and Mary' of the story in the Gospels and the narrative stating that Joseph 'knew her not until she had born a son (read 'sons': Matt. 1:25) was true. The Gospels also stated that they were 'betrothed', meaning that a family-arranged marriage had been established for them. However, when Joseph returned from a trip, he found Mariamne Herod pregnant to Tiberius, 'a son of God' (Emperor Augustus). When the church claimed that 'the brothers and sisters of Jesus Christ were the children of Joseph by a former marriage', it should really have said; 'The brothers and sisters of Jesus Christ were the children of Mary by former partners', Mary of the Gospels being Mariamne Herod.

In the *Latin Vulgate Bible*, Joseph of Arimathea was described as 'Decurio' and in St Jerome's translation, he was given the title of 'Nobilis Decurio' which implied he held the prestigious position of 'Minister of Mines' in the Roman administation. All evidence points to him being affluent and a person of importance and influence within both the Jewish and Roman hierarchies. He was most probably the head of the Essene community in Rome and provided underground support for Judas Khrestus and his followers.

The once-canonical Gospel of Peter recorded that Joseph of Arimathea was a close personal friend of Pontius Pilate and in his younger days was 'a soldier of Pilate for seven years'.[18] The narratives in the Gospel of Peter provided a vital church reference that established that the crucifixion took place in Rome. Christian sources, presumably motivated by a desire to place complete responsibility for the crucifixion of the Gospel Jesus Christ on the Jews, are generally sympathetic to Pontius Pilate. This was in contrast to the account in the Epistle of Agrippa I (Philo), which depicted Pontius Pilate as corrupt, cruel and bloodthirsty. With Joseph of Arimathea's help, Judas Khrestus was exchanged for the 'substitute' under the cover of darkness. Pontius Pilate was in Rome at this time (37AD) for late in 36 he had been ordered by the governor of Syria, Vitellius, to travel to the city to answer for his conduct to Emperor Tiberius.[19] However, Tiberius died on 16 March 37, and just before Pontius Pilate reached Rome.[20] Pontius Pilate remained in Rome and was still there during the reign of Emperor Claudius 41–54.[21]

Pontius Pilate never returned to Judea but at this point he still retained the Procuratorship of Judea and the judgment responsibilities of the area still under his jurisdiction.[22] However he deferred to Herod Agrippa I,[23] who was also in Rome at that time having just received his commission as Tetrarch of Ituraea, Trachonitis and Lysanias (Eastern Upper Galilee) from new Emperor Caligula. Those areas were mostly his late Uncle Philip II's (d. 33–34) territory known also as Upper Galilee. It was no small coincidence that this was the very same territory of Judas Khrestus and his Galilean followers who had their fortress in the rugged hills outside Gamala. It was therefore opportune for Herod while in Rome to be in attendance at the trial and this was recorded in the *New Testament*. However this was not Herod Antipas, but Herod Agrippa I, and when he saw Judas Khrestus he was pleased 'because for a long time he had been wanting to see him' (Luke 23:8). Agrippa I was Judas Khrestus' uncle.

According to the Gospels, Pontius Pilate considered Jesus Christ innocent of any crime, simply because he was referring to the person who became the substitute for Judas Khrestus. Pontius Pilate remarked at the substitute's reticence to speak (Mark 15:5) saying, 'He made no reply, not even a single charge' (Matt. 27:19). Tradition gave the name of Claudia Procula to Pontius Pilate's wife, and she has been identified by some as the Claudia of 2 Timothy 4:21. She also knew the man was a substitute and advised her husband not to 'have anything to do with that innocent man' (Matt. 27:19). Later, the penalty handed to Judas Khrestus was completed with the crucifixion of the substitute.

Crucifixion of Jesus Christ unknown to First Century historians

According to historians Dio Cassius, Plutarch, Strabo and others, there existed in the time of King Herod, a widespread and deep sympathy for a 'crucified King of the Jews'. This person was the youngest son of Aristobulus, the heroic Maccabee, and in 43BC we find this young man, Antigonus, in Palestine claiming the crown, his cause having been legally declared just by Julius Caesar.

Allied with the warlike Parthians, Antigonus maintained himself in his royal position for six years against Herod and Mark Antony (d. c. 30BC). After an heroic life and reign, Roman troops eventually stormed Jerusalem and captured him.

> Antony now gave the kingdom to a certain Herod, and having stretched Antigonus on a cross he scourged him, a thing never done before to any other king by the Romans, and he then put him to death.[24]

The fact that all prominent historians of those days recorded this particular crucifixion showed that it was considered one of Mark Antony's worst crimes and the sympathy for the crucified King was widespread and profound.[25] Some writers think that this crucifixion provided the precedent to an overlaid story in the Gospels but it was probably where the later Gospel writers adopted Jerusalem as the place of the crucifixion of the Gospel Jesus Christ.

There was no verification of a landmark or significant crucifixion of a person called Jesus Christ in the writings of such highly regarded contemporary historians as Philo, Tacitus, Pliny, Suetonius, Epictectus, Cluvius Rufus, Quintus Curtis Rufus, Josephus, Plutarch and the Roman Consul, Publius Petronius. The only conclusion to be drawn is that the historians of the day did not know of any particular or special religious crucifixion worthy of mention. This was a glaring omission from the records of so many noted intellectual writers.

A crucifixion of the Gospel Jesus Christ was also unknown among the early church as late as the end of the Second Century. This was close to 170 years after the church would like the world to think that the brutal death of its god occurred. It must be immediately pointed out that the modern church admitted the records of Bishop Irenaeus (d. 202) created serious problems. They said of him: 'Although of crucial importance in the development of the church's theology, Irenaeus presents problems of considerable difficulty in regard to details' about Jesus Christ.[26] Irenaeus is fondly described by the church hierarchy as 'the depositary of primitive truth',[27] but he denied a virgin birth, never mentioned a trial of Jesus Christ, said nothing of a crucifixion or resurrection and claimed Jesus Christ declined towards old age.

The Gospel burnt by the church

There were attempts by the early church to destroy the documentation recording the 'substitute' of their main Gospel character and it concerned a man called Basilides. Very little was known of him, but it appeared he was a presbyter in Alexandria sometime around 155–160. Of Basilides' writings only scattered fragments now survive. It was recorded he once wrote a twenty-four page document called *A True History* which was later retitled the *Interpretation of the Gospel* (note the singular use of the word 'Gospel'). Basilides' report was later burnt by the church,[28] which makes us suppose that it contained more truthful matter than the church was prepared to deny.

Scholars have suggested that an incomplete account by Bishop Irenaeus (c. 202) in his work Against Heresies[29] summarised the essence of what Basilides wrote. From the central act of Basilides' work, it was claimed that Simon of Cyrene let himself be crucified instead of Judas Khrestus. Under the headline 'Confession of Khrestus but not of Khrestus crucified', Basilides wrote:

> Hence he did not suffer. Rather, a certain Simon of Cyrene was forced to bear his cross for him, and it was he who was ignorantly and erroneously crucified, so that he was taken for Khrestus; while Khrestus for his part . . . stood by, laughing at them.
>
> Therefore people who know these things have been set free from the ruler that crafted the world. One should not acknowledge the man that was crucified (i.e. Simon of Cyrene), but rather the one who came in the form of a man, was thought to have been crucified, was named Khrestus . . .

Basilides' report was also confirmed in the Gospels where it stated that Simon of Cyrene was 'seized as he was coming in from the country' (Luke 23:26) and subsequently 'carried the cross to the hill of Golgotha' (Matt. 27:32).

The Romans spoke of the Zealots as 'Robbers' in order to defame their name and whenever the 'Robbers' were caught they were immediately crucified. Thus it was probable the two *New Testament* men called 'thieves'[30] crucified alongside Judas Khrestus' substitute were actually 'Robbers' which, in centuries of translations, became 'thieves' and were arrested at the same time as Judas Khrestus. They were condemned for the same offence, as crucifixion was not the punishment for robbery. But look what one of the crucified 'Robbers' said (Luke 23:41) about the central player in the crucifixion event:

> We are punished justly, for we are getting what our deeds deserve. But this man has done nothing wrong.

He knew the man being crucified alongside him was innocent because he was substituted for Judas Khrestus. The church claimed the Acts of Thomas contained 'an historical nucleus'[31] and within it was recorded the very words Judas Khrestus was purported to have said, obviously alive:

> I did not succumb to them as they had planned, and I did not die in reality, but only in appearance; I was laughing at their ignorance.

One should also consider the information Mohammed had at his disposal when he wrote the Holy Book of Islam, the Koran (Surah 4), and documented this passage relating to Judas Khrestus:'. . . and they killed him not, nor did they cause his death on the cross'.

The 'redemption' of Simon's body

Examination of the Roman Law of the period revealed that the authorities allowed no burial rights to those who died by crucifixion and violation of this Law brought severe punishment. As the penalty of crucifixion was reserved for rebels, mutinous slaves and other enemies of Roman society, those guilty were simply left hanging naked and rotting, a public and prolonged agony that was a deliberate deterrent to other would-be rebels. It was a custom of the times to post armed centurions (Matt. 27:54) to prevent the removal of the bodies of the near-dead 'unless a rich matron came along and redeemed him'.[32] Unless an Imperial Order was issued, the payment of money to Roman authorities was the only way a crucified man could be released, and Josephus recorded one such instance. Titus, when he was Roman Emperor (79–81), gave instructions to remove three crucified prisoners on the Temple Mount courts and instructed that they should 'receive the best possible treatment'. Two of them, however, later died in the physician's hands, the third survived. They had endured crucifixion for two and a half days and nights. Historical records show that crucifixion was not only the most degrading form of capital punishment, it was also the most prolonged and painful.

According to the Gospels, Simon of Cyrene experienced crucifixion for just part of one afternoon, a few hours. He subsequently escaped its full horrors after Joseph of Arimathea negotiated a financial settlement with Pontius Pilate for his release from crucifixion. The Acta Pilate recorded the long address of Joseph to Pilate, with every clause beginning with the words, 'Give me this stranger'. With the monetary formalities completed, Simon of Cyrene was officially 'redeemed' and now able to be freed from punishment. 'When evening had come',[33] Joseph of Arimathea, went to the crucifixion scene and removed Simon to an adjacent tomb. Joseph then disappeared from the *New Testament* accounts forever, but not from our story. To hide the fact from the Roman authorities, Judas Khrestus and his followers subsequently removed Simon's body from Joseph of Arimathea's private tomb.[34] Additional evidence provided in the Gospel of Peter supported Basilides' record that the body of Simon of Cyrene was removed from the tomb by 'two young men'.[35] The Acts and Gospel of Thomas, the Gospels of Peter and Barnabas and the apocryphal[36] writings provided eleven separate biblical sources recording that Judas Khrestus was living long after the time the church stated the singular Gospel Jesus Christ died.

The trip to India

From the moment Judas Khrestus and Rabbi Jesus were born, they encountered the ancient heritage of the 'first born' with an example seen occurring in the *Old Testament* archetype of Esau and Jacob. Esau sold his birthright for a 'mess of pottage' and Jacob received his father's blessing in his place.[37] Rabbi Jesus Krist, 'brother second in command',[38] now received the blessing of 'the Father' and inherited the title of 'Star', the leader of the Essenes and the rightful king of the Jews, but showed reluctance to assume power. It was recorded in the Gospels that 'perceiving that they were about to come and take him by force to make him king, Rabbi Jesus again withdrew to the mountains by himself' (John 6:15). However, his reticence merely delayed matters for his legal obligations of royal birthright had to be fulfilled and the people wanted him 'made King'.[39] Because Judas Khrestus had drawn upon the 'substitute' advantage of his birthright, the fallen 'Star' was no longer a free man and was sold into bondage by the new 'Star', his brother and 'fellow initiate',[40] Rabbi Jesus.

In a 'relic of the original Greek text'[41] of the Acts of Thomas, Rabbi Jesus 'saw a certain merchant who had come from India whose name was Abbanes, and said, I have a slave that is a good builder and I desire to sell him. And so saying he showed him Judas Thomas (Khrestus) far off and agreed with him for three litrae of silver unstamped, and wrote a deed of sale, saying, "I Rabbi Jesus . . . acknowledge that I have sold my slave Judas by name unto thee Abbanes, a merchant of Gundafor, king of the Indians".'[42] They then 'sailed prosperously till they reached Andrapolis, a royal city'.[43] The church records acknowledged the sale of Judas Khrestus in the Acts of Thomas:

> Rabbi Jesus sold Judas Khrestus to an Indian king (Gundafor) to be his slave and to serve Gundafor as a carpenter. Judas Khrestus undertook to build a palace for Gundafor, but spent the money.[44]

Church records also confirmed the historical existence of a king by that name:

> Now it is certainly a remarkable fact that about the year 46AD a king was reigning over that part of Asia south of the Himalayas. Despite sundry minor variations the identity of the name with the Gundafor of the Acts of Thomas is unmistakable and is hardly disputed. He began his reign during the year 20AD and was still reigning in 46AD.[45]

In this phrase, purported to have been written by Judas Khrestus in India, he expressed remorse, 'But I could not recall my splendor. For, it was while I was still a boy and quite young that I had left it behind in my father's Palace'.[46]

A widespread tradition in both the East and West maintained that Judas Khrestus died of old age at Meliapore in India. Evidence was found in the writings of Ephraem Syrus, Ambrose, Paulinius, and St Jerome and later in Gregory of Tours and others.[47] Gregory of Nazianzus held that Judas the Twin (Khrestus) went to India (Or, 25), a position also found in Acts of Thomas (1). However, John 'golden-mouthed' Chrysostom (347–407) referred to his burial place at Edessa in Syria,[48] a Roman colony that supported a royal residence.[49] Edessa is modern Erfa.

The alleged tomb of Judas Khrestus
© Picture Courtesy of The Great Liberation Library. Tibet. (1927)

According to an ancient Indian legend, Judas Khrestus spent twelve years in villages in the state of Orissa on the Bay of Bengal in India and subsequently died in Kashmir. Catholic missionaries, Francisco de Azvedo and Ippolito Desideri, brought significant accounts from Tibet to that effect in 1631 and 1715 respectively.[50] The claim that Judas Khrestus lived, and eventually died, in India or Tibet strengthened at the end of the 19th Century in documents written by Russian author and researcher, Nicolas Notavitch. He recorded that his personal friend, a Roman Catholic cardinal, confided in him that the Vatican vaults held sixty three complete and near complete manuscripts written in various Oriental languages which confirmed that Judas Khrestus spent many years in India and Tibet and the tomb in Khanyar Street, Srinagar, Kashmir, was actually that of Judas Khrestus. The manuscripts, said Notavitch, were brought to Rome by missionaries from India, China, Egypt and Arabia, and were suppressed. An ornate structure in the Rozabel area of Srinagar (pictured) was held in tradition to be the tomb of Judas Khrestus.

CHAPTER EIGHT

A religion of Galilean criminals

NTIL AROUND THE YEAR 150 THE RECORDS OF TACITUS AND Suetonius mentioning Khrestus were the only examples of any ancient writings having a similarity to the name of Christ. Because the name Khrestus and Christ were pronounced alike, these writings have been critically analysed by researchers for many centuries. The Encyclopedia of Early Christianity said it was 'perhaps a reference to Christ'[1] and the 1908 *Catholic Encyclopedia* also said, 'he may have been Christ'. This could not have been Jesus Christ of the Gospels because, according to the *New Testament*, he never went to Rome.

Why the word 'Christian' did not appear in church testimony until well into the Second Century, has been explained in the very orthodox *Oxford Dictionary of the Christian Church*. With over 480 contributors consisting of leading Anglican, Roman Catholic, Lutheran, Presbyterian, Methodist, Jewish, Orthodox and other clerical experts, they claimed on the cover that they were 'the acclaimed authority on the church'. They made this frank statement:

> Owing to its Pagan origin, the word [Christian] was long avoided by
> Christian writers . . .[2]

The 'Pagan origin' of the word 'Christian'? Surely a stunning admission from such a learned and competent authority. With the new understanding of just who the Galileans were, it is now possible to determine what the church meant.

The word 'Christian' was documented by the church in the Acts of the Apostles and appeared to have been introduced to the world for the first time circa 190 by Irenaeus. That particular narrative said the name 'Christian' originated in the city of Antioch (Acts 11:26) and in the context it was presented, suggested outsiders applied the name disrespectfully to a particular body of people. Religiously, Antioch was a mix of ancient Chaldean, Greek, Roman and Semitic creeds but there was a person (maybe a woman) there called Evodius (Phil. 4:2) connected to the Khrestian movement, and in some way associated with both Simon of Petra and Paul.[3] The death of Evodius was recorded as occurring in 64. Curiously enough, Sabellius, a Third Century Roman orator (c. 260), said 'the word "Christian" was spoken for the first time in Britain'.[4] Whenever it was first spoken, the word had an entirely different origin than subsequently presented by the church.

Tacitus recorded in *Annals* that Khrestus was in Rome leading Jews in a revolt and his captured followers were:

> . . .after having been daubed over with combustible materials, were set up
> as lights in the night time, and thus brightly burnt to death.

The history of Rome also recorded that Emperor Nero (54–68AD) soaked Galilean criminals 'with tar before having them crucified and used them as human torches around his garden at night'.[5] These were the later followers of Judas Khrestus and they were called 'Khrestians'. That word translated in the English language to 'Christians' and the narrative in the Acts of the Apostles (Acts 11:26) was originally written 'Khrestians', not Christians, and used as 'a term of abuse'.[6]

The nature of the Khrestians

To understand the *New Testament* and some of the beliefs it expounds, it is important to acknowledge the people of those early centuries were semi-savages and their religious systems followed the myths of numerous earlier gods and goddesses. It was Pelops, Zeus' grandson, for example, who in childhood was killed and cooked by his father, Tantalus, the son of Zeus, who then served his son's flesh to the gods as the ultimate sacrifice. Thus, the eating of human flesh (particularly children) and the drinking of human blood occupied a foremost place in the rituals of many early religions.

This ritual was supported by the Khrestians, the now-called 'early Christians', and St Justin Martyr, circa 160, recorded that they were 'intolerable atheists'. He said of their unusual nature:

> . . . they met in secret to eat human flesh and once the lamps had been
> upset, to participate in promiscuous incestuous intercourse.[7]

The Romans pronounced the Khrestians 'public enemies' and looked upon them 'as a downright monsterous phenomena, a third race, a destitute and forsaken people'.[8] Emperor Marcus Aurelius (c. 180) said that Khrestians were a strange and distinct class of people given to a 'new and wicked superstition',[9] while Emperor Theodosius I (379–395), almost 200 years later, recorded:

> The mob that gave Khrestians their name hated them for their crimes, their leader had been put to death under Pontius Pilate, but the deadly superstition spread throughout Judea and even Rome. Some confessed their faith and were arrested; on their testimony, a multitude were convicted of arson, but also of hatred of the human race.[10]

The Second Century Christian apologist Minucius Felix,[11] in a writing attributed to him called *Octavius 9*, confirmed the bizarre behaviour of the Khrestians:

> . . . the names of brother and sister hallow fornification as incest. Their foolish superstition makes a boast of crime; a condemned criminal is the object of their veneration. Finally there is infant murder, cannibalism and the banquet with incestuous intercourse.

The cannibalism associated with this ritual intercourse was reported under the name of Agape[12] and translated to 'love-feasts' in the *New Testament* (Jude 12). This drunken cannibalistic orgy was for centuries the early Khrestian/Christian form of the Eucharist, the drinking of human blood and the eating of human corpse flesh.

The Fourth to Seventh Century Christian saints and bishops had great personal problems with the 'love-feasts'. Jerome (347–420), expressed disgust at the Khrestians for their participation.[13] The Bishop of Hippo, St Augustine, in 395, admitted embarrassment that his own mother, Monica, engaged in those macabre festive banquets. She attended meetings in cemeteries under the cover of darkness where human flesh was eaten from the coffins of dead associates.[14] The Bishop of Milan, Ambrose (333–397) unsuccessfully forbade such practices.[15] They were still being condemned as late as the Trullan Council in 692, some 650 years after the death of Judas Khrestus. It was a widespread and on-going animalistic custom and many of the rabble adopted and accepted the Khrestian/Christian name solely to partake in the 'love-feasts'.[16]

To cover-up the true origin of the name 'Christian', the later church reasoned that 'Khrestus was a Pagan substitute for Christus'[17] and are careful to use the name Christus in a favorable sense. In referring to the records of Tacitus and Suetonius the church argued that those historians 'substituted Khrestus for Christus, or anointed, and Khrestians instead of Christians'.[18] This, the church said,[19] made the early Christian movement appear 'a religion of criminals'.

Many of the now-called persecutions of the early Khrestians/Christians were due solely to the fact that they were criminal activists, not religious devotees. As Marcellinus Ammianis (c. 330–400), the famous Roman historian said of them in his time, 'the atrocity of the Khrestians/Christians against opponents surpasses the fury of wild beasts against men'.[20] The Romans were tolerant of any and all religions, excluding Druidism, but very resentful of anything that savored of political rivalry. And much later, when the Khrestians were finally brought to bear, the field for religious propaganda was wide open.

The messiah of Christianity

Judas Khrestus was the Khrestian/Christian messiah in the true sense of the word, the anointed leader of his Galilean apostles. The learned Christian historian Lardner[21] proved that the name 'Galileans' was the primitive appellation of the Christians.[22] St Epiphanius further recorded that 'all Christians were called Nazarenes'.[23] That word was originally written 'Khrestians', meaning the followers of Judas Khrestus the Galilean, an active revolutionist. Those Galileans were the leaders of 'a new and pernicious sect, which was capable of the most horrid crimes'. The original Khrestians/Christians[24] were the militia of Judas (Krist) Khrestus, 'The Galilean', the twin brother of Rabbi Jesus. Here we see the 'Pagan origin' of the word Christian confessed to earlier by the church.[25]

CHAPTER NINE

The Life of Rabbi Jesus

The prophet steps out

KRIST JESUS BEN PANTHERA TRAINED AS A RABBI IN THE SCHOOL OF Rabbi Hillel (Codex of Hillel) who was the most famous Pharisee of the early first century. Rabbi Hillel taught his students to 'seek peace, love all creatures and bring them closer to the *Torah*',[1] the first five books of the *Old Testament*. Rabbi Jesus was a man of pristine virtue and severity, much devoted to the maintenance of the Law of Moses, carried in the *Torah*. It is important to remember that Rabbi Jesus was raised by the Essenes and taught the faith of the Jewish people in some of the 480 synagogues said to have been in the area at the time (Luke 4:44). To play down the importance of the title 'Rabbi' given to Jesus in older *New Testaments*, some newer editions replaced the original word with the less controversial, 'teacher'. However, Rabbi was used in the oldest and most reliable texts of the *New Testament* and was spelt with a capital 'R'.

Like Judas Khrestus, Rabbi Jesus received his religious education into the secret orders of the Essene Initiates and the records of antiquity reveal that they were associated with 'affiliated communities'.[2] Those records also insisted that Jesus spent time as a youth in Druidic communities in Britain and he was there with Joseph of Arimathea.

Regarding British written records, the whole of Britain's history for the first 500 years of the Christian age is almost entirely blank. Gildas, the first British historian, lived between 516–570 but we also glean a few scattered

MARK 9: 2—9

τοῦ θεοῦ ἐληλυθυῖαν ἐν δυνάμει. 2 Καὶ μετὰ
of the God having come in power. And after

ἡμέρας ἓξ παραλαμβάνει ὁ Ἰησοῦς τὸν
days six is taking along the Jesus the

Πέτρον καὶ τὸν Ἰάκωβον καὶ Ἰωάννην, καὶ
Peter and the James and John, and

ἀναφέρει αὐτοὺς εἰς ὄρος ὑψηλὸν
is bearing up them into mountain lofty

κατ᾽ ἰδίαν μόνους. καὶ
according to private [spot] only (ones). And

μετεμορφώθη ἔμπροσθεν αὐτῶν, 3 καὶ τὰ
he was transfigured in front of them, and the

ἱμάτια αὐτοῦ ἐγένετο στίλβοντα λευκὰ
outer garments of him became glistening white

λίαν οἷα γναφεὺς ἐπὶ τῆς
exceedingly such as clothes cleaner upon the

γῆς οὐ δύναται οὕτως λευκᾶναι. 4 καὶ
earth not is able thus to whiten. And

ὤφθη αὐτοῖς Ἠλείας σὺν Μωυσεῖ,
was seen to them Elijah together with Moses.

καὶ ἦσαν συνλαλοῦντες τῷ Ἰησοῦ.
and they were speaking together with the Jesus.

5 καὶ ἀποκριθεὶς ὁ Πέτρος λέγει τῷ
And having answered the Peter is saying to the

Ἰησοῦ Ῥαββεί, καλόν ἐστιν ἡμᾶς ὧδε εἶναι,
Jesus Rabbi, fine it is here to be,

καὶ ποιήσωμεν τρεῖς σκηνάς, σοὶ μίαν καὶ
and let us make three tents, to you one and

Μωυσεῖ μίαν καὶ Ἠλείᾳ μίαν. 6 οὐ γὰρ
to Moses one and to Elijah one. Not for

ᾔδει τί ἀποκριθῇ, ἔκφοβοι γὰρ
he knew what he should answer, quite fearful for

ἐγένοντο. 7 καὶ ἐγένετο νεφέλη
they became. And came to be cloud

ἐπισκιάζουσα αὐτοῖς, καὶ ἐγένετο φωνὴ
overshadowing them, and came to be voice

ἐκ τῆς νεφέλης Οὗτός ἐστιν ὁ υἱός μου
out of the cloud This is the Son of me

ὁ ἀγαπητός, ἀκούετε αὐτοῦ. 8 καὶ
the beloved, be you hearing him. And

ἐξάπινα περιβλεψάμενοι οὐκέτι οὐδένα
suddenly having looked around not yet no one

εἶδον μεθ᾽ ἑαυτῶν εἰ μὴ τὸν Ἰησοῦν
they saw with themselves if not the Jesus

μόνον.
alone.

9 Καὶ καταβαινόντων αὐτῶν ἐκ τοῦ
And going down of them out of the

ὄρους διεστείλατο αὐτοῖς ἵνα
mountain he gave orders to them in order that

of God already come in power." 2 Accordingly six days later Jesus took Peter and James and John along, and brought them up into a lofty mountain to themselves alone. And he was transfigured before them, 3 and his outer garments became glistening, far whiter than any clothes cleaner on earth could whiten them. 4 Also, E-li'jah with Moses appeared to them, and they were conversing with Jesus. 5 And responsively Peter said to Jesus: "Rabbi, it is fine for us to be here, so let us erect three tents, one for you and one for Moses and one for E-li'jah." 6 In fact, he did not know what response he should make, for they became quite fearful. 7 And a cloud formed, overshadowing them, and a voice came out of the cloud: "This is my Son, the beloved; listen to him." 8 Suddenly, however, they looked around and saw no one with them any longer, except Jesus alone.

9 As they were coming down out of the mountain, he expressly ordered them

This is a section of a word-for-word translation into English from an ancient Greek version of the Gospel of Mark (9:2–9). The second line of Mark 9:5 shows one of the thirteen times Jesus is called Rabbi in the New Testament,
(reprinted from the Greek Interlinear with permission).

scraps of information from Taliesin, the Welsh Prince-Bard and authority on matters Druidical.[3] However, there are four separate and entirely independent traditions that present a consecutive story about Joseph of Arimathea, Jesus and Lazarus travelling regularly to and from Britain.

The first was found in Cornwall and was recorded in Barring-Gould's *Book of Cornwall*. He said that 'Another Cornish story is to the effect that Joseph of Arimathea came in a boat to Cornwall, and brought the boy Jesus with him, and later taught him how to extract tin and purge it from its wolfram. When the tin is flashed, then the tinner shouts, "Joseph was in the trade"'. From the earliest times the British tin miners called him 'Joseph de Mar-more of Arimathea'. 'Mar' was an Eastern word for lord, and 'more' signified 'great'. The interpretation of Joseph's title in this example was 'The great lord Joseph of Arimathea'. Curiously, in some ancient writings, he was also called Joseph of Abarimacie.

The second and third traditions were found in Somerset and provided descriptions of Joseph of Arimathea and Jesus sojourning to a place called Paradise. A letter signed 'Glastonian' in the *Central Somerset Gazette* on 7 August 1936, informed that 'Paradise' was also the ancient Celtic Glastonbury but the writer does not give his/her authority for the statement. It was also said that Joseph of Arimathea and Jesus often stayed at the little Somerset village of Priddy on top of the Mendip Hills. The records of Geoffrey of Monmouth stated that Jesus' grandfather, Roman Emperor Augustus, 'equipped' him 'with weapons' for the journey from Rome[4] and this reference placed Jesus in Britain at least once before the age of twenty-three, for Augustus died in the year 14.

It was significant that all four traditions are entirely independent but are synchronically achievable, and it was equally significant that no tradition existed in Devonshire. The name 'British' was derived from two words in the ancient Hebrew language, B'rith meaning Covenant' and 'ish' meaning a man or woman. Joined as one word, British meant 'Covenant man or woman' and the Druids considered themselves Covenanters like the Essenes. An argument in favour of these traditions was that the continental Essenes sent their neophyte priests to 'auxiliary branches' in Britain to undergo special training at the hands of Druid priests, and Jesus was one of them. The Essene doctrine was 'So closely associated with Druidism that its origin may be said to have been Druidic'[5] and the Druid's beliefs were the same as those entertained by the Essenes.[6] 'From a close study of their religious beliefs, everything points to the fact that the Kimmerians (ancestors of the Celts) held fast to the patriarchal faith of the *Old Testament*' and so did the Essenes.[7]

The Essenes maintained mainly secluded communities throughout the whole of the Roman occupied territory 'and in every town the Order had its respective 'house'.[8] Except when toiling in the fields, they dressed invariably in white linen robes. 'They cultivated obedience, truthfulness, continence, justice and temperance. The initiated members ate alone. They laid claim to magical powers and the ability to predict . . . it is enough to say that between Essenism in certain aspects and Christianity there are some points of resemblance'.[9] They were 'a very numerous sect'[10] and Pliny and Philo estimated their numbers at four thousand in the Palestine area alone during the First Century. They were famous not only as religious teachers of the Law of Moses, but were especially noted for their vast knowledge of herbal medicines. Josephus recorded that they:

> . . . have a profound knowledge of the art of healing, and study it arduously.
> They examine herbs and plants, which they prepare as medicine for man
> and beasts. They also know the use and worth of minerals as medicines,
> and do a great deal of good by applying these for healing the sick.

Josephus said that 'many of the Essenes have often stepped forth among the people as healers and prophets' and because of their knowledge of natural therapies they became known as the Therapeute, 'the healers, the ones who laid their hands upon' (applying their herbal ointments). This was part of the role of the pious Rabbi Jesus and many examples of his well meaning can be found in the *New Testament*. Before his official dispatch into the world as a prophet, he was baptized by his cousin, John the Baptist. Baptism, or the application of water, was a rite well known to the general community before the time of the Gospels and, according to Reverend J.P. Lundy,[11] was introduced sometime after the Babylonian captivity (c. 397BC). The Essenes purified themselves frequently, using a ceremony common to many earlier religions. Once they were 'made clean from some supposed pollution or defilement', they hated to be touched by anybody.

> Extreme importance was attached to ceremonial purity, and they followed
> scrupulously the prescriptions against Levitical defilements; even for a junior
> to touch a senior was pollution to the later.[12]

There are references in the *New Testament* to Rabbi Jesus resisting being touched—'Do not touch me', he said in the Gospel of Mark.[13]

It is worth noting the so-called 'Messianic Rule' found among the *Dead Sea Scrolls* recorded all male members of their community were, at the age of thirty years, regarded as mature and ready to serve the public. The *New Testament* revealed, 'Rabbi Jesus, when he began his ministry was about thirty years of age' (Luke 3:23). In the canonical Mark and John Gospels, the 'original Hebrew' version of Matthew's Gospel and the earliest Luke Gospel, it was at this age that Rabbi Jesus' story began and at this time, he would have been a married man. 'Eighteen years is the age of the nuptial canopy', says the Rabbinical text on the stages of life.

Jesus' first two wives

From information given in the Gospels, it was clear that Rabbi Jesus was married. The Jewish records stated that he was a Rabbi teaching and living the religious beliefs of the Law of Moses, which provided for marriage. In fact, it was quite proper within that Law for Rabbi Jesus to have had several wives at the same time, Noah's father, Lamech, being the first polygamist recorded in the Bible. The belief that Jesus was married was supported by his title 'Rabbi', a term that translates as 'My Master'. Jesus was called 'Rabbi' thirteen times in the *New Testament* and therefore he had to be married for the Jewish Mishnaic Law of the time specifically stated 'an unmarried man may not be a Rabbi'. From information recorded in old church writings and other ancient texts, it was possible to determine that Rabbi Jesus was married three times.

His first wife was Princess Cypros, a Nabateean Arab and daughter of Cypros and Alexas. Cypros was also her mother's name and she was King Herod's granddaughter. Rabbi Jesus' first wife was not mentioned by name in the *New Testament* but was recorded in the family tree of King Herod. Her uncle was Joseph of Arimathea who was also the brother of Berenice, the mother of Mariamne Herod and Herodias.[14] Rabbi Jesus and Princess

Cypros had five children, three boys, Adminius, Guiderius and Caradoc, and two girls, Eurgain (Eigan) and Gladys.

Rabbi Jesus' marriage to Princess Cypros was indirectly responsible for the establishment of Christianity today. To determine when, where, and how they met is now almost impossible to establish. There was no documentary church evidence available to assist in providing more detail on this marriage, nor should we expect to find it, but once 'the true name of Jesus Christ' was known, it was possible to establish the historicity of the union. Under Rabbinic law, it seemed certain that Rabbi Jesus was married at, or before, the age of eighteen and this being so, he and Princess Cypros would most probably have lived with one of the Essene sects that Josephus said accepted marriage. The importance of the part played in world history by the children of their marriage will become apparent as the story unfolds.

There is much to be said about Rabbi Jesus' second wife, Mary Magdalene, and support that he was romantically involved with her commenced with some Gospels suppressed early in church history. In the Gospel of Mary, for example, was recorded that Rabbi Jesus 'loved' Mary Magdalene while the Gospel of Philip said he 'used to kiss her often on the mouth'. In an ancient undated writing found by Rev. W. D. Mahon in the St Sophia Mosque at Constantinople in 1883, was told the story of:

> . . . an old man who lived on the road to Bethany who once had been a rabbi, a man of great learning, and well skilled in the Law [of Moses], and that Jesus was often there with him reading the Law; that his name was Massalian, and that I might find Jesus there with him; But he was not there. Massalian said he was often at Bethany with his family, and he thought there was some love affair between him and one of the girls. I asked him if he had seen anything like a courtship between them. He said he had not, but inferred from their intimacy and from his fondness on the woman's part as well as from the laws of nature, that such would be the case.

Mary Magdalene was portrayed throughout the Gospel stories in the constant presence of Rabbi Jesus and as a leader. All four Gospel accounts mention her first when speaking of the group of twelve women associated with the story of Rabbi Jesus. In the Byzantine Chronicles, she was recorded to have been in Rome with Rabbi Jesus at the time of the trial of Judas Khrestus. The records showed she played a leading role in his life, in fact, Mary Magdalene and the other ladies, financed the ministry of Rabbi Jesus (Luke 8:3).

Nowhere in the Gospels of the New Testament does it say that Mary Magdalene was a prostitute. More importantly, the only detrimental Gospel statement regarding Mary Magdalene' reputation was carried in Fourth Century interpolations that make up the last twelve verses at the end of the

Mark Gospel today but are not in the earliest New Testaments currently available. For that reason most modern Bibles delete these narratives, or index them to a special footnote advising readers that they were later interpolations into the Bible. So why did the early church prevent further investigation into Mary Magdalene's activities and why did it wish her discredited in this fashion?

The well-established Christian image of Mary Magdalene as a prostitute is a slander not based on fact and, like so many other stories inspired by a censorious church, has long been proved nonsense. Despite all attempts by Christian historians to cast her as a redeemed prostitute, there is no external or Gospel evidence to that effect. So who really was Mary Magdalene?

The most difficult question in Bible history

The Roman Catholic church has always denied that 'our Lady, the Blessed Virgin Mary' was anything but a virgin, or that she had other children. However, the Gospels recorded that she had seven children and the quality of the evidence to dispute the church claim is relevant to Mary Magdalene.

The Gospels of Mark (6:3) and Matthew (13:55) claimed James the Younger, Joses (Joseph in some translations), Judas Thomas and Simon, were the sons of Virgin Mary and therefore the brothers of Rabbi Jesus. In other areas of the Mark Gospel (3:18) and the Matthew Gospel (10:3), the authors advised James the Younger was the son of Philip (Herod), which implied Virgin Mary had children by a second husband. On this matter, Smith's *Bible Dictionary* admitted that 'This is one of the most difficult questions in Bible history'.

The Gospels also stated that Rabbi Jesus had sisters but only one— Salóme[15]—was named. That there was more than one was clearly stated in the Matthew Gospel (13:56) when discussing Rabbi Jesus the author referred to 'all his sisters'. The brothers of Jesus were married[16] and this chapter shall determine that 'all his sisters' were also married. Just who their husbands were is important in establishing at least one reason why Mary Magdalene was defamed.

Ancient church tradition maintained that one of Rabbi Jesus' sisters was named Maria, or as recorded in some early Gospels, Margi. That this 'Maria/ Margi of Christian tradition' was the 'elusive' Mary Magdalene is a conclusion that can be supported. The names of all Rabbi Jesus' sisters can be determined by combining the incomplete Gospel documentation with the writings of the early presbyters and the suppressed Gospels. But first it is important to clarify a vital Gospel statement, which claimed Lazarus and Martha were Mary of Bethany's brother and sister.

Great artists symbolically depicted the Virgin Mary with seven children. This one is by Jean Fouquet (1415–1484) called 'The Virgin Surrounded by Red Angels'; Antwerp Museum. The 'Red Angels' number 6, and the baby in arms makes 7. See another similar concept painted by Stefan Lochner, c.1451.

© Film Library of Renaissance Art. Italy.

There is substantial reason for regarding Mary of Bethany and Mary Magdalene as the same person. The early presbyters Irenaeus (115–202), Quintus Tertullian (160–210) and Origen (185–251) certainly considered them to be so as did popular tradition at the end of the Second Century.[17] Many biblical scholars of today concur.

Adding further to the biblical construction of Mary's name, Magdalene came to be taken as meaning 'from the area of Magdala'. Today Magdala is presented as a wealthy and depraved First Century Roman holiday resort situated six miles south of Capernaum in Galilee, not far from the famous mineral springs at Tiberius. However, in the Gospel of Mark (8:10), Magdala was curiously called Dalmanutha and this word will shortly be shown to be a secret editorial *New Testament* cipher revealing a far different location for Magdala. However, had Mary Magdalene moved to Bethany, she would traditionally have been called Mary of Bethany, and this is an important point in determining that Mary Magdalene and Mary of Bethany were the same person.

If Mary Magdalene and Mary of Bethany were one and the same person, and the sister of Rabbi Jesus called Margi or Maria in early church tradition was Mary from Magdala (or Bethany), that made Martha and Lazarus half-sister and brother to Rabbi Jesus. If so, this would have meant the so-called Virgin Mary (Mariamne Herod) had four paramours and nine children, including the twins. They were the Roman father (Tiberius Panthera) of Jesus and Judas Thomas (the twins), the unnamed father of Jose and Simon,[18] Philip (Herod), father of James the Younger and Salóme[19] and Cyrus, the father of Mary (Magdalene née Bethany), Martha and Lazarus (Gospel of James).

Mary Magdalene's name was again found in documentation first published in Latin in 1275 entitled 'The Golden Legend' which was compiled from a variety of early Gospels by the Bishop of Genoa, Jacobus de Voragine (1230–1298). Whatever its substance 'The Golden Legend' emanated from a very early source and importantly, for what is being established here, recorded Lazarus and Martha were Mary Magdalene's brother and sister. The canonical Gospel of John (11:5) stated Rabbi Jesus 'loved Martha and her sister [Mary of Bethany, née Mary Magdalene] and Lazarus'. The Golden Legend also provided a reference drawn from the Second Century Gospel of James (Protevangelion) that stated Mary Magdalene was actually a woman of noble birth. A 15th Century English translation of this work said:

> Mary Eucharis Magdalene had her surname of Magdala, a castle and was born of right noble lineage and her parents which were descendant of the lineage of Kings. And her father was named Cyrus and her mother also Mary (Mariamne Herod) Eucharis.

Both Mary Magdalene and her mother's middle names are strikingly similar to the central act of Christian worship, the Eucharist, and the suspicion was that the ancient rites were conducted by those two women and the ceremonies became known as the 'Eucharist'.

There is ever fascination to be found in a name and that of 'Mary Magdalene' is no exception. It seldom fails to intrigue the mind, creating a curious desire to learn what it may mean and how it was derived. In names, as shown herein, invariably is found the key that unlocks the door to an age-old mystery. At the time of the First Century, the Roman words for 'Castle on a Hill' were Margi-dvnvm.[20] Here then we see the origin of the name Margi Magdalene found in some old Gospels. It derived from 'Margi from the Castle Magdala' and supported the Gospel of James (Protevangelion) reference to the royal status of Mary Magdalene. The name Margi Magdala subsequently evolved to Maria/Mary Magdalene in centuries of translation variations. Whatever Berenger Saunière discovered at Rennes-le-Chateau was a secret directly associated with Mary Magdalene, and the castle-like constructions he built and called 'Bethanie' (Bethany) and 'Magdala' seem to point to the fact that he knew the royal nature of Mary Magdalene and the real location of the Magdala Castle.

In this scene from a medieval tapestry portraying Mary Magdalene, the building in the background indicates the Castle Magdala. The curious headgear has remarkable parallels to the draped female figure shown on many First Century royal Celtic coins—see examples later in this chapter. Note the Celtic Cross on the figure on the right.

© The Collected Works; Florence

The renaming of 'Magdala' to 'Dalmanutha' in the Gospel of Mark provided a vital clue in establishing the real location of Magdala. The church extended the opinion that 'Dalmanutha in Mark's Gospel might be a corruption of Dalmantius', who was a nephew of Constantine the Great (d. 337). This was a curious statement, for the church claimed the Gospel of Mark was written 300 years before the time of Constantine.[21] The knowledge that Sir Francis Bacon coded secret information into the Bible provided a more supportable solution, and led to an examination of ancient maps.

The word Dalmanutha was a modern translation variation of Delmetia, sometimes also interpreted Delmethia. It was an area of Britain in South Wales, and then bounded on the south by the 'sea called Severn' and on the west by the Demetian Sea.[22] It was here that the able antagonist of Julius Caesar's invasion (c. 54BC) of Britain, King Caswallon the First (Cassivellaunos to the Romans) had his Castle Magdala. Upon the death of King Caswallon, his nephew, Tenvantius, the son of King Lud and the Duke of Cornwall, became King of Britain. With the multiplicity of names then given to leaders, Tenvantius may also be the person called Addedomaros in the records of that period. It was also possible that he adopted the title

Caswallon the Second, for this person was recorded in one old record as the father of Lazarus. If he was the father of Lazarus, he was also the father of Martha and Mary Magdalene. The name Tenvantius, however, was an ancient variation of Cyrus, recorded in the Gospel of James as being a 'descendant of the lineage of Kings,' father of Mary Magdalene, Martha and Lazarus, and all 'born of right noble lineage'. Mary Magdalene's father was King of Britain and she was a Celtic Princess, and probably a Druid priestess.[23] Prince Lazarus and Princess Martha, Mary Magdalene's brother and sister, were also royal Celts, and half brother and sisters of Rabbi Jesus.

Documented twice in the Bible was the tradition that accepted incest to be approved by God. Moses' parents, for example, were made to be nephew and aunt (Gen. 6:20), and Abraham clearly stated Sarah was 'the daughter of my father but not the daughter of my mother; and she became my wife' (Gen. 20:12). Therefore, under the biblical Law of Moses, it was quite proper and correct for Rabbi Jesus to have married his half-sister, Princess Maria/Margi (Mary Magdalene), and lived with her and several other wives at the same time. This may be the reason why the later church tried to disassociate Rabbi Jesus from Princess Mary Magdalene who, in this premise, was the Virgin Mary's daughter from another marriage. Similar to his first marriage to Princess Cypros, it was possible that it was an 'arranged' royal marriage, as was the well established practice of the time.

The New Testament clearly substantiated the practice of marrying one's sister, 'We have authority to lead about a sister as a wife, even as the followers and the Lord's brothers and Cephas, do we not'.[24]

This narrative clearly stated two of Rabbi Jesus' brothers were married to their two remaining sisters, Martha and Salóme. If this narrative presented a correct picture of what the author originally conceived, it showed a tradition of regal family inter-marrying.

What was generally believed the story of a woman called Mary of Egypt was later adopted and applied to Mary Magdalene as the Gospel stories evolved. Mary of Egypt was a Third Century prostitute from Alexandria who solicited business among the pilgrims en route to Jerusalem. Subsequently she gave up her whore's life, became very devout and lived as a female hermit in the Syrian Desert. She was later canonised for her alleged miracle of walking across the waters of the Jordan to take Holy Communion.

The possibility that the church's Jesus Christ was married many times and fathered numerous children causes Christian believers to react with utter horror. The church defense for such a suggestion was to point out the lack of documentation in the Gospels that specifically said Rabbi Jesus was married. Just as relevant there was no statement in the Gospels that said Jesus was not married either. In fact, there was a deathly silence throughout the New Testament regarding Rabbi Jesus' marital status. Morton Smith, Professor of Ancient History at Columbia University, USA, found a document in the Mar Saba Monastery near Jerusalem in 1958 revealing evidence that Rabbi Jesus' marriages was deliberately removed from the Gospels by church decree at the Fifth Ecumenical Council in Constantinople in 553.[25] The numerous connotations and indirect references in the current version of the Gospels, however, strongly suggested the authors were under the firm impression that Rabbi Jesus was married. Whether the wedding ceremony only found in the Gospel of John was actually one of Rabbi Jesus' could be discussed until the cows come home, but it probably was.

Sex was clearly encouraged by the God of the *Old Testament*, particularly for recreational purposes[26] and Rabbi Jesus and Judas Khrestus did not make celibacy a pre-requisite when commissioning their supporters. Many, if not all, were married.[27] Records established that Simon of Petra married Jotape 'who accompanied him everywhere'[28] and fathered at least two children, a boy and a girl, while Paul said he had been married but was widowed.[29] In the ancient writings of Clement of Alexandria (160–215) he noted that the disciple Philip, as well as Simon, brother of Judas Khrestus and Rabbi Jesus, had married and produced families. Clement's records supported the claims that Rabbi Jesus' brothers married their sisters.[30] In the Gospel of Matthew, Rabbi Jesus himself declared 'a man shall leave his father and mother and be joined to his wife' (Matt.19:5). Given the traditions of the time, Rabbi Jesus practiced what he preached.

St Mary of Egypt, the reformed prostitute. She is shown in paintings wearing nothing but long hair. This one was by Quentin Massys, c. 1510.
© Film Library of Renaissance Art. Italy.

Rabbi Jesus' name changes

In the *British Chronicles*, King Tenvantius was recorded as the father of a man called Cunobeline, the terminology in this application meaning 'absorbed into the family by marriage'. This was a well-established adoptive naming practice of the times (Alford's Regio Fides) and from information available, it seemed that when Rabbi Jesus married Mary Magdalene, he was given the name, Cunobeline. The structure of the title, Cunobeline, represented spiritual renewal over carnal death (Cuno—carnal, death, mortify; Bel–Baal—sun, new-life, re-birth) and may have been applied to Rabbi Jesus during some form of Celtic initiation.[31] Later historians recorded Cunobeline in various languages as Cynfelyn, Cynvelin, Cuno-belin or Cunobelinus, but to avoid confusion we shall call him Rabbi Jesus Cunobeline during this period of his life.

Rabbi Jesus Cunobeline was the 'Cymbeline' of Shakespeare (Act 3, Scene 1), immortalised in the lines, 'The lofty cedar, royal Cymbeline, Personates thee'. We now know this person as Jesus Christ, and the hidden Gospel story was parodied in Shake-speare's Plays. Maybe 'Cym' of Cym-beline was an abbreviated clue leading to 'Cymric', the ancient Celtic language, and 'beline' (Cym-beline), we know, meant 'new life'.[32] If so, the name 'Cymbeline' could be a coded Francis Bacon cipher, meaning 'a new life for Rabbi Jesus with the Celts'.

First Century Celtic coin depicting Cunobeline
© World Coins, Celtic

The name Tascio-vanus was also applied to Rabbi Jesus Cunobeline and was supported by the existence of First Century coins, but a person with this name was 'wholly unknown to history'.[33] Tascio-vanus was an applied term only, 'analogous to the Divine Caesar title of the Roman emperors' and was later expressed by various language experts to mean, Theomantius, Theo-mantis, Theo-man and Toma, meaning 'twin' in Aramaic (twin-man?). The Celtic Tascio-vanus coins directly connected Rabbi Jesus Cunobeline with the Caesar line of Rome.

First Century Celtic coin showing the word Tascio and two heads in profile, one bearded (Twins?)
© World Coins, Celtic

First Century Celtic coins show two differing draped female heads. In Royal tradition, the minting of coins depicted only Kings, Queens, Princesses and Princes. Maybe these particular coins show two of Rabbi Jesus Cunobeline's three Royal wives.
© World Coins, Celtic

Rabbi Jesus Cunobeline, with Mary Magdalene, produced another two children and their names, Princes Cadwalladr and Polydore, are not recorded in the canonical Gospels. In one *New Testament* narrative alone, however, the names of two of Rabbi Jesus Cunobeline's grandchildren are recorded, and they were the inheritors of King Cyrus' ancestral estates in Britain.

The commencement of the British church

The two things that strike the investigator of early Christian history are the rarely discussed records of the exodus of the main Gospel personalities to Britain after the sale and dispatch of Judas Khrestus, and the manner in which the Roman church dismissed the mass departure as insignificant. Ancient church tradition maintained that some primary Gospel characters also settled in the Southern France area:

The evangelization of Gaul has often been attributed to missionaries sent
from Rome by St Clement, a theory which has inspired a whole series of
fallacious narratives and forgeries, with which history is encumbered. Most
likely the first missionaries came by sea, and touched at Marseilles . . .[34]

The first 'missionaries' were not missionaries in the modern church portrayal
of the word. A realistic account of events was recorded in a writing carried
in an 11th Century manuscript[35] that recorded a cumulative French and
British tradition maintaining that after the Roman authorities discovered
the fabricated nature of Judas Khrestus' crucifixion, Joseph of Arimathea,
Mary Magdalene, and members of her family fled 'from the city of Rome'[36]
by sea to Marseilles (Massila) and some re-established their lives in that area.
Tradition also maintained 'Lazarus and some women, and some companions,
landed in Provence at a place today called Saintes-Maries.'[37] From what
records were available, everything associated with their departure pointed
to haste. Mary Magdalene herself was said to have eventually retired to a
hilltop residence at Provence at a place that came to be later called La Sainte-
Baume, where she lived for thirty years until her death in 63.[38] At the
'invitation of certain Druids of high rank'[39] Bishop Eusebius recorded that
some of the group 'passed beyond the ocean to the Isles called the Britannic
Isles.'[40] They were the founders of the Celtic church (c. 37) in Britain that
preceded the establishment of the Roman church by around 300 years.

While there are many learned minds dating from that era onward that
provided a similar record of a curious exodus, there is special advantage in
quoting from a most eminent church historian who used Vatican records to
compile a twelve-volume work called Annales ecclesiastici. He was Cardinal
Caesar Baronius (1538–1607), and was considered the most outstanding
historian of the Roman Catholic church.[41] Baronius, who turned down
two offers to become Pope in 1605, confirmed Eusebius' report:

> In that year the party mentioned was exposed to the sea in a vessel without
> sails or oars. The vessel drifted finally to Marseilles and they were saved.
> From Marseilles, Joseph of Arimathea and some of his company passed
> into Britain and there died.[42]

This event in British history may come as a surprise to many Christians,
but there was substantial church evidence to support the knowledge of the
journey and its outcome.

In Vatican records, the exiles were called the Bethany Group and included
not only Joseph of Arimathea, but 'Martial and Trophimus'. The Recognitions
of Clement recorded that 'the family of Joseph, his servents and twelve others,
including Zachaeus' (father of John the Baptist?) were included in the journey.
'Zachaeus stopped at a place called Rocamadour; Joseph and his household

continued on their way to Morlaix in Brittany, there to wait for suitable weather conditions to cross to Britain . . . four days sail.' Joseph of Arimathea's move to Britain was constantly attested to in church records. It was a subject of debate at various European church councils for centuries, with the English being able to claim an earlier church connection with the family of the royal twin boys long before any at Rome. At the Council of Pisa in 1409 there was even an argument about whether Joseph of Arimathea or Mary Magdalene had come first to Britain.

Old photograph of mystic stone centre in the ancient Celtic world of Brittany, 1909.
© Estate of Cyril L. M. Owen; Wales

It was interesting to note that the Bethany Group was never referred to as Christians, or even later when the name was in common usage. They were called Céli Dé, or Culdich, which was Anglicized to Culdees, as were other members of their group who arrived there some time later. The interpretation of the word 'Culdee' was 'Essene Initiates' or 'Krists', and the Bethany Group subsequently founded a college of twelve holy Druids who came to be called Culdees, the word being purely of the Celto-British language.[43] The Culdee name later was attached to their first given name such as Angus the Culdee and they were generally understood to be Celtic monks expounding a particular brand of esoteric knowledge.

Some of the Culdees traveled back and forth to various parts of Gaul, with Lazarus settling at Marseilles and reputedly dying there early in the second half of the First Century. A 'sister and friends of Lazarus' were said to have 'progressed up the Rhone valley' and established themselves at Lyons, 'but it was not thought necessary [for the church] to enquire why they should be found in France'.[44] The 'sister' traveling with Lazarus was either Mary Magdalene, Martha, his full-blood sisters, or Salome, his half sister. The only record we possess of Lazarus beyond the Gospels is a very ancient British publication called 'Triads of Primitive Britain'. It is difficult to explain how the name of Lazarus could find its way into these peculiarly British memorials except by his presence in Britain. It was also interesting to observe that Irenaeus, one of the earliest church presbyters, 'went to south-western Gaul' before he began his orations at Lyons in France. The conclusion drawn is this: Mary Magdalene, Lazarus and Martha were originally Britons who hastily returned home after supporting Judas Khrestus' uprising and then assisting with the fake crucifixion in Rome. With Princess Mary Magdalene was her husband, Rabbi Jesus Cunobeline, his first wife Princess Cypros, and their seven children, and the possibility exists that most of the children, if not all, were earlier born in Britain.

It was recorded that Emperor Caligula banished Herod Antipas to Lyons, Gaul in 41 and although he permitted his wife, Herodias, Mariamne Herod's sister, to return to her home, she chose to accompany her husband into exile. The Gospels stated that Herodias earlier had a daughter named Salome to her uncle, Herod Philip I (Mark 6:17). The Gospels also stated that Mary (Mariamne Herod), the mother of Jesus, also had a daughter named Salome to Philip.[45] Professor Eisenman revealed that 'Philip in the Gospels is Herod (Philip)'. Therefore, either Herodias and Mariamne Herod both had a daughter to uncle Herod Philip and both named Salome, or one of the Gospel narratives is incorrect. The whole Herod family, however, were now back together and generally based in Southern France. Rabbi Jesus Cunobeline's wives and children, and Martial (eight years old), being some of the unnamed 'twelve others' in the Bethany Group (The Recognitions of Clement), along with Joseph of Arimathea and Trophimus all went on to Britain. There they had a meeting with Mary Magdalene's father, King Cyrus (Tenvantius), who granted them 1920 acres of land that was originally called the Sanctuary of the Krists ('Essene Initiates'). It was later renamed the Isle of the Krists[46] and then, the Isle of Avalon. Today it is called Glastonbury, and there commenced the development of the British church.

The 'twelve holy Druids'

The documentation of events in Britain during the first half of the First Century are so disconnected with the modern day church presentation of the origin of Christianity that few realize the Roman church was still centuries away from being established. 'Three times the antiquity of the British church was affirmed in Ecclesiastical Councila: 1. The Council of Pisa, 1417AD; 2. The Council of Constance, 1419AD; 3. The Council of

Siena, 1423AD. It was stated that the British church took precedence over all other churches, being founded by Joseph of Arimathea.'[47] For early information about Britain, historians are obliged to turn to Julius Caesar, Dio Cassius, Tacitus, Suetonius and other later Roman writers, whom they too often accept as wholly accurate, forgetting that in many cases those writers viewed Britain through enemy Roman eyes. Julius Caesar's description of Britain as 'barbaric' is often taken in the modern sense of the word, but to the Roman of the times, the word applied merely to all who were not Roman, in the same relationship as Gentile to Jew. The available records revealed that Britain, in those days, possessed a highly developed civilization and culture, and excluding the 'warriors of war', was anything but barbaric in the modern sense of the word.

Diodorus Siculus (d. 14AD) described the people of Britain as 'civilized and courteous to strangers. They are of much sincerity and integrity, far from the craft and knavery of men among us, contended with plain and homely fare, and strangers to the excess and luxury of rich men.' From other descriptions of the Britons, we read that their ordinary clothing was of 'tartan, spun, coloured and woven by themselves. The upper classes wore collars and bracelets of gold and necklaces of amber. The chiefs were armed with helmets, shields and cuirasses of leather, bronze or mail-chains, while their many weapons of defence—darts, pikes and broadswords—were often richly worked and ornamented'.[48] This was the Britain with which Joseph of Arimathea was familiar, and where his name had become widely known.

The Bethany Group's connection with the development of the original British church was recorded in the oldest of historic texts and was intermingled with a mass of unique earlier local traditions maintaining Joseph of Arimathea lived a large part of his life in Southern Britain. It was also said that he died there aged seventy-six and was buried at Glastonbury. Those traditions may be summarized and explained as follows—Joseph of Arimathea gained his wealth as an importer in the tin trade that operated between Cornwall and Phoenicia. The Phoenician territory consisted of an extensive coastal strip on the western seaboard of the Mediterranean from the tip of Mt. Carmel to Sidon, 120 miles, and a hinterland of twenty miles stretching to the western slopes of the Galilean hills. Herodotus (445BC) referred to the existence of a long-established metal trade between Cornwall and Phoenicia and called the British Isles the Tin Islands or Cassiterides. Pytheas, circa 352–323BC also mentioned the British tin trade, as did Polybius, circa 160BC. Tin from Cornwall was also shipped around to Colchester and was used in minting British money. The oldest graves discovered in Cornwall at Harlyn Bay, near Padstow, were believed to have been the earliest settlers, and some think the first tin workers.[49] Associated with the mines of Cornwall was the mining of lead, copper and other metals in the Mendips, which formed alloys with tin. An ancient pig of lead found in the area bore the stamp of Britannicus, the son of Roman Emperor Claudius (10BC–54AD), and established that mining of lead in the Cornwall area was being pursued in the first half of the First Century.

Diodorus Siculus also gave a detailed description of the trade, explaining that tin was mined on the mainland and then carried for shipping to an island called Ictis or Mictis, joined to the mainland at low tide, which is generally held today to be Mount St Michael in Cornwall.

From there, it was shipped across the Channel (then called the Gallican Gulf) to Morlaix in Brittany, and then transported overland down through France to Marseilles on packhorses.[50] From Marseilles, it was then re-shipped to Phoenicia. The tin mines of Cornwall were the source of the world's supply in those days, and its export to Phoenicia provided the most suitable outlet for its use in the civilized Grecian world.

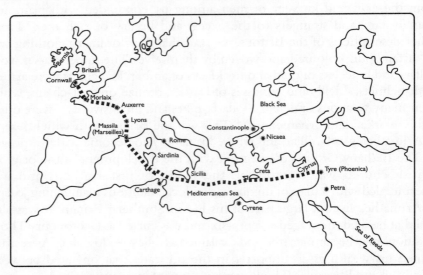

The traditional metal trade route from Cornwall to Phoenicia

Joseph of Arimathea should not be viewed as a lone figure on British shores in pursuit of his mining interests but rather as a rich man of those days travelling with a considerable retinue and with entrée to the Royal Court. By the testimony of ancient Chronicles, he became the ancestor of a long line of British princes and princesses. His marriage to Mariamne Herod produced Jose and Simon[51] and the name Jose, or Josephes in some translations, appeared in several heraldic charts as the husband of a British Princess.[52] There was nothing recorded to indicate whether the high office of 'Nobilis Decurio' was conferred upon Joseph by Pontius Pilate, or possibly one of the Roman Emperors, for he lived in a time when honours were showered upon the families and friends of the leaders at every celebration.

Church writings claimed Joseph owned 'numerous fleets of fine ships'[53] and that he 'lived at a "menage" in Britain that never paid "geld" nor tax'.[54] Cardinal Baronius' records supported a similar statement in the *Domesday Book* of 1086 that said the 'Glastonbury church possesses in its own ville XII hides of land which have never paid tax'.[55] One hide of land equalled 160 acres and was deemed by the King sufficient to maintain a man and his family. The twelve 'Essene Initiates' among the Bethany Group received one hide each (12 X 160 acres = 1920 acres combined) and subsequently founded a college or Celtic monastery of 'twelve holy Druids' on the gifted land at Glastonbury.[56]

The date of 1086 was not the date of the writing of the *Domesday Book* but represented the time in which King William collated a series of earlier writings into one book. The original record of the gift of land was first found referenced in a manuscript called The Anglo-Saxon Chronicle that was created by King Alfred the Great in 871 and now preserved in the British Museum. The *Domesday Book* appeared to be a continuation of The Anglo-Saxon Chronicle that corroborated the original deed of the twelve hides of land and its tax-free grant. Of the gifted land the Anglo-Saxon Chronicle originally stated:

> With this land grant a document was furnished setting forth the legal aspect of the gift, which gave the recipients many British concessions including right of citizenship and all the privileges accorded to the Druidic hierarchy. Every Druid was entitled to one hide of land, free of tax, freedom to pass unmolested from one district to another in time of war, and access to secret ceremonies at Stonehenge.

The words of history recorded that the 'Essene Initiates' were 'joyously invested with all the privileges of Druidism'[57] by 'Druids of high rank'[58] who invited the Bethany Group to British shores.

Jesus adopted the Druidic wisdom

Upon the ceremonial acceptance of the land, Rabbi Jesus Cunobeline forgave his Rabbinic teachings and became a member of the sacred order of the Druidic priesthood. He was now symbolically regarded as 'twice born' or 'born again' into the Druidic life of elevated enlightenment that incorporated the sign of the Sun.

In many pre-Christian secret religious societies, it was customary to refer to initiates as Phoenix's or men who had been 'born again' after agreeing to accept a higher level of knowledge secretly passed down from the first custodians of divine revelation. The Druids had an entry level into their ranks consisting of three separate degrees of training through which their members were required to pass before being allowed access to the most secret religious mysteries. The few who passed the life-threatening third degree were said to be 'born again' and were then permitted to learn the ancient hidden teachings the Druid priests had preserved from antiquity. By accepting the gifted land at Glastonbury, it seemed the twelve Krists were not required to undergo Druid training for they were already high initiates and became honorary 'holy Druids'.

It was said the Druid initiates enjoyed the special favour of the divinities and were thus worthy of the title 'twice born' for they had come to second birth from the womb of the mysteries, and as such, were considered truly evolved human beings. From these high-ranking initiates were chosen many of the dignitaries of the British religious and political world. The Druids had a Madonna with a child in her arms and at dawn on the twenty-fifth day of December, the birth of the Sun god was celebrated. Both the symbol of the cross and the serpent were sacred to the Druids. This very ancient 'born again' concept can now be found in the Gospel of John, 'Unless a man be born again, he cannot see the kingdom of God' (John 3:3). In the words of Rabbi Jesus Cunobeline, a person was not considered 'twice born' until he was initiated into higher levels of esoteric understanding.

Druidism was regarded by the Romans as its greatest religious opponent, partly because its headquarters was Britain, and partly because of its very widespread influence opposed to Roman and Greek mythology. This influence might be summed up in the words of the historian Hume, 'No religion has ever swayed the minds of men like the Druidic'. In the time of Rabbi Jesus Cunobeline, it could claim a past history of at least 2000 years and a familiar triad summarized its ancient principles, 'Three duties of every man; Worship God; be just to all men; die for your country'. It was its religious tenets or philosophy that caused Druidism to be marked for destruction by an empire to universal dominion and to merge all nationalities in one city. The Roman political attitude towards it was evinced by the Edicts of Augustus and Tiberius that clearly proclaimed to 'abolish Druidism'[59] by making the exercise of the functions of a Druid priest a treasonable offence.

The difficulty of admission into the Druidic order was on a par with its privileges and the barriers of admission threw the Order almost entirely into the hands of the aristocracy, making it literally a 'royal priesthood'. Kings, princes, and nobles largely made up its composition. The authority and influence of the Druids were very great, and, overall, as popular as they were great. The extreme penalty lodged in their hands, and the one most dreaded, was that of excommunication which was, in fact, a decree of expulsion from both worlds, present and future. The temples of the Druids were circular and obelitic, i.e. open above and on every side, representing in forms the dome of heaven, on which metal was not allowed to come. The altar in the Druidic circle was called 'cromlech' (stone of adoration) and a nearby hollowed stone captured untouched 'holy water' direct from rainclouds. No Druidic service could be celebrated before sunrise or after sunset. The circular forms of the temples symbolled the eternal cycle of nature and ceremonial avenues leading to and from the temples were sometimes seven miles long. The national religious processions moved slowly through these on the three great festivals of the year.

In the First Century, the Druidic institutions were the largest in the world, both in size and in attendance. In Britain, alone they had a recorded number of sixty universities and over 60,000 enrolled students.[60] When the great range of acquirements that the system included is understood, we can wonder why it required twenty years of time to fully master the circle of Druidic knowledge. Ancient Britain had acquired a stature with institutions of learning that rivalled those of today and many elected to study there. Greek and Roman testimony stated that the noble and wealthy of Athens and Rome sent their children to study law, science and religion in Britain. The determined efforts of the Roman Empire to overthrow its supremacy, and, if possible, suppress it altogether, prove that its rulers had been made practically aware of this fact.

King Jesus Cunobeline

When King Tenvantius died, Rabbi Jesus Cunobeline became 'King of Britain'[61] and the pious domestic name then given to him was Bran the Blessed (Bran ab Fendigaid). Bran originated from the word Bren-line, the 'Brenline Prydian Oll' meaning, from the line of the religious 'Kings of all Britain'. In the records of history we therefore see applied to the Gospel Rabbi Jesus the variant names of Tascio-vanus, Cunobeline and Bran the Blessed. King Bran the Blessed's (Rabbi Jesus Cunobeline, as we shall continue to call him) jurisdiction covered major parts of Southern Britain including the lower portions of Wales to the west and some portions of the east. This included Tri-Novantum and the pre-Latin version of this word was Troynovant (originally derived from New Troy), called London today. Just fifty miles to the northeast was Camulodunum, now called Colchester. In 10AD, Camulodunum was reoccupied for the second time by a powerful group of Belgic people called the Catuvellaum, and King Jesus Cunobeline was their ruler. It was here that he developed a mint and by the year 42, the town had grown to 110 acres. The records of history are sparse in this period but it seemed that a formidable sovereign fighting force was developed by King Rabbi Jesus Cunobeline and/or his sons, due maybe to the fact that Druidism was marked for destruction by the Roman Emperors and invasion was anticipated.

Artist's rendition of Arch Druid Bran the Blessed (née Rabbi Jesus Cunobeline)

The brief four-year reign of Emperor Tiberius' successor, Caligula, was not marked by any serious attempts of hostility towards the Royal Druids in Britain. His projected expedition against them was viewed with extreme distaste by the soldiery, his camp in northern Europe was broken up and they returned to Rome in false triumphal procession on Caligula's birthday, 31 August 40. To save face, he adopted the well-known phrase of Julius Caesar saying, 'Let us, my comrades, leave these Britons unmolested. To war beyond the bounds of nature is not courage, but impiety'. Caligula was assassinated in 41 and was succeeded by Claudius who reigned for fourteen years. He was regarded as but one remove from an idiot. 'He is as imbecile as my son Claudius' was the phrase his mother used when she wished to imply an extraordinary degree of stupidity. Claudius survived the violent reigns of four earlier Caesars, remained Emperor for fourteen years and was thought by his contemporaries to be a fool. 'Tall and full in person, and possessed, when seated, of the external show of dignity, in motion his knees shook, his head perpetually trembled, his tongue stuttered, his laughter was outrageously violent, and his anger marked by profuse foaming at the mouth.'[62] He was married four times and was subsequently poisoned by his last wife and niece, Agrippina.

Increasing hostility towards the Druids marked the early years of Claudius' reign and 'many fled to the ports prepared to go forth to another land in search of freedom'.[63] In the year 42, Emperor Claudius strengthened the Roman resistance to Druidism with the issue of yet another Edict providing for invasion and destruction by force of arms of the Druidic cori, or seminaries, in Britain. In his Edict, Claudius proclaimed in the Roman Senate that acceptance of the British Druidic faith was a capital offence punishable by death and ordered the destruction of the institution and its libraries.[64]

The Romans had not previously held any special enmity to the British. Actually, and perhaps grudgingly, they had held the British in respect but the Edicts against the Druids were politically motivated. Association in commerce and culture had drawn them together for centuries and it was not uncommon for the children of the nobility on both sides to seek education in the institutions of each. The British were a dominating problem. They were a warrior nation skilled in the art of warfare on land and sea. Intelligent rulers and commanders, all of whom were steeped in the invincibility of the spirit created by the passion in their faith, guided them and declared that all men should be free. One of the earliest battle hymns of the Britons was 'Britons never shall be slaves'.

CHAPTER TEN

King Jesus Cunobeline's sons go to war

T HE INVASION OF BRITAIN HAD BEEN DECIDED UPON, AND THE Roman fleet and transports were collecting at the usual northern European rendezvous of Boulogne. The Commander-in Chief selected by Emperor Claudius to carry out his Edict was Aulus Plautius. He stands in Roman history as one of the most brilliant commanders and conquerors in her military record. However, he came up against an obstacle unparalleled in the annals of Roman obedience. His army refused to embark across the Channel, and broke into open mutiny. Appeals to their sacraments, or military oaths of allegiance, failed to move them, the only response they elicited being, 'We will march anywhere *in* the world, but not *out* of it'. The lapse of ninety years had not yet extinguished the memory of the defeat of Julius Caesar's campaigns in Britain. Notification of this alarming state of affairs soon reached Rome by courier, and Emperor Claudius at once dispatched his favourite minister, Narcissus, a eunuch, to the scene of dissatisfaction to motivate the soldiers. It was the first time a eunuch had ever dared address a Roman military battalion. When he exclaimed that he 'would himself lead them into Britain', a universal shout of execration arose, and rushing to the tent of Plautius, they called upon him to give the signal for embarkation. Taking instant advantage of this change of attitude, Plautius dispatched the army in three divisions and landed two days later in Britain, making his headquarters in the area of Chichester. It was now the year 43 and Britain was about to march against the world in arms for the first time.

The 'superfluous population was drafted off as an army, or more generally as a colony' and nobly did they acquit themselves. The Romans encountered an aggressive fighting force consisting mainly of clan members gathered from Welsh Silures, a powerful people inhabiting South Wales, but also included Trinovantes and Atrebatians. They were reportedly hard, cruel, and vicious in battle. At Southfleet, across the Sarn on the flat between the Kentish hills and the Thames, Aulus Plautius found the British army drawn up under Prince Guiderius, one of King Rabbi Jesus Cunobeline's sons (mother, Cypros).[1] During the early stages of the battle, Prince Guiderius (Gwyderius), the Togodubnus of history, attacked the Romans and drove them back to their ships. He was later treacherously slain at Wimbleton Heath by a Roman named Laelius Hamo who disguised himself as a Briton, made his way to the military tent of the Prince and stabbed him while under no apprehension of danger. Prince Caradoc, third son of King Rabbi Jesus Cunobeline, assumed his brother's mantle upon the field of battle, and declared himself the Pendragon, literally the King Commander. He immediately pursued Laelius Hamo, eventually killing the Roman as he was boarding a ship to escape, thus avenging Guiderius' death.

The loss of Prince Guiderius was a heavy blow to King Rabbi Jesus Cunobeline and the unhappy king decided to abdicate in favour of Prince Caradoc. Rabbi Jesus Cunobeline subsequently became Arch Druid of one of three seats of Britain, Caer Troia, or Caer Llud or Caer Llyndain, and then later Arch Druid of Britain. Caradoc, a brave leader feared by the Romans, became the Arvi-ragus, the High King, and carried on the war. In the records of history Caradoc was later known by his Latinised name Caractacus and he was a man of great vigour, intelligent and versed in the arts of politics and warfare.

He was born at Trefan (Trevran) near Llan-Ilid (Wales) and received his education at the Druidic cor of Caerleon-on-Usk, where most of the Silurian nobility were trained in the cycle of Celtic accomplishments. Being raised in a staunchly Druidic household, he had deep religious convictions. Caradoc had two daughters—Eurgain, the eldest, Gladys (named after his sister)— and three sons—Linus, Cyllinus, and Cynon the Younger. Caradoc's name was often mistakenly recorded as Arvi-ragus but this was a title only. 'The alternative title of 'Arvi-ragus' for Caractacus shows that the British kings, like the Early Egyptian kings, were in the habit of using more than one title'.[2] The title of Arvi-ragus was later mistaken for a person's name and written King Arvi-ragus, being confused with the traditional use of tribal titles for leaders of that time. 'Indeed, the identity of the title (Arvi-ragus) with Caradoc was well known and used by contemporary Roman writers.'[3] He has been confused with a large number of legendary characters and even turned up in the Round Table romances. In Chrétien de Troyes' *Perceval*,

Caradoc was involved in an adventure involving a mock execution that had extraordinary parallels to the story of Uncle Judas Khrestus' mock crucifixion. Caradoc proved to be a formidable King and what was to happen in his lifetime had a profound effect on the development of Christianity.

For the first time the Romans found that they were not opposing a race of people who could be terrorized by huge numbers or brutalities. To their dismay, as reported by Tacitus, the Romans found that destruction of British sacred altars increased their anger, making them blind to odds and circumstances. The more destructive the Roman persecution the more determined did the British warriors strike back. Their bravery and disdain of death shocked them. 'The Britons, however, not yet enfeebled by a long peace, are possessed of superior courage.'[4] They were fighting for the defence of their faith, one that taught that the soul does not perish after death but moves from one body to another, or returns and goes on living 'elsewhere'. This belief fostered courage on the battlefield and helped overcome any fear of death. For the first time the Roman soldiery heard the amazing motto of the ancient Druidic priesthood transferred into a clarion battle cry, 'The Truth against the World', referring to their belief of the immortality of the soul. Their saying never died, living through the ages and today is still the motto of the Druidical Order in Wales.

In 45 and after two years of ceaseless warfare, a truce to seek peace through an armistice was eventually established between the warring parties. After the two parties settled upon a six-month 'cease-fire', the British warlord Caradoc was invited to Rome to personally discuss the possibilities for peace with Emperor Claudius. What was then to happen has no equal in the pages of history.

Strange family marriages

During the truce period, Emperor Claudius offered his natural daughter, Venus Julia (Venissa, in British accounts), to King Caradoc and, amidst great celebrations, the couple were married in Rome. Emperor Claudius had earlier sworn to exterminate King Caradoc and now his fiercest battlefield opponent was his new son-in-law. In Britain, and while maintaining the truce on behalf of the Roman Emperor, Aulus Plautius, Emperor Claudius' General, married Gladys, sister of King Caradoc (Gladys was Rabbi Jesus Cunobeline's daughter).

On her marriage, Gladys took the name of Pomponia, according to Roman custom, which was the name of her husband's Plautius clan. Later the name Graecina was added, so that she was thereafter known as Pomponia Graecina Plautius. The added name was a distinctive academic honour conferred upon her in recognition of her extraordinary scholarship in Greek. Like her father, the ex-King Rabbi Jesus Cunobeline and subsequently Arch

Druid of Britain, she was devoutly religious, completing her spiritual instruction at Avalon (Glastonbury) and in succession with some of the Bethany Group. Tacitus referred to her as 'a woman of illustrious birth' and when General Aulus Plautius was eventually recalled to Rome in 47, 'He took his foreign wife with him'. This record clearly indicated that Plautius' wife, the daughter of Rabbi Jesus Cunobeline, was not considered Roman.

The marriage of Gladys and Plautius was brought into Roman limelight by Tacitus in his *Annals* (13:32), wherein he related with some humour the peculiar circumstances and results of a later Roman trial in which Gladys, the wife of Plautius, was accused of being a Druid. She was officially charged with 'embracing the rites of a foreign superstition' and the matter was referred to the jurisdiction of her husband. Plautius then called together a number of Gladys' immediate relations to act in her defence. Evidently, Plautius had a sympathetic leaning to her faith for the group he assembled were all Druids from the Royal Silurian household. Plautius pronounced his wife innocent.

The truce subsequently failed, hostilities resumed and King Caradoc was now the wartime opponent of both his father-in-law and brother-in-law. Ostorius Scapula subsequently replaced Plautius in Britain who returned to Rome, but the war raged for another seven years. It was during this period that the Iceni and Brigantes tribes entered the war, and King Caradoc and the Silures took the war into North Wales. 'The race of the Silures,' observed Tacitus, 'was not to be changed by clemency or severity.' Tacitus recorded that Caradoc was frequently in the midst of his warriors urging them to fight with emotive words about freedom and independence, just as his uncle Judas Khrestus did earlier with the Galileans. The Roman world became fascinated with King Caradoc and his troops bearing the whole brunt of the massive arms of the Empire under a series of its finest generals. 'Every Briton, from the king to the peasant, followed Caradoc when he lifted his spear to battle.'[5] For the first time the Romans met women warriors fighting side by side with their men in combat. Tacitus stated that their long-flowing flaxen hair and blazing blue eyes were a terrifying sight to behold.[6] King Caradoc's military merit won the unstinted admiration of the enemy who named him the 'Scourge of the Romans'. In those years, according to Suetonius, thirty pitched battles were fought, some raging for several weeks. 'The Silures reposed unbounded confidence in Caradoc, enumerating the many drawn battles he had fought with the Romans, the many victories he had obtained over them'.[7] The Roman battlefield chiefs had appealed to Emperor Claudius for reinforcements and he subsequently arrived personally, complete with the Second and Fourteenth Legions and a squadron of elephants. This was the first time these strange creatures had been seen in Britain and it was hoped their size and weight would neutralize the chaos the steel scythes of the British chariots were causing. Finally, the British warriors under King Caradoc met disaster in the year 52 at Clune, Shropshire, by a strange trick of circumstance.

Jesus' third marriage

During this time, Rabbi Jesus Cunobeline remarried for the third time, and his new wife was Queen Aricia (Arèddig), recorded in Tacitus' records as Cartismandus (Celtic for Aricia). She was the former wife of the Brigantes Chief, Venusius, who was an ally of the Romans. After a rift with her, Venusius took up arms not only against his ex-wife but against the Romans as well. Queen Aricia managed to seize his brother and parents by a trick but the deception was discovered and the Brigantes rose against her. In Welsh tradition, Queen Aricia became Aregwedd Voeddawg, 'the Stinking One' and was regarded as a woman of 'seduction, trickery and scheming'.[8]

Queen Aricia became frustrated in her ambitious desire to unite the son of her first marriage, Cloten, to Rabbi Jesus Cunobeline's granddaughter Princess Eurgain, the Imogen of Shakespeare's play Cymbeline. The circumstances were such that Adminius, Rabbi Jesus Cunobeline's eldest son, slew Cloten, with the resultant family tensions causing the estrangement of Adminius. Adminius, sometimes called 'Hugh the Intellectual' in ancient records, was banished by his father, and from then on treated by the family as non-existent or dead (like Judas Khrestus). Adminius then became an insurgent against his father and eventually fled to Belgium where the Romans arrested him. From the scant records available, it appeared he was taken to Rome to be interrogated by the Emperor.

Upon the murder of Cloten, Queen Aricia seized an opportunity for vengeance by betraying Rabbi Jesus Cunobeline's son, King Caradoc, to the Romans. By order of the traitorous wife, King Caradoc was taken prisoner while asleep, loaded down with chains and delivered to Ostorius Scapula. Not only was King Caradoc captured but Rabbi Jesus Cunobeline and his entire family were taken as hostages to Rome.

CHAPTER ELEVEN

The most famous trial in Rome

IT WAS THE MOST COMPLETE SUBJECTION OF ANY ROYAL HOUSE ON record by an enemy. Tacitus wrote that the news of the capture of the famed British warrior 'spread like wildfire'[1] and three million people crowded the streets of Rome to view the captive King's arrival. The record stated that King Caradoc, heavily chained, 'bold and honourable' walked proudly with his relatives and family through the streets of Rome, following the chariot of Emperor Claudius. 'Rome trembled when she saw the Briton, though fast in chains.'[2] Rabbi Jesus Cunobeline was clad in Arch Druid's white linen robes and wore the symbol of the Druidic Trinity around his forehead, a crown of mistletoe with its three white berries. The mistletoe entwined itself around the branches of the sacred oak tree and, to the Druid, represented an earthly parallel to the spiritual incarnation of the Deity in mankind. 'The Druidic cross was wrought in gold down the length of the back of his robe.'[3]

The contemporary Roman historians expressed amazement that King Caradoc was the first captive kingly enemy not cast into the terrible Tarpeian dungeons. Here was the son of the twin brother of Judas Khrestus, the earlier leader of the hated Khrestians, a British warrior King and a man who for nine years inflicted many disastrous defeats upon the mightiest Roman army ever to march onto the field of battle, being treated with utmost respect. Neither he, nor any member of the British royal family was subjected to any physical indignities[4] while being held in custody before the trial. On the day of the commencement of the trial, Gladys refused to be separated from her father, though it was against the Roman law for a woman to enter the Senate. Voluntarily she walked by the side of King Caradoc up the marble steps into the venue in the Forum of Augustus, brave and composed like her royal father.[5]

The Senate was crowded to capacity and here again the historians note another breach of Roman law with the presence of yet another woman. History recorded that the great Queen Agrippina sat on her throne, on the far corner of the Dais, a fascinated witness to the most famous trial in Roman history. She was the mother of Nero[6] and had married Emperor Claudius in 49, although she was his niece. King Caradoc, the man who should have been the most hated as the leader of the British army drew admiration from all sides and he looked poised before his sworn enemy, Emperor Claudius. As the trial proceeded, King Caradoc spoke in a strong, clear voice and replied to his prosecutors with words that have lived down through the ages. Tacitus recorded the Briton's epic address to the Senate, delivered in their own language, Latin:

> Had my government in Britain been directed solely with a view to the preservation of my hereditary domains, or the aggrandizement of my own family, I might long since have entered this city an ally, not a prisoner: nor would you have disdained for a friend a King descended from illustrious ancestors, and the dictator of many nations. My present condition, stripped of its former majesty, is as adverse to myself as it is a cause of triumph to you. What then? I was lord of men, horses, arms, wealth; what wonder if at your dictation I refuse to resign them? Does it follow, that because the Romans aspire to universal domination, every nation is to accept the vassalage they would impose? I am now in your power . . . betrayed not conquered. Had I, like others, yielded without resistance, where would have been the name of Caradoc? Where is your glory? Oblivion would have been buried in the same tomb. Bid me live. I shall survive for ever in history one example of Roman clemency.

Never before had the Roman Tribunal been addressed in such a noble manner. There and then, by order of the Claudian Tribunal, King Caradoc and all members of the royal British family were immediately pardoned. When the decision was announced, the Senate cheered and applauded loudly. Queen Agrippina quickly rose, embraced King Caradoc and each member of his family, and shook hands according to British tradition. Tacitus recorded dismay at this rare display of emotion, citing it as another strange deviation from Roman custom.[7] The only restriction imposed in the pardon of King Caradoc was that he personally remained at Rome in free custody (libera custodia) for seven years, and that he, or any member of his family, was never again to bear arms against Rome. To this King Caradoc agreed and never once thereafter did he break his pledge.

The other Royal captives were free to leave Rome but Rabbi Jesus Cunobeline remained for some time. King Caradoc's eldest son Cyllinus returned immediately to Britain to rule over the kingdom of the Welsh Silurians in the stead of his father. He oversaw the income from the family's rural estates and forwarded monies to Rome to his father and grandfather. Emperor Claudius allowed the family full enjoyment of the revenues of their royal Silurian domains. Under Rabbi Jesus Cunobeline's instructions, another son (of Mary Magdalene), Cadwalladr the Blessed, returned to Wales with half-sister Princess Eurgain and set up an 'inclosure' in the centre of Siluria (Llan-Ilid) as a safe house for Khrestians who had fled to Britain for royal protection (Triads of the Isle of Britain).

While King Caradoc lived in Rome, he enjoyed all the privileges of a free man and resided with most of his family at the palatial royal household called Palatium Britannicum, 'The Palace of the British'.[8] Emperor Claudius gifted 'twenty acres of ground and detached buildings on the crest of the Esquiline mount' (Viminalis Hill) exclusively to King Caradoc and his family, and provided immunity to its occupants. Roman authorities were not permitted to arrest any member or guest of the Palace of the British and the residents were allowed full use of the city provided they obeyed the civil law. For the seven years King Caradoc lived at the Palace (52–59), an official law approved by the Roman Senate provided protection for him and occupants of the property. It was a Khrestian sanctuary in the true sense of the word and the ensuing years would see the most famous of the *New Testament* figures harboured within its walls.

For many years, professors and students of Roman history looked for an underlying reason why the Senate rendered its remarkable verdict. Why did the bloodthirsty Claudius not demand the customary revenge—death by brutal torture and the cruellest means? Was it because King Caradoc was married to his daughter, Venus Julia? Did the strange intermarriage between King Caradoc's sister, Princess Gladys and the Roman aristocrat Aulus Plautius, induce the Senate to make its decision? Historians declared to the contrary and affirmed that the strict Roman law was so embedded in the conscience of the Roman people that neither the Senate nor the Emperor dared to avert traditional ruling. The reason the Claudian Tribunal bestowed such generous clemency upon the Royal Britons can be explained by the fact that, although illegitimate, Rabbi Jesus Cunobeline, the father of King Caradoc, was invested by birthright with the title of 'Caesar'. This honour passed to Rabbi Jesus Cunobeline's descendants, making his whole family Roman royalty of the highest order. The *New Testament* provided confirmation with a direct reference to those 'of Caesar's household'[9] residing at the Palace of the British in Rome. A letter, addressed to the family of Rabbi Jesus

Cunobeline, canonically acknowledged the descendants of the line of Caesar through Emperors Augustus and Tiberius. King Caradoc's address to the Roman Senate confirmed his personal knowledge of aristocratic breeding when he proudly referred to his descent 'from illustrious ancestors' and his 'hereditary domains'. In his speech, he also called himself, 'lord of men'.

CHAPTER TWELVE

The Palace of the British in Rome

OLLOWING THE PARDON OF KING CARADOC, A CLOSE RELATIONSHIP developed between him and his former enemy, Emperor Claudius. Caradoc helped Claudius plan Roman war strategies that did not affect Britain and he became a popular figure with the Roman administrators. Emperor Claudius greatly admired the character and beauty of teenage Gladys,[1] the youngest daughter of King Caradoc (named after Jesus Cunobeline's daughter and Caradoc's sister). It grew into a deep affection with the result that Emperor Claudius adopted Gladys Caradoc as his own daughter and conferred upon her the name, Claudia. The House of Claudius 'used many different forenames and surnames'[2] and through this title, the British Princess and her entire family received additional status, and were now officially, 'of the House of Claudius'.

In the year 53 and at the age of seventeen, Claudia Caradoc married Rufus Pudens Pudentius, a wealthy Roman Senator and former aide-de-camp to Aulus Plautius whom she met at Regnum (the old name for Chichester) as a youngster living in Britain.[3] From the sparce documentation available, it seemed that he owned a residence in Chichester and was in some way an associate or member of the powerful Acilii Glabriones family of Rome. Cardinal Baronius chronicled a curious record about Rufus, saying, 'Rufus the Senator received St Peter (Simon of Petra) into his house on Viminalis Hill, in the year 44AD'. Nine years later, the same Senator Rufus married Claudia at the British Palace in Rome by a man called Hermas Pastore (sometimes translated as Hermes) who was known to both St Paul and St Peter.[4] On the marriage of his daughter to Pudens, as he was generally called, King Caradoc bestowed upon the bridal couple, a gift, the British Palace on Viminalis Hill in Rome. Pudens then forsook his parental home on another section of Viminalis Hill, along with his estates in Samnium Umbria (Italy), and prepared to live at the Palace of the British.

Some conception may be formed of its size and magnificence from the number of servants Pudens brought in to staff the establishment, being 'two hundred males and the same number of females, all born on the hereditary estates of Pudens at Umbria'.[5] Adjoining the Palace were two magnificent thermal baths, the largest and most ornate in Rome. They were later named after the two sons subsequently born to Claudia and Pudens, Timoteo or Timotheus (d. 150 aged ninety) and Novato or Novatian (d. 139). They also had two daughters named Pudentiana (d. 107) and Praxedes.[6] Of Claudia, the witty poet Martial, one of the Bethany Group and resident at The British Palace in Rome, wrote:

> Our Claudia, named Rufina, sprung, we know,
> From blue-eyed Britons; yet, behold, she vies
> In grace with all that Greece or Rome can show,
> As bred and born beneath their glowing skies.

Rufina was the feminine vernacular for her husband's first name, Rufus. It was common custom to refer to a married woman personally by replacing her own first name with his. Names then, were used rather indiscriminately, which tends to confuse us who retain throughout our lifetime our given and family name. Consequently, it can be bewildering to read of the British Princess called by so many names—Gladys-Claudia-Britannica, Rufina-Pudens, Pudentiana and Pudenziana—all before she was twenty-one. The dark-haired Romans admired the golden-haired, blue-eyed, pink-complexioned women of Britain. Again, Martial sang with praise, 'For mountains, bridges, rivers, and fair women, Britain is past compare'. Martial wrote a long poem describing the nuptials of Claudia and Pudens. He also wrote another on the birth of Claudia's daughter, Pudentiana (d. 107). Claudia's first-born son, Timotheus, was named after one of her favourite Khrestians who frequented her home, Timothy from Ephesus (in today's church, St Timothy). Timotheus, later in his life, deeded the Palace of the British in Rome to the Khrestian movement. In the *New Testament* Timothy was associated with John and Paul (St John and St Paul today). Paul referred to Timotheus as, 'The beloved son of Christ' which originally read, 'The beloved grandson of Krist' (Rabbi Jesus Krist).

The occupants of the British Palace

Thus, we see in mid-First Century Rome, the gathering together of particular characters in preparation for the role that they were to subsequently play in what was to later become the greatest misunderstanding in the history of the world. Residing at the Palace of the British at various times during King Caradoc's confinement were:

The Arch Druid of Britain, Rabbi Jesus Cunobeline (Bran the Blessed)

His son, King Caradoc and his wife, Queen Venus Julia, daughter of Emperor Claudius

King Caradoc's daughter, Princess Eurgain and her husband, Salog, the Prince of Old Sarum (Salisbury?)

Princess Eurgain' brother, Prince Linus (King Caradoc's son)

Claudia–Gladys (King Caradoc's daughter), her husband, Senator Pudens, and their four children. (Claudia died peacefully at Umbria, aged sixty-one, in the year 97).

The mother of Pudens and St Paul, Prassede (Priscilla)

Hermas Pastore, kinsman of Pudens

Martial, the poet. He was born in 29 and was only eight years old when he travelled with the Bethany Group to Britain. It was recorded that he moved to Rome in 49 and lived there until 86. He died at Bilbilis in Spain in 104, aged seventy-five.

Going to and from the Palace were the following people, some being next-of-kin of Rabbi Jesus Cunobeline and all connected by marriage or sympathy:

Paul/Saul (St Paul)

Simon of Petra (St Peter)

Timothy (St Timothy)

King Caradoc's sister, Pomponia Graecina (Gladys) and her husband Aulus Plautius, who 'resided in a nearby street' (Tacitus).

Cadwalladr the Blessed and Polydore, the sons of Rabbi Jesus Cunobeline by Princess Mary Magdalene. They lived in Britain and travelled regularly to Rome.

Flavius Justinius, (c. 166). Justinius was a Roman citizen and is today called St Justin Martyr.

There were other *New Testament* characters recorded living in the Palace, (Tryphena, Persis, Patrobas and Julia, for example) but those mentioned here are important figures in unravelling the *New Testament* story. The later church writers attested that 'all' the Pudens household at the British Palace were Christians (Khrestians) but Rabbi Jesus Cunobeline, King Caradoc, Claudia, Eurgain, Salog, Linus and Hermas Pastore were all Druidic emissaries of British royalty, the Royal Silurians. They represented the chief assembly of personalities who were unwittingly responsible for what was to later evolve in the narratives of the *New Testament*.

The true authors of the Epistles

The letters attributed to Paul in the Bible are promoted as 'divine' writings by the church and represent fourteen of the twenty-seven books of the Christian *New Testament*. They were addressed to the Galatians, the Corinthians (the first and second letters), the Romans, the Thessalonians (the first and second letters), the Ephesians, the Colossians, the Philippians, Philemon,[7] Timothy (the first and second letters), Titus and Hebrews. Philemon, Timothy and Titus were the only letters addressed to individuals. Of the collection, the canon of Muratori, a Latin fragment of the canon found by Muratori in the Ambrosian Library at Milan in 1740, recorded that Ephesians (formerly called Laodiceans) was a forgery although it is in the Bible today.

The letters made up about a third of the *New Testament* and the church has always maintained that they represented the personal teachings of 'Paul, the great apostle of the Gentiles'. But archival records said something entirely different, naming Paul as the author of only two epistles and then with some doubt. None of the letters were associated with what is now known as Christianity for the majority were addressed to the major Essene communities of the day.

> They (the Essenes) had missionary stations or colonies of their community established in Rome, Corinth, Galatia, Ephesus, Phillippa, Colosse and Thessalonica, precisely such and in the same circumstances, as were those to whom St Paul addressed his letters in those places.[8]

The original authors of the 'Epistles of Paul' were documented in pre–1900 editions of the Oxford Bible. This is what was recorded:

Romans: This letter was written by 'Tertius' (Romans 16:22) and delivered 'by Phebe' to the Palace of the British in Rome (p.1148). In some translations, Phebe was Paul's sister (Romans 16: 1).

Corinthians: 'The first epistle to the Corinthians was written from Philippi by Stephanas, and Fortunatus, and Acaicus, and Timotheus' (p.1164).

Corinthians: 'The second epistle to the Corinthians was written from Philippi, a city of Macedonia, by Titus and Lucas' (p.1175).

Galatians: 'Unto the Galatians written from Rome' (p.1181). The author was unnamed.

Ephesians: 'Written from Rome unto the Ephesians by Tychicus' (p.1186).

Philippians: 'It was written to the Philippians from Rome by Epaphroditus' (p.1190).

Colossians: 'Written from Rome to the Colossians by Tychicus and Onesimus'.

Thessalonians: The first epistle unto the Thessalonians was written from Athens (p.1197), as was the second epistle (p.1199)—in both cases, the author was unnamed.

Timothy: 'The first epistle to Timothy was written from Laodicea, which is the chiefest city of Phrygia Pacatiana' (p.1203). The author was unnamed. 'The second epistle unto Timotheus was written from Rome, when Paul was brought before Nero the second time' (p.1206). The church claimed that because Paul was in Rome, he was the author.

Titus: 'It was written to Titus, ordained the first biscop (bishop today) of the church of the Cretians, from Nicopolis of Macedonia' (p.1208).

Philemon: 'Written from Rome to Philemon, by Onesimus, a servant' (p.1209).

Hebrews: 'Written to the Hebrews from Italy by Timothy' (p.1220).[9]

Church records showed that the authors of all but two of the epistles reproduced in the *New Testament* were: Tertius, Stephanas, Fortunatus, Acaicus, Timotheus (1), Titus, Lucas, Tychicus, Epaphroditus, Tychicus, Onesimus (1), Nicopolis, Onesimus (2) and Timothy (2). The epistles that may be attributed to Paul are:

Galatians: Cardinal Baronius wrote that it was written to 'the Gauls' (or the Galileans), and 'must be corrected'.

Timothy: a relative of Paul, also a resident at the Palace of the British.

The church admitted that some of the *New Testament* Epistles were forgeries, and those that were genuine, were later falsified:

> Even the genuine Epistles were greatly interpolated to lend weight to the personal views of their authors.[10]

The Epistles of the *New Testament* are heavily interpolated and doubtful works. Over and over again in the *Variorum Teacher's Bible*, verse after verse, referring particularly to the Epistles, was pointed out as being corrupted or suspected of being corrupted, 'not original' or 'embellished', with some translations being described as 'conjecture only'. It makes truly extraordinary reading and the express findings of those theologians unquestionably established that, with the Acts of the Apostles, James, the letters of Peter and John and Jude, all the Epistles are heavily edited and forged documents.

By the end of the Second Century, the Ebronites (Ebionites in some translations), one of the most powerful of the early sects, totally and constantly rejected all Epistles. They said the original letters had received 'numerous modifications' and disregarded them. The church itself expressed further serious doubt about the validity of the Epistles, particularly the three known as the 'Pastoral Epistles'[11] for it constantly used the words 'if genuine' when referring to those documents. It admitted those letters may have been 'written by a disciple of Paul'[12] and if that was the case, only one *New Testament* Epistle can be attributed to Paul (Galatians). In Galatians, Paul acknowledged three Galilean apostles, Simon of Petra, James Herod, the half-brother of Judas Khrestus and Rabbi Jesus, and Barnabas.

Recognizing the facts, we can well understand why the ancient writers affirmed that Paul spent most of his time in Rome at the sanctuary of the British Palace. Paul was, 'the ringleader of the Nazarenes',[13] a subsiduary offshoot of the Essene movement. Bishop Tertullian confirmed again that Paul was the 'chief' of the Nazarenes[14] and was 'constantly pursued' by the military. St Epiphanius said that 'all Christians (Khrestians) were called Nazarenes'[15] and Dr Lardner[16] established that the name 'Galileans' was the original name of the early Khrestian/Christian movement.[17] Judas Khrestus and Simon of Petra were Nazarenes leading the Galilean sect, and from the brief records available, it seemed that Paul, while continuing their work (Acts 9:25), was captured, and returned to Rome, 'a prisoner on parole'.[18] While in Rome, he 'deprived Nero of his favourite concubine, and seduced his ablest secretaries. That is why they kept him so long confined in the Marmertine [dungeon]'.[19]

The Bible recorded that Paul was 'a pestilent fellow, and a mover of sedition'.[20] He was a major leader of the active Khrestian revolutionist sect and was continually 'being hunted and stoned'.[21] Paul eventually fled to Britain for Royal Druidic protection at the 'inclosure' built under Rabbi Jesus Cunobeline's instructions at Siluria in Wales.[22] Addressing the Mayors of Bath, Colchester and Dorchester at the Vatican in 1931, Pope Pius XI said that St Paul went to Britain some twenty years after Joseph of Arimathea, circa 57.[23] An ancient manuscript in Merton College, Oxford, purported to contain a series of letters written by St Paul supporting that he had once resided in Siluria.

Paul was known by a variety of appellations and his name 'often appears in distorted form'.[24] Paul, which meant 'little man', was a nickname. He was sometimes called Elisha ben Abuiah in the *Talmud*. The *Talmud* said of Aher (Paul) in the Yerushalmi, that 'he corrupted the work of that man', meaning Rabbi Jesus.[25] Paul's nickname was supported with a peculiar description of him in the Acts of Paul. He was described as 'a little man with a big bold head . . . his legs are crooked . . . his eyebrows grew close together and he had a big nose'. It was said that at one time he had his head shorn at Cenchrea because 'he had taken a vow'.[26]

The common inference was that Paul returned to the bosom of the royal

British family in Rome in the year 58, but St Jerome said he returned in 'the second year of Nero' which was 56. Nero succeeded Claudius as Emperor of Rome. Before Paul returned, he instructed Tertius, the author of the letter to 'those at Rome',[27] to pass on Paul's greetings and best wishes.[28] 'Those at Rome' were the occupants of the Palace of the British and not a new Roman church professing a developing Christian faith. Paul's salutations extended to more than thirty people including Stachys, his 'beloved',[29] Phebe, 'our sister'[30] and Quartus, 'a brother'.[31] He also offered praise to his mother: 'Salute Rufus and the mother of him and me'.[32]

In this greeting, Paul was referring to Rufus by his domestic and family name, that being Rufus Pudens Pudentius (d. 96) and Paul's statement made the mother of Rufus and Paul the same person.

The history of Paul's mother was recorded in an 'old and secret tradition':

> The grandfather of Saul/Paul was a very wealthy Benjamite of Tarsus, capital of Cilicia, the rocky province in Asia-minor, due north of Syria. A Romano-Graeco Hebrew he had purchased for himself 'with a great sum' the Roman citizenship for himself and family, and added a Roman name to his Hebrew patronymic. His son, Davidius Paulus [Paul's father], as usual, added a Roman nomen, Appius Tullius, took service in the army and rose to be a centurion. His wife, Prassede [senior—Paul's mother] was left a wealthy widow, cultured by a Roman education.[33]

At the time of Saul/Paul's return to Rome, his mother was married to Pudentius the Patrician, the father of Pudens. Pudentius was on duty in Rome as a high civil servant when he met and married the wealthy widow. Her marriage to Pudentius appeared to have been very displeasing to Paul who refused to accept Pudentius' name, proudly proclaiming his father' name Paulus, hence Paul today.[34]

Paul and Rufus Pudens were half-brothers, and Rufus was married to Jesus Cunobeline's granddaughter, Princess Claudia. Paul's mother was living at the British Palace and the biblical writings show that Claudia was Paul's sister-in-law. When Paul arrived in Rome, his abode was with his entire family at the British Palace. It was interesting to note that the Bible recorded Paul had many other relatives in Rome, notably Andronicus, Junea and Herodian. Recorded in the Roman Martyrologies, this interesting phrase: 'The children of Claudia were brought up on the knee of St Paul'.

He was their uncle. The records stated:

> The sister of Prassede, Paul's mother, was named Mariamne, but on marriage with another Roman patrician, she assumed the name of Priscilla.[35]

If this Mariamne was Mariamne Herod, Paul was Rabbi Jesus and Judas Khrestus' half brother, and the Priscilla in the *New Testament* was Mariamne

Herod. Priscilla was also a resident at the British Palace in Rome. Prassede was the sister of Mariamne Herod therefore she was Herodias of the *New Testament*.

The church said that St Paul wrote two letters to Timothy (Timotheus) but doubts their authenticity.[36] However, those two letters contained the names of certain people that can be supported historically from references external to church writings. The second letter was written locally in Rome, and delivered to Timothy at the Palace of the British while Paul was before Emperor Nero the second time.[37] The following statement was recorded: 'Eubulus greeteth thee, and Pudens and Linus, and Claudia.'

The records of history identify the following:

> Eubulus—Claudia's cousin, a Druid from Avalon (Glastonbury).
> The 'greeting' was the welcome received by Paul upon his arrival at the British Palace in Rome.
> Pudens—the husband of Claudia, daughter of King Caradoc and the half-brother of St Paul.
> Linus—a son of King Caradoc and grandson of Jesus Cunobeline.[38]
> Claudia—King Caradoc's daughter (Gladys), and Jesus Cunobeline's granddaughter.

In this *New Testament* narrative, the names of two of Jesus' grandchildren—Linus and Gladys—are recorded (King Caradoc's children). The thoughts expressed by Paul in his letter to the Galatians stated that he was continuing 'the traditions of my fathers'[39] and appeared to be transferring his traditional Nazarene ideals into the letter he wrote that is now in the *New Testament*. Those ideals were Essene ideals, for the Nazarenes were one of the sects recorded by Josephus as being an independent Essene-derived body of fighting men from Galilee. That Paul was recorded in the *New Testament* as a Nazarene obviously connected him, like Judas Khrestus and Simon the Zealot,[40] to the family's resistant movement operating at that time. Paul today is the most revered of all the early Christian churchmen and promoted as one of the spiritual giants by the church, but records revealed that he was a Nazarine fighting for Khrestian ideals.

In the years following the marriage of Pudens and Claudia, Hermas Pastore used the Palace of the British for conducting secret Druidic services and it seemed his name became the origin of 'Pastor' in the Christian church today. Later, Novatus made the 'Bath' building or guest house 'a Title', and called it 'Titulus Pastore' after Pastore, and some records say Pastore eventually inherited the property from Novatus. It was later renamed St Pudentiana, the name the building retains today.

Today the Basilica of St Pudentiana stands on Via Viminalis Hill Urbana, Rome, and is built over the ancient Palace of the British which is approximately nine metres below the surface. A series of underground rooms that made up the original Roman home of Rabbi Jesus Cunobeline and his son, King Caradoc, can be reached through a door situated in the left-hand corner of a chapel now called 'Caetani'. In some of the rooms below, the remains of mosaic floors can be seen; among them being a very rare type known as 'Lithostraton' where fragments of different coloured marble have been placed between the weavings.

Basilica of St Pudentiana at Rome. This photograph shows the main door of the 11th Century. It was believed the bell tower in the background was built in the 13th Century.
© St Pudentiana's Rectorate, Roma.

Underground details of the latticed walling in the Palace of the British. The remains of the piping for baths, and large pieces of Roman bastolato, can be seen.
© St Pudentiana's Rectorate, Roma.

Remains of the home given to King Caradoc and his family in the middle of the First Century. Major personalities of the New Testament lived here (St Pudentiana at Rome).
© St Pudentiana's Rectorate, Roma.

Underground substructure tunnels. This building is today known as Termae Novatii and may have been an extension of the Palace of the British in the year 139.
© St Pudentiana's Rectorate, Roma.

Between 1960 and 1964 underground rubble was removed and this courtyard was discovered adjoining previously unknown rooms.
© St Pudentiana's Rectorate, Roma.

Catholic historian, Cardinal Baronius said, 'Of all our churches the oldest is that which is called after the name of Pudens'. However, it was not a Christian church in the manner now presented, but a Druidic establishment for its Royal British occupants. The Gospels had yet to be written and Christianity was still 300 years from being established.

King Caradoc returns to Britain

Upon King Caradoc's return to Britain, he lived at Aber-gweryd in Glamorganshire 'on the north bank of the Bristol Channel between Cardiff and Swansea' where remains of a Romano-British villa—*More Romano*—were found.[41] A farm-house a mile or so down the road from Trevran was said to be the Manor of Bran the Blessed. This was traditionally the place where Bran (Rabbi Jesus) spent summers, and nearby was Llan-Ilid. 'Ilid' (or 'Illid') seemed to have been the Welsh name of Joseph of Arimathea 'who established his mission under the protection of Bran'.[42]

The majority of King Caradoc's family were attached to literary pursuits. Rabbi Jesus Cunobeline introduced the use of vellum into Britain from Rome[43] and copies of writings of the best Roman authors were circulated in Siluria and deposited in the principal receptacles of Druidic learning by the younger members of his family. Claudia herself wrote several volumes of odes and hymns.

With King Caradoc now back in Britain, Emperor Claudius sought to make a permanent peace with the British people by offering him the hand of yet another of his daughters, Genuissa. Initially, this was unacceptable to Caradoc, but he was later persuaded by the nobles to accept the offer for marriage was a well established practice in mending internal and family disputes. The marriage proved entirely happy and King Caradoc built a castle for Queen Genuissa at Gloucester. This was a compliment to her father Emperor Claudius, whose name in the Celtic tongue was Glouster. The couple had four children, but only two of their names appeared to be recorded. The eldest was Eudaf Marius, and another was Eudal Marius, meaning fair-haired, with 'Marius' being simply a title and typical of the common use made of titular designations by the ancient peoples. The Chronicles stated that Caradoc '. . . governed his kingdom in peace and tranquillity. In war none more fierce than he, in peace does none more mild, none more pleasing in manner, nor in his gifts, more magnificent. When he finished his course of life, 80AD, he was buried at Gloucester'.[44]

Upon his death, Cyllinus, his eldest son by Venus Julia, succeeded to the Silurian throne, 'Cyllinus ab Caradoc, a wise and just king . . . He, first of the Cymry, gave infants Krist names; for before, names were not given except to adults, and then from something characteristic in their bodies, minds, or manners' (Gwehelyth Iestyn ap Gwrgant). Today, they are called Christian names, originally deriving from Krist, the title of the Essene initiates.

CHAPTER THIRTEEN

The stoning of Rabbi Jesus Cunobeline

RABBI JESUS CUNOBELINE SPENT A CONSIDERABLE AMOUNT OF TIME at the Palace of the British and sometime around 48 he left Rome for Egypt to pursue his greatest esoteric goal. The spiritual knowledge from his secret learnings in the Essene and Druid movements was soon to be elevated to the highest level possible—initiation into the innermost rite of the Egyptian Temples.

In the oldest temples there was always a twofold plan in the architectural arrangement, and every temple had two divisions; one for ordinary religion (Exoteric) and the other for secret mysteries (Esoteric). The public performances were symbolical and sacred, but did not reveal any hidden secrets to the audience. The initiation into the real Mysteries, however, was never performed publicly and was a most secret rite. The supernormal character of the Greater Mysteries was hinted at by various initiates, as one once declared, 'Thanks to the Mysteries, death for mortals is not an evil but a good'.

The Egyptian Mysteries were for long kept sealed from foreigners, and it was only in latter times that a few were admitted and initiated. The regulations covering entrance were strict and severe and those who received the greatest mysteries were trusted to keep their vows of secrecy.

The earliest recorded account of the Egyptian Mysteries was that given by Herodotus, a highly regarded historian who traveled to Egypt in 440BC for his initiation. He spoke of his learning there with great reverence:

I impose upon myself a profound silence in regard to the secret of the
Mysteries of which I am acquainted.

It was probable that Rabbi Jesus Cunobeline's earlier initiation into both
the Essene and Druid schools played a major part in his acceptance into the
Egyptian school. The Druids could claim a very early origin and the essence
of their wisdom was also that of the Essenes. In the case of the Essenes, it is
possible to show that their movement was specifically established to preserve
secret information, for they knew and used the sacred writing of the Initiates.
This is but a hint, but the full meaning of the point being made is that in
the case of all Secret Schools, the inner and ultimate Mystery was revealed
only to a High Initiate.

Masonic secret symbols

Jewish literature stated that Jesus was 'around life's half distance' when he
became a Rabbi. The author of the Codex Nazaraeus said, 'John [the Baptist]
had baptised for forty-two years when Yesu [note the spelling of Rabbi
Jesus' name] came to the Jordan to be baptised with John's baptism'. Assuming
John the Baptist was around twenty years of age when he commenced
baptising, this statement if reliable, would show Rabbi Jesus to be
approximately sixty years old when baptised, for the Gospels made him but
a few months younger than John. The present copy of the Codex Nazaraeus
dates from 1042, but Bishop Irenaeus quoted from it and cited ample
references to it. The material common to Irenaeus and the Codex Nazaraeus
therefore was at least as early as the compilation of the canonical Gospels,
sometime during the second half of the Second Century.

A statement in the Gospel of John (8:57) had Jews saying to Rabbi Jesus,
'you are not yet fifty years old', an indication that the twin brothers were
considered by the people who compiled the John Gospel to be men much
older than Jesus Christ as portrayed in modern church literature. Both the
documentation of Irenaeus and the internal evidence in the Gospel account,
placed Rabbi Jesus still alive around twenty years later than the time the
church said he died.

The records of Irenaeus (115–202), Bishop of Lyons, revealed that Rabbi
Jesus:

> On completing his thirtieth year he suffered, being in fact still a young
> man, and who had by no means attained to advanced age. Now that the
> first stage of early life embraces thirty years, and that this extends onward
> to the fortieth year, everyone will admit; but from the fortieth and fiftieth
> year a man begins to decline towards old age, which Jesus possessed while
> he still fulfilled the office of a Rabbi, even as the Gospel and all the elders
> testify.

In this passage, Irenaeus clearly stated that Rabbi Jesus suffered in his 'thirtieth year' yet still 'possessed' the latter years of his life to fulfill an office of spiritual teaching. The suffering was the ordeal of one of at least two initiations during which a long period of deprivation was an essential part of the process.

It should be noted that Bishop Irenaeus purposely prepared 'Against Heresies' to contradict another statement current in his time and to the effect that the ministry of Rabbi Jesus lasted one year. Irenaeus, writing about ninety or one hundred years after the death of John the Baptist consistently stated Rabbi Jesus declined towards old age and 'the Gospel and all the presbyters testify'. That timeframe was confirmed because Roman Emperor Trajan came to power in the year 98 (98–117 was his term) that made John, on the authority of Irenaeus, a man of around one hundred years old. From Irenaeus' writings it was evident the first missionaries of the Christian church were far more willing to admit the truth than their successors.

St Austin (c. 380) asserted that it was generally known in church circles that Rabbi Jesus had been initiated in Egypt, and that 'he wrote books concerning magic'.[1] In the Gospel of Nicodemus the Jews brought the same accusation before Pontius Pilate, 'Did we not tell you he was a magician?'[2] Celsus (c. 178) spoke of the same charge. In the *Clementine Recognitions*[3] the accusation was brought against Rabbi Jesus that he did not perform any miracles but practiced magic and carried about with him the figure of a seated skeleton.

This is one of the Masonic symbols used in secret correspondence and fits the description of the ancient sacred logo recorded to have been carried about by Rabbi Jesus.[4]

Jewish tradition invariably asserted that Rabbi Jesus learned 'magic' in Egypt. The kernel of this persistent accusation may perhaps be reduced to the simple historical element that Rabbi Jesus went to Egypt and returned with far wider and more enlightened views than those of his former religious associates. The accusations against the result of Rabbi Jesus Cunobeline's

Egyptian trip were numerous and one of the most enduring charges of the Jews. 'They even ventured to call him a magician and a deceiver of the people', complained St Justin Martyr.[5] It is a matter of interest in this premise that the word 'Druid' partly derived from 'dru', which also meant 'a magician, sorcerer, druid'.[6]

It was indeed strange to read yet another revealing passage in the writings of Justin Martyr. Justin, giving as his authority Trogus Pompeius, showed Joseph of Arimathea, the 'father' of Rabbi Jesus Cunobeline, as having acquired a great knowledge in magical arts with the high priests of Egypt.[7] This assertion bears more the evidence of fact on its face than the transparent fabrications concocted by the later presbyters. Interestingly enough, the church again recorded the word 'magician' in relation to Rabbi Jesus, this time by Bishop Eusebius in the Fourth Century. He said that Hierocles, Governor or Bithymia (c. 303) claimed the First Century sage, Apollonius of Tyana had done works far greater than had done Rabbi Jesus, who Hierocles described as 'a magician and a robber'.[8]

One of the best and most unquestionable proofs of 'Jesus the magician' assertion was found in the Gregoriana Museum in Rome. On a sarcophagus panelled with bas-reliefs representing the miracles of the Gospel Jesus Christ may be seen the full figure of Rabbi Jesus, who, in the depiction of the resurrection of Lazarus, appeared beardless and equipped with a wand in the received guise of a necromancer, whilst the corpse of Lazarus was swathed in bandages as an Egyptian mummy. This sarcophagus was placed among the earliest productions of that particular form of art which later inundated the world with mosaics and engravings representing the events and personages of the *New Testament*.[9] 'The name of Lazarus suggests symbolism', said the *Encyclopedia Biblia*. Bishop Irenaeus (c. 200) agreed:

> And he that was 'dead' came forth bound with bandages, feet and hands.
> This was symbolical of that man who had been bound in sins.[10]

Simon, also of *New Testament* fame was, like Rabbi Jesus, called a 'magician' and some Bibles actually recorded his name, Simon Magi. It was possible that Simon the Magician was the same Simon recorded as Rabbi Jesus' brother,[11] and he was called a 'magician' because he too had been initiated into the Mysteries of Egypt.[12] It was with Simon Magi we see one of the earliest clashes between Christianity's exoteric (external) doctrines and the esoteric (spiritual) teachings of the Mystery Schools. An interesting legend concerned Simon Magi and told of his theosophical contests with Simon of Petra while the two were said to have been promulgating their differing doctrines. In relaying this story, it should be remembered that Simon Magi was a High Initiate and knew the Secret of the Ancient Mystery Schools, whereas Simon of Petra appeared to have been only aware of a lesser understanding.[13]

According to a story the church wrote some 400 years after his death,[14] Simon Magi was to prove his spiritual superiority by ascending to heaven in a chariot of fire. In the story he was made to be picked up and carried high into the air by unseen infernal spirits. When Simon of Petra saw this, he cried out with a loud voice ordering the invisible spirits to release their hold on Simon Magi, and they obeyed. Simon Magi fell a great distance and was killed, decisively proving to the 'rabble' when told, the superiority of the Christian saint's powers. This story was undoubtedly manufactured out of whole cloth, as it was only one of many accounts concerning Simon Magi's death, none of which agreed.

The initiation of Rabbi Jesus into the Greater Mysteries

Those who were initiated into the Ancient Mysteries took a solemn oath never to reveal what had passed within the sacred walls. Every year only a comparatively few Egyptian initiations were conducted, and the number of persons who knew their secrets was never at any time large. The initiations always took place with the onset of darkness and the candidate was entranced for periods of varying lengths, depending upon the level of the degree for which he had entered.

The first initiatory step involved a forty-day procedure that basically involved purification, not only in physical form, but dissolving all tendencies to evil thoughts, purifying the mind as well. He fasted, alternatively on vegetables, juices and very special herbal concoctions. The *New Testament* recorded that this happened to Rabbi Jesus who 'was led into the desert . . . and he fasted forty days and forty nights' (Matt. 4:1–2). There are two important matters arising from this Gospel narrative. Firstly it was recorded that Rabbi Jesus 'was led' into the desert, he was led by the person or guide who was to see him through his initiation into the knowledge of the Mysteries. Secondly, the number 'forty' used in relation to Rabbi Jesus can be found many times in the Bible. Bishop Augustine of Hippo (354–430) expressed amazement about this number when he said, 'How then, is work perfected in the number forty?'[15]

When analyzed, the number forty was used in both the *Old* and *New Testaments* as expressive of a particular period of probation or trial. The Israelites, for example, wandered forty years in the wilderness, and forty years of bondage they also had to serve under the hard yoke of the Philistines. Moses was made to spend forty days on the Mount of Sinai and both David and Solomon were made to reign for forty years each.[16] Elijah was forty days in hiding. For forty days the deluge fell and for yet another forty days Noah was shut within the ark. The men of Ninevah had a like period of probation under the preaching of Jonah. The punishment of scourging of criminals was limited to forty strokes (Deut. 25:3) so when Rabbi Jesus

Cunobeline entered into his probation period it had to be for forty days, such was the tradition of the times. This trial period involved more than just fasting. During the forty days and nights of ordeal, the candidate was required to study astronomical charts to supplement his skills in astronomy and memorize charts of the heavens. They were also given a particular ritual from which to memorize certain passwords, secret signs and handclasps, skills that are still practiced to this day in Freemasonry.

Nor were these initiations limited to Egypt. The ancient civilizations inherited these Mysteries from a remote antiquity and they constituted part of a primitive revelation from the gods to the human race. Almost every people of pre-Christian times possessed its institution and tradition of the Mysteries. The Romans, the Druids of Britain, the Greeks, the Cretans, the Syrians, the Hindus, the Persians, the Maya and the American Indians, among others, had corresponding temples and rites with a system of graduated illuminations for the initiates.

The modern world knows little of these ancient rites yet they were conducted in a huge variety of buildings the world over. Dozens of hypotheses are resorted to, for example, one more unlikely than the other, as to the sixty-two 'Round Towers' of Ireland. Those cylindrical edifices with a single door around three metres from the ground, were built for no other purposes—they were sacred places of initiation. The 'Towers' which are also found throughout the East in Asia were directly connected with the Mystery-initiations.[17] The candidates for initiation were placed in them for three days and three nights, whenever there was no temple with a subterranean crypt close at hand.

In this aspect of the initiatory procedure we again see a direct Gospel parallel with Rabbi Jesus saying, 'After three days I shall rise again',[18] for he knew the finishing process he was to undertake would take three days—being a symbol of the period of time required to complete a condition of development. The ancient Egyptian hieroglyphic texts speak of an initiate as 'twice-born', and he was permitted to add to his name the words 'he who has renewed his life', so that on some ancient tomb-inscriptions, archaeologists still discover these phases descriptive of the spiritual status of the deceased person. So little did the later Gospel writers understand the initiatory process that they never perceived they were developing a story that included a Rabbi's (and Arch Druid of Britain) experience in an Egyptian Mystery School.

The place of the skull

Using Gospel narratives and combining them with what was recorded about the Mystery Schools and their initiatory process, we learn what the 'place of the skull' really was. Church dictionaries defined Golgotha as the place of the crucifixion of Jesus Christ. However, the oldest Gospels used the word 'skull', and 'gol-go-tha' was simply the Greek word for 'skull'.[19] In the Fifth Century it came to be taken to mean a barren craggy, oval shaped hilltop outside the city of Jerusalem. Such a physical place as Golgotha was not documented in any historical records and was only found in the *New Testament* where it was later interpreted as a place or location.

The 'place of the skull' was a reference to the display of a human skull in the initiatory process and has been used by the Mystery Schools in such a manner for thousands of years.[20] For them, it was symbolic of Mortality and was used to connect the initiate with a higher awareness of his purpose that cannot be reached with words.

This painting of the crucifixion was from the School of Jean Fouquet, c.1485. Note the human skull at the base of the cross.
© Medieval Painters

It appeared the word Golgotha was sometimes associated or confused with a Gilgal, a megalithic circle of vertical stones, also called a cromlech. It was probable that initiations were carried out at these Stonehenge-type structures. They were mentioned in the *Old Testament* when Joshua set up 'a Gilgal' with twelve vertical stone pillars after crossing the River Jordan[21] and, interestingly, both Elijah and Elisha were also associated with 'a Gilgal'.[22]

The ancient Egyptians introduced a full skeleton at their feasts to impress the idea of the evanescence of all earthly enjoyments. In early times, the 'death's heads' appeared on heralds to denote that the deceased person was the last of the family. The Masons subsequently adopted the symbol, and in all degrees where it was necessary to impress the idea of mortality, a skull or a skull and crossed bones, were used for that purpose. If we wonder why 'the skull' is so important in Christianity today, it was simply a reflection of its vital and compulsory use in ancient (and modern) initiatory rituals. In many old Christian paintings, particularly those in St Catherine's Monastery (Mt Sinai), a skull can be seen depicted in association with famous churchmen. Orders of monks, such as Dominicans and Franciscans were always associated with human skulls. One of the several mysterious and ancient crystal skulls was actually called 'The Jesuit' because it had been associated with the Jesuit priests of Italy. Paintings of St Francis of Assisi often showed him reverently holding a skull in front of him and the Knights Templar are known to have worshipped a mysterious head. Some say this was actually the mummified head of Rabbi Jesus Cunobeline but this was pure assumption. In old engravings of Masonic ceremonies the skull is displayed in the final stages of initiation.

The story of the missing Torah

Tradition clearly held that Rabbi Jesus Cunobeline had been initiated into the Egyptian Mysteries and that he had brought the substance of privileged information back from Egypt. Later church writings also established that the mysterious Secret was well known to Rabbi Jesus. This interesting passage was recorded in the *Clementine Homilies*:

> And Peter said; We remember that Jesus and Rabbi, as commanding said to us, guard the Secret for me, and the sons of my House [Royal?]. Wherefore also he explained to his disciples, privately, the Secret of the Kingdom of the heavens.

Some of the followers of Rabbi Jesus expressed surprise to find him using unusual forms of expression with the people. 'Why speakest thou unto them in parables?' they often inquisitively inquired (Matt. 10:13). Rabbi Jesus answered them:

> To you it has been given to know the Secret of the Kingdom of heaven, but to them it has not been given.

According to Young's *Analytical Concordance*, the exact meaning of the word 'secret' as used in the *New Testament* was, 'that which is known only to the initiated' and the reply of Rabbi Jesus was that of one initiate speaking to another. Other *New Testament* statements such as 'It is given unto you to know the Mysteries', 'we speak the wisdom of God in a Mystery' and 'we are stewards of the Mysteries of God and understand all Mysteries' clearly showed that Rabbi Jesus and some of his associates were in possession of particular secret knowledge.

The custom of communicating only to a portion of the community was known among early Christian writers as 'Disciplina Arcani' or 'The Discipline of the Secret'. That Secret was guarded with the utmost care from the obtrusive eyes of all who had not been duly initiated into the sacred rites that qualified them to be present. Johann Mosheim, the great Christian historian (c. 1755) said, 'The [Christian] religion having thus, in both its branches, the speculative as well as the practical, assumed a twofold character . . . one public or common, the other private or mysterious'. The term used by the initiates to dismiss those ineligible to hear or see their performance was, 'Holy things for the holy, let the dogs depart'. The Gospel accounts of Rabbi Jesus' ministry provided a number of cases where he taught an open exoteric message in parables to the rabble and then privately instructed others in deeper esoteric or secret meaning.

It is no longer possible to exclude from research into the story of Judas Khrestus and Rabbi Jesus any document that may hold out the faintest hope of throwing even a sidelight on the countless obscurities of the church texts. Most opportune for our inquiry, then, was the recent publication of a curious ancient writing called *The Narrative of Joseph of Arimathea*. This very concise old document has been given only brief treatment by church historians in the construction of their exhaustive dictionaries and encyclopedias. For the thesis presented in this book, however, it sheds a whole new light on the Gospels and their development. Therefore, it compels the setting forth of the substance of the whole matter as it was found recorded in this writing.

As with many Christian writings, including the Gospels, there was a dispute as to the likely date when this document was written, although general academic belief dates it at sometime around the beginning of the Third Century. The genesis of the story was obviously much earlier and what was recorded in this old document failed to capture the attention of most researchers of the *New Testament*. The manuscript generally related to a fascinating account of the only *Torah* Scroll at Jerusalem being stolen and, because of this, the Jews were in a state of despair because they could not conduct a Passover. This was significant in our study because it was Rabbi Jesus Cunobeline who was accused of stealing the *Torah*. A woman called Sarra publicly accused Rabbi Jesus of this act and the Jews said to her, 'We believe you for they held her as a prophetess'.

> At the fourth and fifth hours they went out and found Jesus walking in the street. Towards evening they obtained a guard of soldiers. They came to Jesus and saying, 'Hail Rabbi'. They took Jesus to the High Priest who examined him. Jesus was held captive upon Sarra's word.
>
> On the next day, being Wednesday, at the ninth hour, they brought him

(Jesus) to the priest's hall and asked, 'Why did you take away the Torah?'
He was silent.

The story of the missing Torah finds a parallel account in traditional Rabbinic and Jewish literature. Many readers may say, 'Why did we not know even so much as that there was a recorded Jewish life of Rabbi Jesus'. There certainly was, and one of the most persistent charges of the Jews against him was that he had learned something 'special' in Egypt. This statement has puzzled researchers of the story of Jesus Christ for centuries and the overriding importance it assumed in Jewish tradition supported the fact that it may have actually happened. In the 'Toldoth Jeschu', while we still hear of Jesus learning something supernatural in Egypt, its main feature was the recording of the robbing of the Torah (and the Divine Name) by a 'strange device' from the Temple of Jerusalem. This 'strange device' may have simply been a cunning manoeuvre, for in the several variants of the story, we can actually see the evolution of the tradition whereby Rabbi Jesus was said to have outwitted the guardians of the Torah Scroll. The Talmud, however, knew nothing of the robbing of the 'Name of God' from the Temple, but in recording the tradition of bringing 'a magic secret' out of Egypt, it added details of the means whereby it was said to have been conveyed out of that country. Thus in the Palestinian Gemara was written:

> He who scratches on the skin in the fashion of writing is guilty, but he who marks on the skin in the fashion of writing, is exempt from punishment—Rabbi Eliezer said to them: 'But has not Jesus brought "magic" out of Egypt in this way?' They answered him: 'On account of one fool we do not ruin a multitude of reasonable men.'

The fact that the Rabbis called Jesus a 'fool' for 'making marks on the skin in the fashion of writing' is extremely relevant to this discussion. However, Rabbi Jesus was not the 'fool' his associates thought. As little known as it is, there are several Jewish traditions of Jesus bringing writings from Egypt on his skin, but the one recorded here was the closest in time to the original story. It was interesting to note that Rabbi Eliezer met with the objection that Rabbi Jesus brought something mysterious from Egypt by 'marks' on the skin but not by 'scratching' (tattoos). The marks were presumably not letters proper—the writing of words in Hebrew—for the discussion was not of writing, but of 'marks in the fashion of writing'. Did it refer to diagrams of sigils, or drawings of some kind, or to hieroglyphs? It certainly did—it referred directly and only to the Secret in the *Bible*.

In discussing this complex line of tradition, all that need be said is that ancient Jewish belief seems plainly to have preserved a strong account of the inscription of curious marks on the skin of Rabbi Jesus. The idea in the mind of the Rabbi was presumably that the Egyptians were known to be very jealous of their 'mystical lore' (secrets) and did all they could to prevent writings revealing what was being taken out of their country. Rabbi Jesus then, according to the oldest Rabbinic tradition, was said to have circumvented their vigilance by subterfuge of the kind recounted in the Palestinian Gemera.

In considering the preservation of these peculiar descriptions of the *Torah* being stolen in both Jewish and Christian tradition, we may possibly be provided with the answer to a major unknown Gospel problem.

It was the Sanhedrin who subsequently tried Rabbi Jesus for stealing the *Torah*, not the Romans.[23] They were the supreme Jewish religious, political and legal council in Jerusalem, at and before, *New Testament* times. Before the beginning of the Christian era the Sanhedrin became sufficiently confident in its authority that the high priest, Hyrcanus II (63–40BC), summoned Herod to stand trial on capital sentences he had passed without the Sanhedrin's authority (Josephus). At this particular time they had four species of capital punishment, all just as cruel as Roman crucifixion. They were stoning, burning, beheading and strangulation.

When Herod took Jerusalem in 37BC he retaliated by killing the entire membership of the Sanhedrin (Josephus). Under the Roman procurators (6–41AD) the Sanhedrin's power increased once again, so when the Gospels started to come into existence in the second half of the Second Century, the writers represented the Sanhedrin as the supreme court of justice.[24] The chief priests were the key figures in the Sanhedrin. They were probably the former high priests and members of the priestly aristocracy from which the high priest were chosen. According to the historian Josephus, they were 'the leading men of the people, the leading people of Jerusalem, the powerful and the dignitaries'.

The real grievance against Rabbi Jesus by the Sanhedrin was hinted at in the Gospel of John (11:45–53). Here it was said that the Jewish high priests, meeting informally, decided to try Rabbi Jesus. Members sat in a half circle so they could see each other. Before them stood two scribes, one writing down what was said for, and the other what was said against the accused. The high priests 'questioned' him about 'his teachings' (John 18:19) and Rabbi Jesus replied that he had 'said nothing secretly' (John 18:20). If the Sanhedrin believed Rabbi Jesus has stolen the precious *Torah*, they would indeed have had a reason to bring him to trial, for the theft of their most valued document prevented them from keeping the Passover and partaking in the consumption of the obligatory four chalices of wine. Not only had they lost their *Torah*, they also had lost access to the very sacred Secret it contained.

In connection with the charges against Rabbi Jesus, there was a remarkable passage preserved in the Babylonian Gemara that demanded attention. This recorded the essence of the original charge against Rabbi Jesus and it ran as follows (in part):

> . . . that thou shalt not have a son or disciple who burns his food publicly, like Jesus the Nazarene . . .[25]

The main point of the accusation was contained in the word 'publicly'. It was the doing of something or other 'in public' which apparently might not only have been tolerated privately, but which was presumably the natural thing to do in private. The main burden of Christian tradition was that Rabbi Jesus went out and taught the people the Law of Moses . . . the poor, the outcast, the oppressed, the sinners, to all of whom, according to Rabbinic law, the mysteries of the *Torah* were not to be expounded unless they had first of all purified themselves by the long process of initiation. These so-called 'ignorant and unclean' persons were 'Amme ha-aretz' (men of the earth) and the Secret in the *Torah* was certainly not for them.

The strict fold of Rabbis charged Jesus because 'he burnt his food publicly'. That is to say, Rabbi Jesus was about to renounce openly what he had learned in Egypt—he was about to reveal the Secret in the Bible, that sacred Mystery of the Ancient Schools and, more importantly, the highly confidential Divine name of God. He said so himself:

> Nothing is covered up that will not be revealed, or hidden that should not be known. Therefore whatever was said in the dark shall be heard in the light, and what was whispered in private rooms shall now be proclaimed from the rooftops. (Luke 12:2)

The disclosure of secret information blatantly violated the Ancient Rule of the Order of High Priests and they had to stop him. It was evident that the whole point of the story of 'burning food publicly' had to do with some scandal or breaking of the established rule or order of things, or with paving the way for doing so, and was the downfall of Rabbi Jesus. The main point here, however, is the question of why would Rabbi Jesus want the *Torah*. He said:

> Think not that I have come to destroy the *Torah* and the Prophets [the additional *Old Testament* books]. I came not to destroy but to complete. (Matt. 5:17)

From the evidence of both the early church and Rabbinic records, one of the most tenacious charges against Rabbi Jesus was that he had learned 'something special' in Egypt. What this meant was that he had traveled to an Egyptian Mystery School, learned the 'Secret', and returned to Jerusalem with 'marks in the fashion of writing' on his skin. With these inscriptions, he then needed the *Torah* (and there was only one at Jerusalem)[26] to publicly demonstrate to the uninitiated the Secret that it held, an act most stringently forbidden by the initiates. This attempted disclosure of age-old hidden information offended the priestly line 'for one is wholly forbidden to reveal their mysteries; rather one must keep them secret in silence'.[27] For this reason he was arrested by the Sanhedrin, charged, and tried. 'The chief priests accused him of many things' (Mark 15:3), found him guilty and sentenced him to die by stoning for attempting to make public the essence of the hidden Mysteries.

The Gospels recorded that the Rabbis 'took up stones to throw at him, but Jesus hid' (John 8:59). On a later occasion, he was captured and attempts were made to throw him 'headlong off a cliff' but Jesus managed to again flee unharmed (Luke 4:29). Yet another attempt to stone him failed, he 'escaped' and went into 'hiding' (John 10:31). It is impossible now to recover accurately the subsequent movements of Rabbi Jesus but a combination of writings indicated that he entirely left the area with the *Torah*, returned to Britain, but was pursued.

The stoning at Lud

The early church knew the real story of the death of Rabbi Jesus. In the research for this book an ancient document titled the Arethas Codex became available. This writing appeared to have had at least two previous titles but in its current form it purported to be the works of the Second Century presbyter, Bishop Clement of Alexandria. This writing stated that, 'In his sixty-third year of his age [Rabbi Jesus] was stoned to death . . .'

Another of the early presbyters also confirmed Rabbi Jesus was killed by stoning. Writing about 197–198, the Bishop of Carthage, Tertullian, rhetorically addressed the Jews stating, 'ye stoned him'.[28] Tertullian spoke of the stoning of Rabbi Jesus not as the invention of an enemy, but simply as a genuine piece of accepted church history.

The Rabbinic records confirmed the church accounts and stated that Rabbi Jesus Cunobeline was eventually captured and stoned to death by a person called Pinhas at a place called Lud.[29] Both the Palestinian and Babylonian *Talmuds* contain a precise description of his death that, in both cases, was appended to the following passage from the Mishna:

> . . . and to bring him forward to the tribunal and stone him. And thus they have done to Jesus at Lud, and they hanged him on the day before Passover.[30]

But where was Lud? Some have suggested that maybe it derived from Lydda to Ludim to Lod.[31] However, this was not so for the origin of the name was recorded in rare old documents. The name Lud (sometimes Llud) derived from 'the great burh, Lundunaborg, which is the greatest and most famous of all burhs in the northern lands'.[32] Both name and town alike are popularly accounted for in the wonderful legend of Geoffrey of Monmouth[33] that found credence in the Middle Ages. According to this story, Brutus, a descendent of Aeneas who was the son of Venus, founded this city after the fall of Troy, circa 1100BC, and called it Troynovant, or New Troy. About one thousand years later (c. 41BC), there reigned in the same town King Lud, the father of Tenvantius, Mary Magdalene's father, who built walls and towers to his city, and renamed it Cáer Lud. Thus Lud's Town became Londinium in the Fourth Century and then London, the capital city of England today and chief city of the British Empire.[34] King Lud's name still lives in London today and is encompassed in one of the seven double gates called Ludgate, the location of St Paul's Cathedral and the probable site of the stoning of Rabbi Jesus Cunobeline.

Both these ancient Rabbinic accounts are part and parcel of the Lud tradition and the death of Rabbi Jesus in both writings was by stoning in Britain, clearly inferred from the Babylonian *Talmud*. Stoning, and then the hanging of the body of Rabbi Jesus, was recorded in Jewish history, and Jesus Christ 'hanging on a stake' was also preserved in the canonical Christian writings today.[35] The word 'stake', not 'cross', was found in all oldest Christian Gospels and the 'cross tradition' did not enter the *New Testament* until centuries later. The church admitted that 'there is no proof of the use of a cross until much later' than the Sixth Century.[36] The word 'cross' was later substituted for the word 'stake' in the rewriting of the Christian texts.[37]

It was recorded in Christian archives that the general use of the crucifix became ratified at the Sixth Ecumenical Council in 680 (Canon 82). The council decreed that 'the figure of a man fastened to a cross be now adopted'. The new church logo was later confirmed by Pope Hadrian 1 (772–95).[38] About a century afterwards, the first pictures of Jesus Christ standing against a cross slowly started to appear, mainly in Syrian art. In these depictions, he was always of ripe age, 'utterly divested of all circumstances of suffering'[39] and generally clothed in a long sleeveless tunic, called a 'colobium'. Earliest illustrations dates from the end of the Eighth Century and probably the very first was called the Palatine Crucifixion, discovered in 1856 as a *graffito* on a wall in the page's chamber of the Imperial Palace on the Palatine Hill in Rome. It showed a cross against which Jesus stood upright, unbound, with arms flung wide apart as if praying. But Jesus had an ass' head. In the left foreground was a much smaller man in an adoring posture, and a Greek inscription which read: 'Alaxamene worships his God'.

Rabbi Jesus Cunobeline wished to help people's spiritual development by disclosing the ultimate Secret he had learnt during the Egyptian process of initiation.[40] The Rabbinic records of Rabbi Jesus said of him, 'In the beginning a prophet, in the end a deceiver',[41] the deception being Rabbi Jesus' desire to reveal to the world the forbidden sacred Secret. That mysterious information is revealed in this author's next book, 'The Secret in the Bible'.

The role of Pontius Pilate.

The Romans had nothing to do with the punishment of Rabbi Jesus Cunobeline. No doubt it would be convenient to bring Pontius Pilate into the Jewish *Talmud* stories of Rabbi Jesus but they are conspicuous by their absence. The Christian and Jewish descriptions of Jesus Christ's life were totally at a variance with each other. That was because they were both talking about different men. When compared with the *New Testament* there was an obvious conflict of testimony because the Christian writings subsisted around a crucifixion and the Jewish writings around a stoning. The Second Century historian Celsus provided a hint when he referred to the 'alleged crucifixion' of Jesus Christ. The church later burnt his books.

Death by stoning.
Etching by W. Palmer. © A.C. Bushby. 2001

It was probable that the parchments that stunned parish priest Berenger Saunière and his church associates around 1886 contained this information, and it was also probable that it was Saunière who created the headstone at Bingerbrück in Germany. It was said the scrolls provided evidence that the crucifixion was a fraud and Rabbi Jesus was still alive in 45. The reference here to the staged crucifixion was to that of Judas Khrestus who had given up his birthright to save his life. Due to the discrepancies that commonly exist concerning the dating of this era, it was not possible to establish exactly when Rabbi Jesus was stoned, but what was revealed about the scrolls found at Rennes-le-Chateau determined that both Judas Khrestus and Rabbi Jesus were still alive after 45.

According to a Jewish legend, three boatloads of Jews arrived in Arles (Southern France) circa 53AD, and the theory proposed is that this group were pursuing Rabbi Jesus Cunobeline. They eventually captured him in Lud's Town to where he had fled and reunited with his son, King Caradoc and other close family members. At this stage in his life he was approximately sixty-three years of age, which confirmed the records of Bishop Clement of Alexandria.

CHAPTER FOURTEEN

The expansion of the Krist knowledge

JOSEPHUS RECORDED THAT THE SANHEDRIN CONDEMNED JAMES HEROD, the Gospel brother of Judas Khrestus and Rabbi Jesus, to be stoned to death, but he escaped punishment. In 62 James arrived to settle in Britain[1] just a year or so before Rabbi Jesus Cunobeline's death, and their Druidic beliefs were developed and expanded under his guidance. From around that time onwards, the Celtic church reaffirmed its doctrines, using the basic Essenic and Druidic traditions that were concerned primarily with education, agriculture, an ethical code, a strong sense of fraternity among its participants, and the transmission of the secret Krist knowledge. Their order was strictly monastic and was essentially based upon the teachings and social codes of Rabbi Jesus Cunobeline.

At this time, the Gospels we know today were yet to be written and therefore unknown to the early church in Britain. Although considered austere by the somewhat ostentatious Roman church, the Celtic church, in time, became popular throughout Europe and many Celtic priests later took up church positions in Europe.

The Celtic church became an hereditary institution, with the high bishops in Britain being drawn generally from a dynastic family, and their office passing from father to son in many instances. Certain British gods and goddesses were subsequently incorporated into the structure and the Celtic church sponsored its own saints independently of the Roman church. Through the ages they included such well-known characters as St Bridget, St Patrick, St David and St Columba. Although now generally perceived to have been part of the overall Christian movement, the ministry and doctrines of the British saints were totally divorced from what is now called the Roman Catholic church.

It was not until the Eleventh Century that the Western church became subjected to Roman influence through the marriage of an hereditary Celtic priest to a Catholic heiress to the Saxon House of England. This affected certain aspects of the Celtic tradition and eventually led to the establishment of a British Bible (*King James Version*) that differed substantially from the Roman Bible (*Vulgate*).

Emperor Vespasian proclaimed "messiah"

About twelve years after the stoning of Rabbi Jesus Cunobeline (c.66), Emperor Nero Claudius Caesar (54–68) sent Flavius Sabinus Vespasian to the East to conduct a war against the Jews. His conduct of the conflict raised his reputation, and Vespasian was proclaimed Emperor at Alexandria on 1 July 69, and soon after all through the East. He traveled to Rome in the following year, leaving his son Titus to continue the war against the Jews. Josephus, the Jewish historian, was present with Titus at the siege of Jerusalem, and in 71 accompanied him to Rome where both father and son triumphed together on account of the conquest of the Jews.

Emperor Vespasian took possession of all Jewish religious artifacts that had previously been safely stored in the Temple, including the precious Torah, and stored them in the Capitoline Jove in Rome. He then proclaimed the entire Jewish territory the Roman Emperor's personal property, and had his decision officially ratified by the Senate. He also ruled that the half-shekel yearly contribution of Jews the world over to their Temple be redirected into a special fund, the Fiscus Judaicus, and paid into the Capitoline Jove. Josephus recorded that Vespasian personally kept the Torah, revealing that it had at sometime been recovered from Rabbi Jesus Cunobeline and replaced in the Temple. Vespasian also took the coloured priestly robes from the Jerusalem Temple and stored them in a special room in his own Palace on the Palatine Hill. The Roman empire now owned the entire collection of Jewish religious artifacts that had been built up over many centuries, the great Temple of Jerusalem was no longer, and the Jews had been disposed of their land, their treasure and the physical substance of their religion.

At a gala public forum, Josephus then applied the Essenic messianic prophecy to Emperor Vespasian and proclaimed him the 'Deliverer' ('Redeemer' in some translations) of the people, for which Josephus received the freedom of the city from Vespasian. Josephus then assumed the name of the Flavian family (Flavius), and was treated with great favour by Vespasian and his successors, Titus and Domitian. From that time on, and by legal inheritance, all subsequent Roman Emperors were messiahs, 'but the Jews, referring it [the messianic prophecy] to themselves, rebelled'.[2] This was the beginning of a major religious problem that would not even start to be resolved until 325, the time of Emperor Constantine and the first Christian council at Nicaea.

CHAPTER FIFTEEN

The Mystery Schools knew about Rabbi Jesus

S IR FRANCIS BACON AND THE MYSTERY SCHOOLS KNEW THE FULL
story of Rabbi Jesus Cunobeline's royal family adventures some 400
years ago. Not only was the knowledge that Rabbi Jesus Cunobeline
was initiated in Egypt and later stoned in Lud also known amongst the
gatherings of the Secret Societies of the Middle Ages, it was secretly coded
into the Shakespearean plays.

Throughout the Shakespearean 'Folios' and 'Quartos' are scores of hidden
acrostic signatures, some of which are ingenious in their design. The simplest
form was called 'The Capital Initial Code' whereby a name (in this instance,
Francis Bacon's) was concealed in the first few letters of consecutive lines.
In *The Tempest* appeared a striking example of Bacon's acrostic:

> **B**egun to tell me what I am but stopt,
> **A**nd left me to a bootelesse inquisition,
> **CON**cluding, stay; not yet . . .[1]

Here the initial letters of the first and second lines, together with the first
three letters of the third line (initialled) formed the word 'Bacon'. It was
not so much the word 'BACON' that was of concern here. The shape in
which those letters were formed was the important issue. When drawing a
line around the design of Bacon's name, the letter 'L', like this, was revealed:

> **B** egun to tell me what I am but stopt,
> **A** nd left me to a bootelesse inquisition,
> **C O N** cluding, stay; not yet . . .'

This letter connected with other letters following on in the writings until 33 consecutive letters are combined. Those letters then created full words that spelt out particular statements. For the purposes of this exercise, this 33 letter acrostic is simply called 'Bacon's Code'. It appeared in both the Shakespearean Plays and the *Bible*, and an example of its application is now given.

What was Sir Francis Bacon trying to say in using the cipher number 33 in the Bible? In the Preface to a book he wrote called *Advancement of Learning* (1640), Sir Francis gave a clue when he wrote that 'the glory of God is to conceal a thing and the glory of the Kings is to find it out'. This leads to the *Old Testament* Book of 'Kings' where further ciphers using the number 33 are found, and here an explanation of what he wanted known could be established. The first Temple of Solomon stood (in the biblical timetable) for 33 years in its pristine splendour, an allegory if there ever was one. King David was made to rule for 33 years in Jerusalem, just as Jesus Christ was made to be crucified in the 33rd year of his life.

Yet the Gospels and the early church movement recorded that Rabbi Jesus Cunobeline was much older than 33 years (John 8:57). If church records revealed that Rabbi Jesus lived to an advanced age, why was the mysterious number 33 arbitrarily chosen to symbolize the duration of his life? That question is easy to answer.

In the Mystery Schools, 33 mystical years are required to obtain Mastership. The passing of seven major initiations, the last being life threatening, requires 33 actual degrees or transformations of consciousness. Sir Francis Bacon was recording the fact that he, the Knights Templar, and the Secret Societies of his time, knew Rabbi Jesus was a 33° Initiate into the Sacred Mysteries. It should not come as any surprise to learn that the 'Spear-shaker' also received a mention in Sir Francis Bacon's editing of the *New Testament*. In the final chapters of the Gospel of John, Sir Francis had the suffering Jesus Christ prodded in his left side by a 'Spear-shaker'. This verse is not recorded in the oldest versions of the first Gospel written.

It is difficult to approach any phase of the life of Sir Francis Bacon without being confronted with what appears to be evidence of careful preparation to reveal, yet conceal, secret information. This observation does not result from imagination or prejudice. Much of his coding was centred directly on the Masonic number 33. An example was found in the SHAKESPEARE FOLIO OF 1623, THIRTY-THREE that was strangely enough 'Dedicated' to 'The Pair of Brethren' (Mariamne Herod's twins?). The vital clue here is the 33 letters making up this sequential coded statement, and that points the enquirer directly to page 33. When unravelling 'Bacon's Code' in the 1623 Folio, it is almost impossible to comprehend what can be found, but it is there for the whole world to see. Hidden in Bacon's favourite cipher system can be found 33 consecutive letters (on page 33) which spell out the words, JESUS CHRIST, INITIATION, GREAT PYRAMID. The existence of this cipher in the Shakespeare Folio of 1623 is sufficient indication to prove Sir Francis Bacon's editorial connection with both the King James Bible and the Shakespeare plays.

The fact that the name Jesus Christ was found secreted in the Shakespearean writings was not the only amazing thing about the coding of Sir Francis Bacon. Other examples are found in the *Old Testament* that he began editing upon his appointment as Solicitor-General in 1607. An example can be found by turning to Psalm 46, and then counting 46 words from the beginning until arriving at the word, 'Shake'. Count then 46 words from the end, and the word there is 'spear'. There are 111 words between Shake and Spear, which was the numerical signature of 'Bacon' by the method numerologists call, the 'K. Count'. 'Shake-speare' Bacon was 46 years of age when he structured in this cipher and the year was 1607.

All mixed up on the way to the 'place of the skull'. In this Twelfth Century fresco we see several major elements of initiation applied to Rabbi Jesus. Of particular interest is the cable-tow around Jesus' neck. This procedure was (and still is) used in leading a candidate through various stages of initiation. The important numbers used in initiations are secretly ciphered into this fresco. There are 33 persons shown in this drawing, as there are 33 dots around Rabbi Jesus' head. The 'spear-shakers' are present (seven in number) with one blade nearing Jesus' left chest. Whoever engraved this picture knew the truth about the story in the New Testament.[2]

The hidden clues continue. In 'Hamlet', for example, the page number 100 has been omitted, 257 follows 156 and other errors are clear, obviously made in order to deliberately obtain a particular result on the last page. One could go on and on, but the most startling example of 'Bacon's Code' affecting the current work was found on page III of the Shakespeare Folio 1623. T. Tenison, author of Baconiana, recorded the following clue in 1679:

> And whosoever would understand the Lord Bacon's Cipher, let him consult
> that accurate Edition in Latine, in Folio, Anno 1623 for the form of the
> Letters of the Alphabet, in which much of the Mysterie consisteth.[3]

The ingenuity displayed in the manipulation of words and numbers to create this cipher is almost beyond the comprehension of the human mind. The 33 letter coded message was intentional, having a cryptic meaning that concealed specific information that Sir Francis Bacon wanted discovered at a later time. It said:

JESUS CHRIST STONED DEATH LUNDUNABORG.

It is deeply significant that the original edited manuscripts of the King James Bible are, like the Shakespearean Plays, 'LOST'. Sir Francis Bacon encoded this information in capital letters into both the Bible and Shakespearean Plays.[4]

Whoever unravels the *Shakespeare Folio 1623* may well make the greatest literary discovery of all time. The wonder is how it will be possible for anyone to pierce the veil and reveal the secrets of this volume. One thing is for sure—when the codes in this document are deciphered the value of the *Shakespeare Folio 1623* will certainly be enhanced and it will stand alone as the greatest monument of achievements of the human intellect.

CHAPTER SIXTEEN

The early churchmen

FTER THE LIFETIMES OF THE TWINS HAD PASSED, THE UNUSUAL circumstances of their existence led to considerable excitement amongst the simple population and elements of Judas Khrestus and Rabbi Jesus Cunobeline's very different lives made their way into the discourses of the public orators. These men were called presbyters and they wandered around the district spinning the public an assortment of yarns 'full of the boldest metaphor and rhetorical artifices of the age'.[1] They knew that Rabbi Jesus Cunobeline was a King and 'a son of God' and they also knew that Judas Khrestus was seen alive after he was believed to have been crucified. The essence of the story that eventually became the Christian religion developed with these two factors and this curious body of men were directly responsible. An ancient manuscript supported this assertion.

While making copies of rare books in the Library of the Christian Israelites, New York, in 1904, Dr Elise Louise Morris came across an untitled lengthy Latin manuscript written as a letter by an Essene Elder in Jerusalem to his brother in Alexandria. This old parchment roll had been previously preserved for centuries in the monasteries of the Grecian monks[2] and, apart from a pre-1900 attempt to burn it, this document still exists and is presently stored in a humidor in a private library north of London. Its entire contents were translated into English and subsequently published in 1919 under the commercial title, *The Crucifixion of Jesus by an Eyewitness*.[3]

The simplicity and candor of the essence of the narrative provided an overwhelming impression of truth and added a new dimension to the evolvement of the Christian texts. It was recorded that the simple people in the city, after hearing news that Judas Khrestus, 'a doomed man', was seen alive after he was thought to have been killed by crucifixion, assumed that 'he had risen up by the hand of God . . . and imagined him to be a supernatural being, and therefore throwed themselves down, believing a miracle had happened'. The Gospels confirmed this account, stating that 'when they saw him [after the crucifixion] they worshipped him, but some doubted' (Matt. 28:17). Whether they actually saw Judas Khrestus or mistook for him his twin brother, was impossible to determine, for both Judas Khrestus and Rabbi Jesus were at the crucifixion scene. The presbyters are today called the 'founding church fathers' and they subsequently expanded and developed the 'miracle' into something it never was. Knowledge of the peculiar nature of these men provides an understanding of the origin of the Christian texts, and the development of the early church.

Just who were 'the early church fathers'?

On no subject has the world been more blinded or deceived than that of the church's portrayal of the character and integrity of the presbyters. In spite of the existence of over-enthusiastic priesthood interpretations of the nature of the early clergy, there seems little doubt the prestigious modern-day titles created for them do not reflect a true portrait. Documentation suggests that they became regarded more honorably and grew in stature the farther they receded into the past.

It is of great importance to illustrate the intellectual condition that prevailed during the development of the church texts and correct some of the misunderstandings about the character of the men who set in motion one of the greatest frauds ever perpetrated. This chapter provides background information about the real nature of the men involved in the establishment of the Christian 'religion' (from the Latin word 'religio' meaning 'awe', 'scruple' and 'superstition') and deconstructs the facade built up around them by the church. The existence and character of the men we today call the 'early church fathers' was extensively recorded by earlier Christian historians and validated in the more comprehensive and older editions of the *Catholic Encyclopedias* (1908–1914).

The first Christian bishops

There is a common belief among Christians today that the apostles passed on Jesus Christ's message to bishops of the early church. This cannot be validated. Up until the Third Century, the word 'bishop' was unknown in the primitive church. The term used was 'presbyter' in Latin or 'presbyteros' in Greek. These people were also anciently known as 'capella' and 'capilliatus or capilliatum', depending on which translation and tense was adopted. In those formative years the transmission of both the *Old* and *New Testament* was oral. Rhetoric was the art of the public speaker and church writings were publicly 'read out loud'[4] by the presbyters to gatherings now called churches, and exactly as Matthew, Mark, Luke and John are read in churches today. During their time, the presbyters or capilliatum were beggared entertainers of the public and nothing more.

A study of Christian records showed 'it was those who received the gift of public speech who possessed all authority in the primitive church'. For the first 300 years 'the primitive church had no organization' and the clergy 'did not have a special title . . . they were generally called presbyters'.[5] The original meaning of that name shed light on these men. The word 'presbyter' simply meant 'old man' and a contraction of it resulted in the Old English word 'preost' which today is 'priest'. The word 'capilliatum' translated as 'having long hair' and 'capella' meant 'a dim, dirty fellow'.

The three presbyters generally accredited with founding the Christian religion were Irenaeus (115–202), Clement of Alexandria (160–215) and Tertullian (160–210). In *The Canon of the Bible*, Professor Samuel Davidson[6] said of them:

> The three presbyters of whom we are speaking had neither the ability nor inclination to examine the genesis of the documents . . . No analysis of their authenticity and genuineness was seriously attempted . . . The ends which they had in view, the polemic motives, their uncritical inconsistent assertions, their want of sure data, detract from their testimony . . . The very arguments they use to establish certain conclusions show weakness of perception.

Professor Davidson noted the type of men the early church fostered 'was, in general, very inferior intellectually . . . inhabiting a different mental universe'.

In the early Third Century writings of Tertullian, son of a Roman centurion, it stated that he and an array of other orators gave 'readings' from their writings at late afternoon receptions in the town square while standing on a speaker's box (pulpit). Tertullian went on to say, 'for where two or three people are gathered, there is a church (originally written 'chiche'), even if they are only lay people'. It was expected that the 'holder of the manuscript' would deliver his discourse interestingly, persuasively, with emotion and usually with a lesson. His main aim was to convince the audience of the validity of the story he expounded. In the contest for mastery, he was expected to make a point and prove a case.[7]

The best of the presbyters could read and write. They were called in Greek 'episkopos', which meant 'an overseer or watcher' of other orators who were illiterate and learnt their trade by rote. This word subsequently became 'biscop' in Old English and 'bishop' today. Thus, by the end of the

Third Century 'the title of bishop (biscop) came at length to be appropriated to the chief among them . . . one of these presbyters became the ruling bishop'.[8] He 'was essentially itinerant' and when he moved on, he left behind copies of his manuscripts and nominated another overseer to take over his position to orate those stories to the community left behind. In those early Christian years there was a great diversity of opinion amongst the orators about which of these various writings should actually be 'publicly read'.[9] They debated for centuries until they found they could not agree and then held councils and still could not agree. The resulting scandals were a huge embarrassment for the later church hierarchy with many records of these deliberations suppressed.[10]

In discussing matters associated with the development of the early clergy, the church itself admitted, 'One might indeed be curious about the interval between the time of the apostles and the beginning of the Third Century AD'.[11] The most prominent early presbyter, Irenaeus, said the body of church orators at his time numbered less than 100 people and 'they are as much above kings as the soul is above the body'.[12] By the year 253 its number had increased to 154. In a letter written by a presbyter named Cornelius to an associate called Fabius who lived at Antioch, he recorded the existence of '. . . forty-six presbyters, seven deacons, seven sub-deacons, two-two acolytes, and fifty-two exorcists, lectors and porters'.[13]

By the time of the first Christian council at Nicaea in 325, the number had increased to 'two thousand and forty eight presbyters, deacons, sub-deacons, acolytes and exorcists'. The number of actual presbyters was 318, mainly 'preosts' but amongst them several 'chief orators' or bishops. The exorcists 'said prayers for pretend exorcism' and the acolytes or 'door-keepers', as they later became called, were illiterate assistants who followed the presbyters.[14]

It was around this time, the beginning of the Fourth Century, that the bishops first received their special power. It was officially given to them during the years 320–323 when the Emperor of Rome, Flavius Constantine (272–337), issued legislation that 'permitted all Christians to carry their lawsuits before the biscop'.[15] With this permit, the biscop soon became an influential and powerful personage in the community, the judge and the jury, the voice of Roman authority, and one not entirely of an ecclesiastical nature. 'They tended to regard themselves as superior to the highest authorities in matters ecclesiastical and to think of the church as a department of the State.'[16] The cast-off purple togas and shoes of Roman emperors became the clothing of the biscop of Rome, the presbyters wore the 'toga picta' bearing a red stripe and their followers opted for either black or brown togas. 'They were a conceited body of people and the abuse of their religion dangerously undermined the foundations of moral virtue'.[17] Many of the biscops 'were given up to worldliness and gain, and we hear of worse scandals'.[18]

Eusebius (260–339) was one of them. Scarcely a pious figure, Eusebius was a notorious early presbyter and became one of the earliest and most influential biscops of the Christian church. He is on record as saying, 'It is an act of virtue to deceive and lie, when by such means the interests of the church might be promoted'.[19]

The Christian writer, Dr Donaldson,[20] said this of biscop Eusebius, 'My first, my best, and almost my only authority, is Eusebius'. He continued:

> Like all the rest of the Christians of his time, Eusebius was utterly unethical in his estimates of evidence, and where he, as it were, translated the language of others into his own, not using their words but his own assumption of their meaning, he is almost invariably wrong. Every statement which he makes himself is unreliable.

The curious stories about the early priesthood abound and church historian, Sozomen, related the nature of Athanasius, a biscop living at Alexandria. He was charged at the Council of Tyre in 355 with breaking a mystical chalice, smashing an episcopal chair, false imprisonment, deposing an opposing biscop, unlawfully placing him under military guard and torturing him, striking other biscops physically, obtaining his bishoprics by perjury, breaking and cutting off the arm of one of his opponents, burning his house, tying him to a column and whipping him, and putting him in a cell illegally; all this in addition to teaching a false doctrine. Gregory, a presbyter from Nazinanzus (c. 390) said it was common in his time for 'thugs' to be appointed biscops who were drawn 'from the army, the navy, the plough or the forge'.

Marcellinus Ammianus (330–400) wrote a history of Rome providing a further insight into the character of the early biscops. Once in office, he said:

> . . . they are free from money worries, enriched by offerings from women, riding in carriages, dressing splendidly, feasting luxuriously . . . their banquets are better than imperial ones.

The desert hermit today called St Jerome (died c.420), confessed that the majority of men entering the church were amateurs in theology. He said:

> One who yesterday was a catechumen [beginner or new convert] is today a biscop; another moves overnight from the amphitheatre to the church; a man who spent the evenings in the circus stands next morning at the altar; and another who was recently a patron of the stage is now the dedicator of virgins.

He went on to say that biscops:

> . . . gain admission to aristocratic houses and deceive silly women . . . who seek ordination simply to see women more freely. They think of nothing

but their clothes, use scent, and smooth out the creases in their boots. They curl their hair with tongs, their fingers glitter with rings . . . they are bridegrooms rather than clergy.

And for the 'bridegrooms' were many wealthy widows. Again quoting Jerome, was revealed the motivation of these men. He described the widows as dressed in:

. . . red cloaks, with fat bodies, a file of eunuchs walking in front; they have not so much lost husbands as seek them. They fill their houses with guests and flatterers. The biscops . . . kiss these ladies on the forehead and putting forth their hands as though to bless, take money for their visits . . . after a vast supper, these ladies dream of the apostles.

Over 1700 years later the monastic monks retrospectively applied the word 'bishop' to the majority of the Second, Third and Fourth Century orators when they rewrote fading church writings. Sometime around the period of the Reformation (14th–17th Centuries) the more accepted presbyters posthumously received the supernatural appellation of 'divines'.

The word 'presbyter' became synonymous with 'bishop' and then 'Bishop'. The presbyters of a lesser standing were simply assumed to be priests of the church and sub servant to the bishop. This eventually gave each 'dim, dirty, long-haired old man' a special sense of religious importance never originally existing. They later came to be called the 'older' men, subsequently 'elders', and by the mid-1500 the church insisted upon calling them 'the reverend fathers'. The word 'reverend' was an epithet of respect applied to the *Old Testament* God and was 'never applied to man'.[21] This word expanded to the Most Reverend, Right Reverend and Very Reverend and has been used as a title prefixed to the churchmen's names ever since.

The word 'fathers' became 'Fathers' and then to the 'Divine Fathers of the Church', a title falsely giving the biscops and presbyters the status of special and dignified founders of the Christian church. Today this process is called 'ecclesiasticism', which simply means 'an exaggerated attachment to the practices or principles of the Christian church'. These men were simply opportunists, accepting such favours as food, wine, corn, olive oil, wool, shelter and sex in return for their soapbox performance.

In 1882, the author T. W. Doane published a 589-page book titled *Bible Myths and Their Parallels in Other Religions*. Of the presbyters and biscops, he commented:

Besides forging, lying and deceiving the people for the cause of Christ, the church fathers destroyed all evidence against themselves and their religion they could find.

Doane commented that none of the early presbyters were Christians, but Pagan opportunists. This assertion was fully verified by St Justin Martyr in his *Apology to Roman Emperor Adrian*, when he admitted that those who stood the highest in the church maintained earlier heathen beliefs.

The church of the 15th Century developed an official policy of publicly presenting the original presbyters as learned and dignified men, worthy of the highest respect. So vigorously was this opinion enforced that one of the charges upon which Michael Servetus was burnt to death by John Calvin at Champel, on 27 October 1553 was that he had spoken disrespectfully of the original Christian presbyters.[22]

Charlatans in the church

This wandering group of 'town criers' had many detractors, the most vocal being Celsus. His sense of fair play won the respect and admiration of many of his contemporaries. He wrote a work called 'True Discourse' which was subsequently destroyed by the Fifth Century church (Augustine). Celsus was an acknowledged expert on biblical writings and the most important intellectual opponent of Christianity during its early years. He threw the early presbyters into perturbation when he accused them of accepting the worst superstitions of Paganism, and then interpolating passages into various writings without understanding the meaning of what they created. His accusations were so plausible that for a long time no Christian writer ventured to answer the challenge. He branded the presbyter's orations on the miracles attributed to Jesus Christ as absurd and called them 'charlatans and vagrants, dangerous to the civil ideals of the Roman state'.

His writings were sincere in his wish to 'help all men' and bring the populace to the idea of 'one religion'. He was remarkably well read and informed on all points of religion. The 1908 Catholic Encyclopedia (under 'Celsus') confirmed:

> His knowledge of Judaism and Christianity was such as could not have been obtained from books alone. He must have consorted with Jewish and Christian teachers . . . He knew the writings of the early presbyters . . . And he is unquestionably conscious of his knowledge of early Christianity.

Some forty years after his death, the eunuch named Origen (185–251), at the fervent request of his friend Ambrosias, refuted Celsus' charges in writings called 'Against Celsus', a total of eight books which were eventually completed some seventy years after Celsus' death. It is not known who finished the work.

Origen's attempts to dispel the accusations of Celsus failed and the only remedy was to destroy the writings of Celsus. Many copies of Celsus' original work had been read and studied by such presbyters as Eusebius[23] and Augustine.[24] If no copy of 'The True Discourse' (sometimes translated 'The True Doctrine') is available to this generation it is because the monks of an Oriental church on Mount Athos will neither show nor confess they have at least one Greek copy in their possession.[25] However, around ninety percent of 'The True Discourse' was reconstructed by Jackman (1836) and Keim (1873) using extracts, arguments and whole pages cited verbatim in Origen's condemnation. Origen recorded that Celsus said of the original Christian presbyters:

> . . . you utter fables, as if in a drunken state, producing self-induced visions, and you do not even possess the art of making them likely. You have altered three, four times and oftener, the texts of your manuscripts in order to deny objections made to you.[26]

Those who understand the importance of the vision–factor in the evolution of Christian dogma and 'history' will thank the presbyter Origen, for preserving this expression of his opponent. From these ancient words it is apparent that even towards the end of the Second Century it was commonly accepted that the orators' manuscripts, now called Gospels, were shallow, manipulated transcripts and had already been altered on many occasions.

Celsus, when speaking of the presbyters said that they were made up of:

> . . . weavers, tailors, fullers and the most illiterate and rustic fellows, teaching strange paradoxes. They openly declared that none but the ignorant were fit to hear their discourses and that one of their rules was 'let no man that is learned come among us'. They never appeared in the circles of the wiser and better sort, but always took care to intrude themselves among the ignorant and uncultured, rambling around to play tricks at fairs and markets.[27]

Celsus, in common with most of the Grecians, looked upon the presbyter's preachings as a 'blind faith' that shunned the light of reason. He said:

> [The presbyters] are forever repeating, 'Do not examine. Only believe and thy faith will make thee blessed. Wisdom is a bad thing in life; foolishness is to be preferred'. They teach men to believe without examination.[28]

It was hardly surprising then to read of the early presbyter's constant attempts to present a particular untrue storyline. Origen, for example, was quoted by Jerome[29] as advising anyone in authority in the developing church who was 'forced by circumstance to lie' of the need to observe the rules of the art of lying and to use the lie when arguing with a disbeliever in order to win that person over to the most important Christian points. This was the church tradition confessed to by Eusebius, now called Bishop Eusebius, and others. St Jerome, the author of the official Catholic Vulgate Bible used today, claimed to write in this lying manner [30] and cited in support the practice of numbers of Greek and Latin Christian writers before him. He even named St Paul a liar.[31] St Jerome described the Book of Revelation as 'unintelligible nonsense', and when he wrote to biscops Chromatius and Helidorus towards the end of the Fourth Century, he said:

> . . . a disciple of Manichaeus named Seleucus wrote falsely the 'Acts of the Apostles' which exhibited matter not for edification, but for destruction, and that this book was approved in a synod which the ears of the church properly refused to listen.[32]

Such confessions cause grave doubt about everything recorded in the Christian texts.

There was never any recorded form of ordination from a supernatural Jesus Christ or Simon of Petra (Simon Peter) to the presbyters. They appointed themselves and continually restructured their own writings to further appeal to the rabble without understanding the meaning of what they were compiling.[33] Their good tales are now called Gospels and used by the church to establish the validity of the Christian story.

Yet, these men were self-confessed liars and thieves. Aurelius Augustine (354–430), today honored with the titles Saint and Bishop, himself recorded he 'lusted to thieve and did it'.[34] Such records are contrary to the idealised picture of the early church movement portrayed by the church today. He also frankly admitted between his 'indistinct ravings' he was 'unable to produce any uncorrupted copies of the Gospel'.[35] The bishop revealed in his own writings how he had reveled in the fleshpots of Carthage and Rome and described 'sex as his particular compulsion'.[36] He led a riotous life and fathered an illegitimate son called Deodatus.

Around the middle of the Third Century a Christian sect, the Manicheans, was founded by Mani (Manes in some translations). Through the hostility of the Magi, he was put to death as a heretic and flayed, and his head was set up over a gate still known by his name in the 11th Century. However, his sect continued and taught that '. . . Krist is the glorious intelligence which the Persians call Mithras . . . his residence is in the sun.'[37]

The now highly regarded saint and Bishop of Hippo Augustine was an avid Manichean for nine years before 'adjusting' his belief.

Augustine lived around four hundred years after the canonical time of the Gospel Jesus Christ and believed that Christ (Krist) resided in the Sun. Many other church presbyters of the same time taught the Sun was Jesus Christ 'driving his chariot across the sky'. The Bishop of Troy was one who confessed to this belief and also said he had always secretly prayed to Jesus Christ in the Sun.[38]

The stories related by the early ecclesiastics show how untrustworthy these men were. In his 33rd Sermon, for example, St Augustine said:

> I was already biscop of Hippo when I went into Ethiopia with some servants of Christ . . . in this country we saw men and women without heads, who had two great eyes in their breasts; and in countries still more southly, we saw people who had but one eye in their foreheads.[39]

Towards the end of his 'life of debauchery' (Butler), St Augustine confessed that Christianity was 'a religion of threats and bribes unworthy of wise men'.[40] Today the Christian hierarchies proudly present him as 'the eagle of the fathers' and 'Doctor of the Church'.[41]

St Jerome was born in the town of Stridon on the north coast of what is now Italy and was a man of contradictions—generous towards his friends yet merciless with his enemies. His real name was Sophronius Eusebius Heironymus with 'Jerome' deriving from 'Jaruh of Rome'. He lived in a cave for many years on the barren plains of Chalcis in Syria[42] where he was taught to read and write Hebrew by an old monk. Jerome's desert years ended unhappily, with him at the centre of a religious dispute in nearby Antioch, accused of heresy because he 'preferred Pagan literature' (Ciceronians es, non Christianus). Because of his knowledge of Hebrew, biscop Damasus offered Jerome the commission to revise both the *Old* and *New Testament* manuscripts, the purpose being to end the great differences in the wording of particularly the Gospels. Jerome, 'urged on by Pope Damasus' offer of money',[43] traveled to Rome in 382 and commenced work. His two decades of intermittent work eventually created the Vulgate Bible so special to Roman Catholics today.

He described himself as 'a great favorite with the ladies' and dressed like them. St Jerome was a self-confessed transvestite.[44] Some of the points made about Jerome in this work are extracted from his own writings. He was probably the only male saint to appear in church wearing women's clothes. The explanation offered by the church was that friends of Jerome jokingly placed ladies red clothing in his bedroom while he slept. Next morning Jerome arose in the dark and failed to realize he was donning female attire.[45] It appears that Jerome's dress became the origin of the cardinal's garb today.

Jerome was described by his opponents as 'free with his tongue, uncharitable, sly, a hypocrite, the arch monk'.[46] Today he is called 'the most holy one' and, like Augustine, 'Doctor of the Church'.[47]

Curious beliefs of the early clergy

Here follow a few examples to illustrate strange church beliefs up until the Sixth Century. The Phoenix, a fabled bird said to renew its life every 500 years, was believed real by Clement (sometimes called Clemens), a Roman who died in the first quarter of the Second Century.[48] The church said Clement was a bishop of Rome but 'no evidence' exists to verify this claim.[49] Clement asserted the Phoenix was typical of reincarnation.[50] Tertullian of Rome thought the same thing[51] but confessed to never having seen the bird as it was '. . . away building a pyre' in readiness for its next incarnation.[52] The anti-Christian writer, Celsus, used this fact to illustrate the credulity of the early Christian presbyters.

As highly regarded as Tertullian, Irenaeus and Clement are by the present day church so to be Origen. He defended the fable of the Phoenix and believed the sun, moon and stars were living creatures, endowed with reason and free will, and occasionally inclined to sin.[53] He believed they were rational living creatures because they moved across the sky. He was not certain, however, whether the souls of the stars were created at the same time with their bodies or at the end of the world. Because they were alive, but unseen in daylight, he preached the air was peopled with demons. Their light, he said, was from knowledge and wisdom reflected from the eternal light. That they had free will he 'proved' by quoting from the *Old Testament* book of Job (25:5).

Bishop Cyril of Jerusalem (386) quoted from Clement the story of the Phoenix and declared God had created the bird expressly to enable men to believe in reincarnation. He said it was a wonderful bird and yet it was irrational . . . it did not sing Psalms to God[54] and it knew nothing of Jesus. This was the same Cyril who said, 'Thou must hate all heretics',[55] heretic simply meaning, holding a different view.

The writer of the Epistle of Barnabas believed an ancient superstition that the hyena changed its sex every year, alternately male and female.[56] He also believed a hare had as many young as it was years old and a weasel conceived with its mouth.[57] St Justin Martyr believed in the existence of demons and said they were the offspring of angels who had sex with the daughters of men.[58] He went on to record that insane people were possessed and tortured by the soul of the wicked who had died in their sins and this was sure proof of the immortality of the soul.[59] A presbyter at Antioch, Theophilius (169–177), to whom the Gospel of Luke was addressed, claimed the pains of women in child-birth and the fact serpents slither on their bellies were proof of the fall, as given in the *Old Testament* book of Genesis.[60]

Tertullian too believed the hyena changed its sex[61] and the stag renewed its youth by eating poisonous snakes.[62] He claimed eclipses and comets were signs of God's anger and forerunners of natural disasters[63] and 'the chirpings of birds were prayers'.[64] In the opening words of one of his papers he stressed volcanoes were openings into hell and the volcanic condition was a punishment inflicted on the mountains to serve as a warning to the wicked.

Further, he believed demons sent diseases upon the bodies of humans, blighted apples and grain and produced accidents and untimely deaths.[65] He invited the heathen magistrates to:

> . . . summon before their tribunal any person possessed with a devil; and if the evil spirit, when exorcised by any Christian whatsoever, did not own himself to be a devil, as truly as in other places he would falsely call himself a god, not daring to tell a lie to a Christian, then they should take the life of that Christian.[66]

Clement of Alexandria said hailstorms, tempests and plagues were caused directly by demons[67] and credulity was necessary to render faith easily.[68] He kindly allowed that Jews and Gentiles would have the Gospel (singular) preached to them in hell.[69] Clement's imagination was naturally lascivious. His chapter on the immodesty of rich Pagan women washing naked in the bath[70] portrays the hatred of the 'canaille' (the vulgar multitude) for the upper classes, and showed he must have been from the very lowest grades of society. 'While indignant at the supposed wickedness of the heathen, he wrote a book so unseemly[71] later English churchmen did not bother to translate it until the 19th Century.'[72]

St Jerome said this about the church belief of the soul:

> As to the origin of the soul, I remember the question of the whole kuriakos [church]; whether it be fallen from heaven, as Pythagoras and the Platonists and Origen believe; or it be of the proper substance of God; or whether they are kept in a repository formerly built by God; or whether they are made by God and sent into bodies according to that which is written in the Gospel.

Many of Jerome's writings were abusive, confrontational and full of bitter invective. This passage was more civil and in it Jerome questioned the origin of the soul and whether souls were 'sent into bodies according to that which is written in the Gospel'. This particular narrative was not found recorded in modern Gospels. However, it was written in the oldest Bibles currently existing today, the Sinaiticus, Alexandrius, Vaticanius, Bezae and Syrian.

Justin Martyr, Hippolytus of Rome (176–236), Theophilius of Antioch (c.180), Athenagoras (late Second Century), Tatian (late Second Century), Minucius Felix (d. c. 211), Cyprian of Carthage (c. 258), Origen, Tertullian, Irenaeus, Jerome, Lactantius (245–323), Eusebius and Augustine—in fact all the early Christian presbyters believed in the physical reality of demons. At first, since Christianity presented angels as bodies of air and light, its demons were supposed to have similarly ethereal bodies. According to St Augustine this gave extraordinary powers of perception and enabled them to move through the air at high speed.[73] Over the centuries, however, they appeared to have shed their bodies and become purely spiritual. How else, asked the priests in the 12th Century, could a legion of 6,666 demons be contained in the body of a man? So universal was the belief in demons by the clergy that in 1484 Pope Innocent VIII issued a papal bull against them. The *New Testament* writers believed in them.[74] They believed their evil was offset by the existence of goblins and elves and every fountain, tree, stream, and grove had its sprite. Everything that was done had to be a miracle with the almighty invoked to perform the simplest things.

The Christian audience

For centuries the bishops and presbyters continually referred to their audience as 'rabble' and 'fools', people we today call the 'early Christians'. These early congregations were described by the Bible writers as 'not so many wise'[75] and were held in low esteem by the presbyters. Tertullian said of them, quoting verbatim from the *Old Testament* preacher,[76] 'of fools the number is endless'.[77] This phrase obviously proved embarrassing and was 'adjusted' in 1592. At that time it was made to read, 'those who are lacking cannot be numbered'. It was again 'refined' in 1881 and now reads, 'that which is lacking cannot be numbered'.

As the presbyters orated their stories they interpolated contemporary events and the exploits of various folk heroes into their discourses, embellished the story with 'splendid exaggerations' and created curious scenes to entertain the gathered flock.[78] Paul of Samosata (260–268), for example, went about attended by bodyguards, consorted freely with women and preached to his audience while clapping his hands and stamping his feet from a high throne.[79] 'The mob or confused rabble collected together and called out', and from those assemblies came the Greek word, 'church'.[80]

The simple audience did not know about fraud and dishonesty in religious claims. They were never suspicious of fantastic stories and did not know the difference between truth and fiction. Their gullibility can be seen in the example of Bishop Tertullian telling a group of local residents that while walking past the cemetery, he had seen a corpse kindly move over to make room for another corpse to be laid beside it. The mob rushed to the cemetery and 'gazed across it in awe', believing what they had been told was true and accurate.[81] 'Such was the kind of food with which early Christians were feed a volume could not contain the records.'[82] They also believed Tertullian when he said the devil placed a red or blue mark upon the body of a witch to more easily recognize his property. Such was the simplicity of those people.

It should be remembered when discussing the origin of Christianity we are dealing with a period of time when dragons roamed the earth, according to Pliny the Elder (23–79AD). In his book *Natural History*, which made references to the Essenes, he recorded that a man called Thoas of Arcadia was saved from harm during a robber's attack by his pet dragon. Pliny added a few more details and said the dragons in Ethiopia were thirty feet long. The dragons of India, however, were 'so enormous a size as easily to envelope the elephant with its folds and encircle them with its coils'. Pliny also said the dragons inhabiting Africa had 'crests on their heads'. Pliny perished in the eruption of Vesuvius in 79, which destroyed Pompeii, Herculaneum and Stabial. The reference source of Pliny's information is not known.

The general populace of those primitive times lived in an environment of ignorance and excessive superstition and their knowledge of the world was very limited. Less than one in 10,000 could read or write (Josephus). When a presbyter from Carthage called Cyprian told a gathering of rabble he saw 'an infant vomit the Sacred Species it had received into the holy chalice', they believed him.[83] Alexander, a presbyter at Abonuteichus was 'a religious huckster who created a huge puppet of a snake that awed those who saw it'.[84] It has been argued that the imperial edict[85] of Roman Emperor Antoninus Marcus (121–180) against 'those who terrify by superstition, the fickle minds of men' was specifically directed against the church presbyters.

Another example of their intellectual limitations can be found in the writings of Tertullian who told how he again deceived the simple-minded.[86] He recorded telling a gathering of people, while he was exorcising 200 demons from a young man, how one particularly violent demon struggled very fiercely, and passed out through the young man's eye, knocking the eyeball from the socket. It fell on his cheek, and hung there by a vein until Tertullian replaced it and then held his right hand over the man's eye for seven days and nights until it was entirely healed. The rabble dropped to the ground '. . . and kissed and worshipped Tertullian's hand and called him God Almighty'.

Tertullian is today highly regarded by the priesthood and apart from being called Bishop Tertullian he is fondly referred to as 'the Father of Latin Theology'.[87]

The crass superstitions found in church writings reflected the mental characteristics of those people and substantiated the opinion that the early Christian presbyters and their audiences were collectively 'a parcel of fools'.[88] At the time of Justin Martyr (c. 166) the presbyters used a 'tasteless and infected language with its tendency to exaggeration and used it to clothe the poverty of their own thoughts'.[89] Theodotus, 'the leatherworking presbyter' from Byzantium (c. 200) was severely stung by certain criticisms, which the famous Greek author and physician, Galen of Pergamum (d. c. 199), leveled at the naivety of many early Christians. In his writings Galen considered the infant church gatherings to be 'a place of resort to the curious, the speculative and the idle'. A Greek satirist named Lucian of Samosata (115–200) attacked early Christians as being '. . . misanthropists, who practiced atheism, ritual murder, cannibalism, incest and magic'.

Lucian depicted Christians as an 'ignorant body of people' who had been 'duped by rogues and charlatans' and continually scoffed at their simplicity. Roman orator Marcus Fronto (c.170) in the Second Century, Porphyry, a philosopher from Tyre (232–305), in the Third Century and Emperor Julian in the Fourth Century all made similar comments. A highly regarded, late Fourth Century chronicler named Pelagius, opined the texts read out by the Christian presbyters contained 'a series of strange hallucinations which only a few weak women believe and perhaps a few womanly men'.

To illustrate the highly superstitious condition of the people of these days, it is timely to note their bizarre belief that animals were gods and were worshipped as such. They 'served the creature', worshipping 'four-footed beasts and crawling things', and 'dishonored their bodies' having sex with them. This information is recorded in the Epistle to the Romans.[90] During these times these 'wicked'[91] semi-savage people were charged with 'a depraved and excessive superstition'[92] upon which presbyters established the basis for official Christian writings.

Not lawful for a Christian to doubt

As to the Pagan notion that the earth was round, St Augustine, Lucius Lactantius, a Roman Latin apologist,[93] and other presbyters violently opposed the theory. In quotations, particularly from Lactantius, they explicitly recited their arguments to prove the world was flat, 'a rectangular place', being 'twice as long as broad. The heavens come down to the earth on four sides like the walls of a room. The earth lies in the centre, with the ocean all about it'.[94] This became the 'official' church description of the universe, 'concerning which it is not lawful for a Christian to doubt'.[95] The church's ongoing belief had been the earth 'was flat and rested on the back of a turtle, the turtle on the back of a snake, and the snake on the back of an elephant'.[96]

Lactantius, in *The Divine Institutes,* asserted:

> Is there anyone so senseless as to believe that underneath us are men whose footsteps are higher than their heads; how can crops and trees grow downwards, that the rains, and snow and hail fall upwards to earth.[97]

Cosmas Indicopleustes, an Egyptian, asked exultantly, if the world were round how were the people on the other side to see the Lord Jesus descending through the air on the last great day?[98] The Christian religion staked it's all on the flatness of the earth's surface. When science proved the earth's rotundity the church never attempted to apologise for its flawed instruction.

Supposedly great thinkers

These men were utterly ignorant and incompetent to deal in any way with the issues and questions they handled. They cited irrelevant matters as evidence of a theory. They would look directly into the face of evidence that established theories they did not endorse, and refuse it.

Surely, if the early church was composed of such great scholars it is extraordinary to read how persistently they were wrong. The only excuse offered to explain such errors was 'spiritual insight'. Christian defenders said that, while the men of the early church were renowned as simpletons, ignorant and superstitious, they were yet 'gifted with great spiritual insight'. That 'spiritual insight' did not apply to the accuracy of their writings . . . their imagination supplied the facts. Not only in nature, but also in literature, the presbyters were ignorant and unscholarly. Justin Martyr quoted from Jeremiah and called it Isaiah.[99] Clement of Alexandria quoted scripture passages not in the Bible.[100] He also credited Paul for writings not in Paul's writings.[101] In quoting from an opponent he would insert words not in the original,[102] and he even did the same in quoting from the Bible.[103]

Tertullian quoted as Leviticus a passage not in that book[104] and he frequently misquoted history.[105] He cited as Isaiah a passage in Revelation.[106] Bishop of Caesarea, Eusebius quoted Daniel 13 as scripture[107] and so did Ephraem (306–373). In Protestant Bibles, Daniel does not have a thirteenth chapter and if it did, the church has taken it away. Just as remarkably, Tertullian said he eliminated from the Gospel of Luke the saying that Rabbi Jesus 'came not to destroy the Law (of Moses) and the prophets . . . but to fulfill them'. Tertullian admitted on three subsequent occasions that he removed this verse.[108] That passage is not in today's version of the Gospel of Luke, but can be found in the Gospel of Matthew (5:17).

How reliable these men were in their explanations of heresies may be illustrated in the case of the Bishop of Salamis, St Epiphanius (315–403), who mistook the Pythagoras Sacred Tetraktys—a special seal or signet supposedly having magical powers—for a heretic leader. This extraordinary mistake showed how little these writers knew of what they wrote and the one ignorantly followed the other. Such involuntary blunders and deliberate falsifications; the canonisation of the mythological Aura Placide (gentle breeze) into Christian martyrs St Aura and St Placida; the deification of a spear and a cloak, under the names of SS Longimus and Amphibolus; the quoting of nonexistent words from the *Old Testament*—these all cast doubt on the religion and the sanity of the men who promulgated it.

A perfect example of this conclusion can be found in a church document called *Dialogues*, written by Gregory the Great, circa 600. It is filled with lurid narrations of 'marvelous fictions'[109] a child today would think it a fairytale. Gregory added a new dimension to patristic thought when he declared Jesus Christ created dreams, and the hourly miracles Gregory performed were accomplished with the help of bees humming hymns to the Virgin Mary. Henry James Coleridge, his Christian biographer said of Gregory, he was 'a great man', a 'great saint' and he 'towered above his contemporaries and their immediate predecessors and followers'. Anybody reading Gregory's words could come to only one conclusion—he was either a compulsive liar or insane, and probably both.

Lactantius also penned a document just as weird but more bizarre. Called 'Morbid Persecutions' (De Mortibus Persecutorum) he described with a wealth of gory detail, the supposed 'frightful' mutilation deaths of many of the so-called persecutors of the early church. 'His lurid and grotesque description of Galerius' death was particularly effective.'[110] Galerius was a Roman emperor who opposed the Khrestian/Christian movement. Lactantius' words and thoughts suggested he reincarnated in the 19th Century as Jack the Ripper. The church said 'his writings exhibit many short-comings'.[111]

It may be said these early churchmen were as good as their times but it cannot be maintained. They were not as good, and they and their age were not competent to form a Bible for this or any age. They could not see the truth as easily as other people around them did. Their decisions were much more the result of pious frauds, and once they realised they had erred, they defended one foolish thing by another. In this day and age, should a person publicly express such erroneous and grotesque beliefs it would be attributed to the vagary of an unbalanced mind. Yet these men are the acknowledged founders of the Christian church.

Strange things to say

A glamour attached to the written word saw the rabble revere the manuscripts carried by the presbyters. The texts were invested with an importance and impressiveness that did not attach to spoken words. The precise relation to the persons who wrote them and the nature of their composition was unimportant or obscured. The presbyters were, however, regarded in awe by the ignorant masses who thought these men held some great written secret promising them a better life and 'sought their society'.[112] Today those writings are called the *New Testament* and are the official and only texts of Christianity.

The 'barbarous, uncouth' Bishop Tertullian[113] condemned early church congregations who renounced the presbyter's writings:

> I hope to see them all in the fire of Hell. What shall be the magnitude of that scene! How shall I laugh. How shall I rejoice! How shall I triumph when I see so many illustrious kings who were said to have mounted into

heaven, groaning with Jupiter, their god, in the lowest darkness of hell!! Then shall the soldiers who have persecuted the name of Christ burn in more cruel fire than any they had kindled for the saints.[114]

Later Tertullian said of the Jesus Christ story, 'I believe it because it is absurd'. Another of his famous quotes was made when he tired of the church and called the leading presbyter 'a shepherd of adulterers'. Interestingly enough, later in life Tertullian became a member of the Montanist sect, renounced the Christian faith and disappeared from the scene.[115]

'Hot headed' Tertullian was not the only churchman to display such a 'loving' attitude. The sainted bishop Augustine said of his enemies some two hundred years later:

> Wondrous depth of my words! Whose surface, behold! Is before us, inviting to little ones; yet they are a wondrous depth, O my God, a wondrous depth! It is awful to look therein, yes; an awfulness of honor, and a trembling of love. My enemies thereof I hate vehemently; Oh, that thou would slay them with thy two-edged sword, that they might no longer be enemies; for so do I love to have them slain.

This from a Manichean converted to a religion which preached to pray for your enemies. Such cruel and murderous expressions illustrate the church's forefathers.

St Augustine wrote several books for the church and his most honest was called 'Confessions'. In another of his writings he questioned whether 'the records of Jesus' miracles are lies'.[116] The similarities between Christianity and Mithraism in the Fifth Century were so striking that St Augustine grudgingly confessed the priests of Mithra worshipped the same deity as he. He displayed his naiveté by declaring, 'I believe that Christ was born of a virgin because I have read it in the Gospel'.[117] But it didn't say that in the 'original' Gospel, nor was it in any of the earliest Gospels of the Christian church.

ϧow the Gospels came into being

IT WAS THE PRESBYTERS OF THE SECOND, THIRD AND FOURTH CENTURIES who developed the Christian texts and the initial reaction of most non-church people who read their writings is usually one of bewilderment. Many people are unlikely to have studied the works of Justin Martyr, Irenaeus or Tertullian, or any of the writings of the other early presbyters for that matter. With good reason, as many are almost unreadable and much of what they say is a hotchpotch of crude superstition, credulity and ignorance. By stripping away the naivety behind these writings, they become simply a series of curious passages 'full of the silliest superstitions'.[1] Dr Constantine Tischendorf said:

> We must frankly admit that we have no source of information with respect to the life of Jesus Christ than the presbyters' writings.[2]

In spite of the known origin of its texts, the church today insists on the validity of its writings, particularly the Gospels, citing them as evidence for the essence of its claims. When the facts are determined and examined even casually, these claims prove unconvincing, indeed the church for many centuries itself questioned the authenticity of the Gospels.

The story of Mariamne Herod's twin boys provided the answer to one of the great unknowns in Christian history, the origin of the first Gospel. The later church took the position that the story of Jesus Christ was orally transmitted for decades and eventually written down. This theory does not explain how or why dozens of First Century chroniclers never mentioned

Jesus Christ, the Christian religion or any persons associated with the *New Testament* story, including the Virgin Mary and the apostles.

Church speculation suggested a primitive handbook was later composed which subsequently became the primary source for the Gospel of Mark. Orthodox experts confirmed that the Gospel of Mark was 'the second in the four canonical Gospels but the first of them in sequence of composition . . . and inevitably it set the standard for the later Gospels'.[3] Modern critical analysis showed the present canonical Gospels of Matthew and Luke were dependent upon the Mark Gospel and later derived from it. The Gospel of Mark was almost entirely duplicated in Matthew's Gospel with 606 of the 661 verses appearing word-for-word in Matthew's Gospel. Likewise, sixty-nine percent of Luke's language was derived verbatim from Mark's Gospel while only thirty-one of Mark's verses are omitted from the text of both the Gospels of Matthew and Luke.

The Gospel of John was independent of the synoptics (synoptic meaning, similar in content), the entire Gospel being clearly recognisable and acknowledged as a later production. One thing the church has made clear was that the Gospel of John was the last to have been compiled.[4]

The dependence on the Gospel of Mark writings is of fundamental importance to the interpretation of the synoptic Gospels. With Mark being the original church writing, its importance cannot be rated too highly, even though many passages are quoted in an abridged and garbled form. However severely limited it is, this far from perfect and meager writing was, in its earliest form, the most important aspect of the Christian religion for it was the oldest and purest text and one that comes nearest to the real story.

The Gospel of Mark in the oldest existing *New Testaments* started its story when the twins were 'about thirty'. There was no mention of Mary or a virgin birth, or the now-called *Old Testament* 'messianic prophecies'. It omitted the words 'Son of God' after Jesus' name, excluded a family tree tracing Jesus' bloodline back to King David (the now-called messianic bloodline) and contained a different version of the events surrounding the 'raising of Lazarus'. It also revealed an extraordinary omission later to become the central doctrine of the Christian faith—the resurrection appearances of Jesus Christ and his subsequent ascension into heaven. Yet this first church Gospel was the very basis of the canonical Gospels and forms the whole and only teachings and beliefs of the Christian religion. But who wrote it, and why?

The origin of the first Gospel

Rabbi Jesus could not be tried and condemned to death unless there was some written record made of it by the Rabbinic authorities. Such public acts *had* to be officially recorded upon Sanhedrin dockets under their constitution. Justin Martyr confirmed this policy.[5] It was also a Rabbinic requirement set down in the First Century 'Code of Jewish Law'. As it was the Sanhedrin elders themselves who pronounced the death sentence on Rabbi Jesus (Matt. 26:57) the Head of the House of Justice Rabbi Hillel, was personally responsible for completing the paperwork.

The Sanhedrin was composed of two sections, one of seventy priests (The Greater) and twenty-four priests in the other (The Less). These two legislative bodies had jurisdiction over the entire Jewish commonwealth and although possessed of great power it was not absolute. The highest authority of the nation was the court of the Elders and it consisted of twelve men, the chairman being the High Priest. It was the supreme judicial and ecclesiastical council of the Jews and it conducted its affairs in a temple chamber called 'The Hall of Hewn Stone'—the temple being the Temple of Jerusalem. Its decisions were absolute and it was this court which eventually tried Rabbi Jesus. Its High Priest and President at that time was Rabbi Hillel and he was responsible for the origin of the Gospels of the *New Testament*.

To record the actual trial proceedings of Rabbi Jesus, the Gospel of Mark (14:53) stated that 'scribes were assembled', suggesting there was some written record. The premise offered is that Rabbi Hillel's record of Rabbi Jesus' ministry and trial before the Sanhedrin was originally a major part of the document that eventually became the Gospel of Mark.

The actual time Rabbi Hillel lived is a vital matter in the presentation of this argument. The Christian dictionaries documented his lifespan as 60BC–9AD(?)—a question mark indicating an actual unknown lifetime. However, dictionaries referenced from ancient Jewish sources more precisely record that 'he was born early in the First Century AD and died circa 72AD'. The deliberate changes by the church to its history make it not improbable to suggest that the 'unknown' date of Rabbi Hillel's birth and death in Christian literature was a deliberate editorial adjustment to distance him from the major Gospel events. Synogogal records stated he was born shortly after the time of Mariamne Herod's twins and died circa 72. To clarify, author Norm Segal's extensive research on the subject published in *Good News of the Kingdoms* is referenced.

Hillel the Elder was born into the House of Boethus in Babylon (present-day Iraq) about the year 75BC and died in 23AD. He was the father of Rabbi Gamaliel Hillel who was to become the president of the Sanhedrin in the First Century. Rabbi Hillel fathered a son called Gamaliel of Jabneh—a town later called Jamnia—who was the grandson of Hillel the Elder. (Later historians sometimes referred to Gamaliel of Jabneh's father as Gamaliel the Elder.) It is recorded in the Encyclopedia Judaica[6] that Gamaliel of Jabneh fathered a son curiously named Jesus, who was appointed High Priest of Jerusalem by King Agrippa II (d. c. 92–100AD) in either 63 or 64. Some modern commentators have advanced the theory that the High Priest Jesus, son of Rabbi Gamaliel of Jabneh, was the 'real Jesus'. The birthdate of Rabbi Gamaliel of Jabneh is unknown. However, it was recorded he died of a great age in 115AD.[7]

This famous Rabbi, at whose feet Paul learned the *Torah* (Acts.22:3) was one of the most important scholars of his generation, being responsible for the final version of the 'Eighteen Benedictions'. He conducted debates with Roman philosophers, the Essenes and anybody interested in the Law of Moses (The *Torah*). That Rabbi Gamaliel's death is recorded as occurring in 115 provided a *New Testament* reference giving the approximate dates of the lifetime of Paul. This biblical connection between Rabbi Gamaliel and Paul has, for some reason, been long overlooked by *New Testament* analysts. During their long association could not Rabbi Gamaliel of Jabneh or his High Priest son Jesus have handed to Paul the official Rabbinical records of Rabbi Jesus? But why? Paul, at this time, was the leader of the Nazarenes and was closely associated with the whole royal family of Rabbi Jesus.

Marcellus of Britain

After the death of Paul, history recorded that the untitled Rabbinic record and ten letters[8] were then in the possession of the son of an elderly noble Briton called Marcellus who was born circa 96. This name subsequently developed into Marcus or Marcion, and from the brief writings about him, it appeared that he was a Druid at Tongres. Sometimes he was called Marcellus of Britain[9] and it was probable he was related to Rabbi Jesus Cunobeline's family. He was part of the community at Trevran in Wales that was traditionally the place where Rabbi Jesus Cunobeline and his family spent a lot of time. Marcellus was one of those who exercised the chief influence in the development of the Celtic church and his family was closely associated with Prince Linus, the son of King Caradoc and grandson of Rabbi Jesus Cunobeline. Prince Linus was the same person mentioned with 'all the brethren' in the second letter to Timothy[10] in the *New Testament*. Marcellus was married to Julia and they had two sons, one of them also named Marcellus, after his father. It was variously recorded that Marcellus died sometime between 164 and 168. In his work, he founded a belief system that spread rapidly throughout the Roman Empire and continued for more than six hundred years after his death.

How the ten letters in Marcellus' possession had been recovered from the addressees was something that was never recorded. It was possible that they were never dispatched, supported by the fact that they were all in the possession of Marcellus. Marcellus said he wrote a Prologue or Introduction for each of the letters, which can be read in the *New Testament* today. According to early churchmen Tertullian, Irenaeus and Clement, Marcellus was in Rome during 137–138 and 'orated his tale to those that would listen'.[11] This statement was taken to mean that Marcellus orated from the untitled text in his possession, that being the record of the teachings, trial, escape, capture and death of stoned Rabbi Jesus Cunobeline. Marcellus' influence must have been strong, as St Epiphanius, writing more than two centuries later, said the followers of Marcellus were to be found throughout the whole world.[12] Marcellus' religious rituals were so similar to that of the later Roman church that some 250 years after his death, Cyril of Alexandria (387) found it necessary to warn congregations not to enter a Marconian church by mistake.[13] It was through the corruption of Marcellus' name that he was later called by the church, Marcion. This removed the embarrassing evidence that the writing that later became the first Christian Gospel was originally in the possession of a British Druid.[14]

The Ebronites and the genuine Gospel of Matthew

The several scattered sources from which knowledge of the sect called Ebronites was derived cannot be quickly or easily harmonised. They are probably best described as one of a group in the Second to Fourth Century community who constantly denied the divinity of the presbyters' Jesus Christ. The Ebronites were mentioned in the writings of Justin Martyr, Irenaeus, Tertullian, Hippolytus and Epiphanius of Salamis. The important thing was the Second Century patristic mention of a Rabbi called Ebron (or Ebion) being the author of the Gospel to the Hebrews. Those who subsequently followed him and his Gospel came to be called Ebronites.

It seemed that in Rome, Marcellus' Gospel went off in two separate directions. The presbyters had a copy that they falsified and later it was named the Gospel of Matthew. Another copy was made by Rabbi Ebron for the Essene movement and that was called the Gospel to the Hebrews, the Hebrews being the Essenes. When Jerome read and translated this Gospel towards the end of the Fourth Century, he wrote to a friend and said:

> In the evangel which the Nazarenes and the Ebronites use, which recently
> I translated from Hebrew into Greek, and which is called by most persons
> the genuine Gospel of Matthew . . . the Jews have the truth.[15]

St Epiphanius wrote, 'the Ebronites number among their sect all the surviving relatives of Jesus'. It seemed that Rabbi Ebron preserved for Rabbi Jesus Cunobeline's family a copy of Marcellus' original synagogal manuscript.

Rabbi Ebron's document was the 'original Hebrew' language version of the now-called Matthew Gospel. It did not include the first two chapters there today, nor the resurrection description, nor the so-called *Old Testament* prophecies, nor the family genealogy tracing Rabbi Jesus back to King David. In other words, that Gospel in its earliest form was a direct copy of Marcellus'

Gospel that was the earliest witness to any Christian writings in the records of mankind. Therefore the Ebronites practiced the purest form of primitive Christianity using a Gospel which basically taught a Code of Ethics for the communal living of the Essene and Druid holy men—the balance of prayer, work and study, the care given to the body with time divided between rest, exercise and proper food, and courtesy given to each and every guest.

The *Catholic Encyclopedia* openly discussed 'the major problems posed by the artificial structure' of the canonical Gospel of Matthew.[16] It also stated that the whole of the first two chapters were added in 'the early Third Century AD'. In the way the Gospel of Matthew was originally written, it began, 'In those days came John the Baptist . . . and then Jesus came . . . to be baptised by him',[17] at about the age of thirty years.

When Jerome said the Jews had the 'genuine Gospel of Matthew' he meant that document was considered the 'real' Gospel of Matthew, not the forged version that went into his *Vulgate Bible*. The Hebrew version was considered to be authentic, and the version that became the canonical one today, was not.

The small collection of writings Marcellus (Marcion) used in his orations was never considered the inspired word of God.[18] The main manuscript that Marcellus used was the subject of controversy for centuries. The orthodox church said it became the Gospel of Luke. Others denied this and claimed that it was a collection of anecdotes from which the Gospel of Mark evolved. However, what was known was that the Rabbinic record held by Marcellus originally carried no title[19] and because it was in his possession, the suspicion exists that Marcellus' name became attached to it and it evolved to Marcion, Marcus, Marc and then Mark in subsequent English translations.

A rumour emerged within later church circles that Marcellus had, as a youth, seduced a virgin. This rumour was dismissed as the 'malicious gossip of St Epiphanius'[20]—a later slander set against Marcellus for not accepting a virgin birth narrative in a writing compiled late in his lifetime called the Gospel of Cerinthus (c.164–168). This document also included a genealogy of Jesus Christ and was soon renamed the Gospel of Luke after the 'beloved physician' (Therapeute), described in the ancient Syriac texts of the *New Testament* as 'Asaia, the Essaian' or Essene. It was addressed under this name to Theophilius, a presbyter at Antioch in the year 169, (note the closeness of the dates). It seemed that Cerinthus, an Egyptian Jew, was an associate of Rabbi Ebron and a member of the Ebronites (Ebionites) and directly associated with the Essenes and Nazarenes. The Gospel of Luke, one of 'many' (Luke 1:1), was the longest of the four canonical Gospels because it contained a major and late addition of approximately ten pages[21] now called by the church 'The Great Insertion'. Marcellus argued that the 'virgin birth' and 'family genealogy' were forgeries and had to be removed from the later document. 'Marcion (Marcus) rejected the first two chapters and some shorter passages . . .' of the writing today called the Gospel of Luke.[22] Marcellus also bitterly denied the link between Jesus Christ to the so-called messianic prophecies, because there were no 'prophecies' in the original document in his possession. They were built-in into Matthew's Gospel in the reconstruction during the Third Century.[23]

Dionysius, Bishop of Alexandria (d. c. 264) recorded that the Gospel of John was 'the forgery of an Egyptian Jew named Cerinthus', a statement later supported by Eusebius, Bishop of Caesarea (260–339).[24] When analysing the Gospel of John, there are so many conflictions between it and the earlier Gospels of Mark, Matthew and Luke, it is difficult to understand why Christian researchers have not given the origin of this document more attention. Readers of the *New Testament* can see that the portrait of Jesus Christ in the first three Gospels differs fundamentally from that in the fourth. One who approached the four books for the first time would find it difficult to believe the writers of the Gospel of John and the first three Gospels were talking about the same man. The reason for this was apparent—they were talking about twins.

The Gospel of John is the most problematical of the Christian texts and biblical analysts noted its insincerity. The learned church authorities that contributed to the Ninth Edition of the Encyclopedia Britannica said:

> It (John) has been severely edited, as its closing words make clear; and there is evidence of heavy tampering in the earliest manuscripts, obviously glosses and so forth, as well a sheer muddle. Thus Chapter Five should follow Chapter Six and the final chapter is clearly an addition.[25]

The existence of interpolated material in the John Gospel substantiated the claim that the original document was written without reference to the brothers, Judas Khrestus and Rabbi Jesus. The statements accredited to them in a reconstruction of the original document appeared at a much later date, sometime towards the end of the Second Century. As remarkable as it may seem, even the Bishop of Rome, Callistus I, (217–222) knew of the pre-Christian existence of the substance of the writing to become called the Gospel of John. He declared it was originally discovered sealed in an urn '. . . in a cavern under the Temple of Jerusalem, having been placed there in secret long anterior (previous) to the Christian era'.[26]

Indeed, the early church itself confirmed the fabrication and recorded that this pre-Christian document was 'written over' during the latter years of the Second Century by Cerinthus.[27] The Gospel of John was not mentioned by any Second Century presbyter or historian before the time of Bishop Irenaeus, circa 180–190. Some 8000 church consultants named in 200 opening pages of the 1967 edition of the New Catholic Encyclopedia said of the Gospel of John: 'some of the irregularity undoubtedly stems from the history of editing'.[28]

Yet still the church insists this Gospel is the unadulterated word of God. The New Catholic Encyclopedia further acknowledged that '. . . there was a series of subsequent authors who added material to the body of the Gospel narrative'.

The fabricated nature of this Gospel, and the embellishments it was known to have received, makes it difficult to determine whether any narratives reflect a piece of tradition or not. The church, in reference to the Gospel of John, agreed and stated in the 1910 edition of the *Catholic Encyclopedia*, 'the correct reading of the text is in many places doubtful'.[29]

In its rawest form, John, like Matthew, Mark and Luke, did not record a virgin birth or any aspect of the infancy narratives which established the church later used forged passages as evidence of the virginal birth of Jesus Christ.

After the time of Irenaeus (c.202) the Gospels were regularly quoted by such as Tertullian, Origen and Eusebius but they all lived during, and after, the first half of the Third Century and at a time when the Gospels circulated under their present names. However, the later presbyters knew less of the authorship of the texts than we do today for they had not the critical ability of this age such as infra-red light-testing. Origen, in 237, for example, said of the letter of Barnabas: 'but who it was that wrote this letter, God only knows'.[30]

Fauste, the Third Century Manichean, wrote, 'Everyone knows that the Evangeliums [Gospels] were written by neither Yesu [Rabbi Jesus], nor his apostles, but long after their time by some unknown persons, who judging well that they could hardly be believed when telling of things they had not seen themselves, headed their narratives with the names of the apostles or of disciples contemporaneous with the latter'. The editors of the official Christian reference sources agreed, and admitted that 'The titles of our Gospels were not intended to indicate authorship'.[31]

This knowledge was again supported in the internationally acknowledged directory of the teaching and history of the Christian church, the Catholic Encyclopedias. The Editorial staff diplomatically said, 'It thus appears that the present titles of the Gospels are not traceable to the evangelists themselves'.[32]

Church experts admit to no evidence of the existence of the Gospels for at least a century after the time it said Jesus Christ was born in a manger. The most ancient literature fails to show any trace of acquaintance with, nor the use of, the Gospels we know today. It is not possible to find in any writings compiled between the beginning of the First Century and the middle of the Second Century, any reference to Jesus Christ or the Gospels of Matthew, Mark, Luke and John. Indeed, the 1909 edition of the *Catholic Encyclopedia* stated the Gospels 'do not go back to the first century of the Christian era'.[33]

The *Encyclopedia Britannica* confirmed the late appearance of the Christian texts. It stated:

> No *New Testament* canon, except a partial and unauthorised one existed until the latter half of the Second Century AD, that is, till the idea of a universal church began to be entertained . . . One hundred and seventy years from the coming of Christ elapsed before the collection assumed a form that carried with it the idea of holy and inspired.[34]

Surprisingly, many of the texts written during this time were originally included in the emerging *New Testament* collection but were later removed from the canon and suppressed, the Gospel of Peter being one example. Serapion, a presbyter operating at Antioch (c.190) recorded the Gospel of Peter being in church use during his time but around 140 years later biscop Eusebius said it was 'withheld' because 'it contained some heresy'. Previous to its suppression it was in use in the church at Rhossus in Cilicia, as well as in several other churches.[35] Thus, church history recorded at this time the suppression of a primary Christian Gospel.

It was recorded Marcellus of Britain wrote a work called *Contrasts* in order to outline the differences between his earlier original document and later church writings.[36] The whereabouts of 'Contrasts' is today unknown. In 374, St Epiphanius restructured Marcellus' original Gospel listing 118 passages where the later Gospels differed from the original Rabbinic manuscript.

Long after Marcellus' death, he was labeled a 'heretic' by the church. The intriguing question arises, how does it happen that a 'heretic' was in possession of the first Gospel before the Christian church itself was founded? The answer is simple—he received it from the Nazarenes.

> They [the Nazarenes] elected Marcellus for their biscop . . . At his persuasion the most considerable part of the congregation renounced the Mosaic Law, in the practice of which they had persevered above a century. By this sacrifice of their habits and prejudices, they purchased free admission into the colony of Hadrian [Roman Emperor 117–138], and more firmly cemented their union with Rome.[37]

The documents in the possession of Marcellus of Britain were the first recorded mention of ancient texts that can be associated with the *New Testament* of today, and thus, Christianity. The church claims the Mark Gospel 'was originally written in Rome'.[38] However, the writing Marcellus had in his possession was a shorter version than the today's canonical Gospel of Mark. Using available documentation, it was apparent Marcellus' Gospel was added to in Rome.

The 'Rabbinic record' illustration of the emergence of the first Gospel appeared to be supported in the writings of the early church itself. 'Then came to Rome Justin Martyr, and had lodgings by the "Bath" (building or guest house) in the grounds of the Palace of the British'.[39] Substantiating that Rabbi Hillel's report was known, there exists today a Second Century document called *Dialogue with Trypho*, written by St Justin Martyr circa 160. For the present discussion, *Dialogue* is of supreme importance in two vital matters for it recorded what was basically an extensive argument Justin Martyr had with a Jewish gentleman called Trypho. In this document, Trypho mentioned a 'groundless report' and also clearly and unequivocally stated the early church had 'invented' Christ. In the famous Ante-Nicene Library can be seen this passage which reads:

> But Krist, if he has indeed been born and exists anywhere is unknown . . . And you, having accepted a groundless report, invented a Kristo for yourself.

It was highly likely that Trypho's reference to 'a groundless report' was the official Sanhedrin report of Rabbi Jesus compiled around one hundred years earlier. The fact that Trypho accused St Justin Martyr of inventing 'a Kristo' confirmed that the presbyters had already begun to develop stories for their own 'Krist'.

It was a curious *New Testament* fact that the ten letters attached to Marcellus' Rabbinic record never mentioned or supported any of the most important events recorded in the later Gospels about Jesus Christ's life. The vital omissions are extraordinary and by comparing what the first Mark Gospel *did not* say with what the Epistles *did not* say, the parallels are striking. The oldest Mark Gospel said nothing of a virgin birth, failed to record any physical characteristics, manners, moods and habits and revealed nothing of the lives of either of the twins before they turned thirty. Nothing was mentioned of their education, environment or Rabbi Jesus' first efforts as a preacher. More importantly, there was no mention of a crucifixion and resurrection or ascension into heaven.

The Epistles said Jesus Christ was 'born of a woman' and neglected to mention the parents, where he was born or where he died. The spectacular Gospel miracles applied to Jesus Christ were not mentioned, neither was John the Baptist nor Judas Iscariot. The trial and crucifixion, the empty tomb and the bodily resurrection of Jesus Christ were conspicuous by their absence in the Epistles. Nor was there any mention of Jesus' dealings with family associates like Mary Magdalene and Lazarus. For centuries now, scholars pointed to the Epistles' complete lack of reference to a supernatural Jesus Christ as clear evidence that the presbyters had not yet created the story.

CHAPTER EIGHTEEN

Forgery in the New Testament

I N THE LATTER PART OF THE SECOND CENTURY AND PARTICULARLY during the Third Century, various elements of Judas Khrestus' story merged into Rabbi Jesus' synagogal record and both individual life stories gradually became diffused into the presbyter's handwritten manuscripts. Their growing body of writings was influenced by current ideas about what a god-man should be and do. To qualify, a god had to come from heaven to be born of a virgin, perform many miracles, make mystic utterances, raise the dead occasionally, and then himself die, rise again from the dead, and ascend to heaven, thus 'proving' his deity from advent to ascension. Those were the standard 'signs' by which a new god could be recognised, and these ancient beliefs were gradually attached to the persons of Judas Khrestus and Rabbi Jesus as the circumstances of their life stories became jumbled. The evidence to support this conclusion is substantial.

Everything supernatural the presbyters wrote about their developing god could be traced to earlier religious beliefs. There was hardly a detail of the Gospel birth, the miracles, the mode of death and the resurrection as now told about Jesus Christ not told about the God-men who preceded the presbyter's time. Christianity's essential features and phases depict an outgrowth and remodeling of earlier religious beliefs current among presbyters, 'whose imaginations were familiar with the reputed incarnation of heathen deities. That God should, in some extraordinary manner, visit and dwell with man, is an idea, which, as we read the writings of the ancient heathen, meets us in a thousand different forms.'[1]

The change of names and places, with the mixing up of various sketches of Indian, Egyptian, Phoenician, Greek and Roman mythology, was all that was necessary. The presbyters had an abundance of material with which they built their stories. During the course of two hundred years, the story of the twins became so interwoven with images from myths of bygone ages as to conceal forever any perceivable fragments of an ascertainable history that may lie beneath them. 'The researches of the learned,' said Mosheim, 'though long and ably conducted, have been unable to answer the history of the multitude of earlier cases of legends of immaculate conception, crucifixion and ascension into heaven . . . one might almost be mistaken for the other.'[2]

Earlier virgin births

There were numerous virgin births recorded in the early religious history of mankind. In the classical myth of Hercules, for example, the Supreme God of the ancient Greeks Zeus, 'visited' Alcmene the virgin, in the guise of her husband. Hercules was born as a result of this 'union'. Perseus, also of Greek myth, was said to be divine from the virgin Danae, fathered also by Zeus, 'the father of all gods'. It was of more than casual interest to read verses in the canonical Acts of the Apostles (14:12–18) fondly referring to Judas Khrestus' associate Barnabas as 'Zeus' after the famous Olympian god. The people called Paul 'Hermes' after Zeus' messenger, and in his letter to the Galatians, Paul mentioned that he traveled with Barnabas to Jerusalem (Gal. 2:1). Barnabas was the brother of Aristobulus (Romans 16:10), the father-in-law of Simon of Petra, who went to live in Britain around the time of Paul.[3]

It was said that the founder of Buddhism, Gautama Siddhartha, who came to be known as Buddha, was also virginally conceived after a sacred white elephant pierced his mother's left side (around 500BC). On the wall in a temple at Thebes in Egypt is to be seen a picture representing the god Thoth telling a maiden, Queen Mautmes, that she is to give birth to a 'divine son' who is to be King Amunothph III. Also in ancient Egypt, the Goddess Isis was believed to have conceived her son Horus, a solar god of Egyptian mythology, as a virgin, while in Mexico, the Sun god of the Aztecs and Toltecs Quetzalcoatl, was the result of an immaculate conception. Before he eventually departed from his people, he solemnly promised he would return. His birthday, like Mithra, also born of a virgin, was celebrated on 25 December.

The birth of the Chinese philosopher and teacher of righteousness, Confucius (c. 551BC), was attended by angels. Around one thousand years later, the birth of the prophet and founder of Islam, Mohammed, was said to have been promised to his mother by an angel in a vision. It should therefore not surprise that the annunciation by an angel to Joseph 'in a dream' was directly copied from the message of Apollo to Ariston, Periktione's husband, which said the child born to her was Apollo's offspring.

So, how did the non-historic and formerly insignificant Gospel Mary come today to hold the status of Queen of Heaven, mother of all Christians, the mother of God? The church said, 'there is perhaps ground for surprise if we do not meet with any clear traces of the cultus of the Blessed Virgin in the first Christian centuries'.[4] Why, when the early churchmen never mentioned the mother of Jesus Christ, do their modern-day counterparts extend such reverence to his mother? The mother of God concept certainly captured the hearts and imagination of men and women, particularly during the last five hundred years or so, and writers and artists have vied with each other in paying her homage. Yet in Christian history she was not honoured for hundreds of years and prayers were not addressed to her until 593.[5]

What remaining documentation exists of the Council of Nicaea referred to the Egyptian virgin Isis, her spouse, Osiris and their baby boy, Horus but not to Mary—an extraordinary fact of Christian history. This suggested Isis was the original virgin mother. She was considered by the early church to be the supreme 'mother of God' and in this high-ranking capacity she virtually displaced God as the originator of 'all things'. For some of the earlier presbyters it was Isis, not God, who created the world. Some four hundred years after the canonical time of Jesus Christ, Bishop Augustine, actually dedicated himself to be 'a servant of Isis', not Mary.[6] So strong was the respect for Isis that the title of the first book of the Old Testament, Genesis, was derived from terminology associated with her name. The Gene-of-Isis thus became Genesis—the beginning of everything and therefore, all that Is, is (ISIS).

The mothership of Mary was first raised at the third Council of the church at Ephesus in 431 where it was proposed that she be posthumously accorded the status of the mother-of-God. The idea was fiercely resisted by Nestorius, the then Patriarch of Constantinople, and his followers, for they only saw the Gospel Jesus and Mary as mortals. In records of that Council, Nestorius candidly stated, 'Let no one call Mary the mother of God . . . For Mary was but human'.

The resolutions of that 'awful, brutal assembly'[7] were simply an act of religious power politics. At this meeting, the murderous Cyril, Bishop of Alexandria, openly embraced the cause of Isis, and then anthropomorphized her into Mary. Not only was the adoration of Isis under the new name of Mary confirmed, but also her image of standing on the crescent moon reappeared. Subsequently, the 'superstition of the Latin's almost exalted her (Mary) to the rank of a Goddess'.[8] Sir James Frazer, the author of The Golden Bough made this rather thought-producing comment:

Certainly in art, the figure of Isis suckling the infant Horus is so like that of the Madonna and child that it has sometimes received the adoration of ignorant Christians.

Idealized depiction of rejoicing in the streets on 22 June 431. 'Town criers were sent through the city to announce that the churchmen had decided to make Mary the mother of God. The bishops were then led to their abodes for wine with women marching before them burning incense. A large crowd of excited rabble followed.'[9]

© Copyright. A. C. Bushby, 2001

Other crucifixions

The diversity of earlier religions was truly staggering and legends surrounding the birth and death of a significant central figure abound in masses of sacred writings. Virgin births and crucifixions occurred in numerous ancient mythologies and the number of god-men known to religious history comes to thirty-four. Of these, sixteen became saviour-gods through stories remarkably similar to the one developed for Jesus Christ.

Those sixteen slain saviour-gods, believed by their followers to have lived and died for the sins of the world, together with their countries of origin and approximate dates were: Osiris, Egypt 1700BC; Bel, Babylon 1200BC; Atys (Attis), Phrygia 1700BC; Tammuz, Syria 1160BC; Dionysius, Greece 1100BC; Krishna, India 1000BC; Hesus, Europe 834BC; Indra, Tibet 725BC; Bali, Asia 725BC; Iao, Nepal 622BC; Alcestis, Pherae 600BC; Quetzalcoatl, Mexico 587BC; Wittoba, Travancore 552BC; Prometheus, Greece 547BC; Quirinius, Rome 506BC; Mithra, Persia 400BC.

This engraving from a stone seal-cylinder shows a crucified Orpheus on a cross 400 years before the commencement of Christianity. He was the founder of Greek theology and one of the many who sacrificed themselves that mankind might have the wisdom of the gods. The seven stars represent the 'Lyre of Orpheus.' The inscription, 'Orpheus Bakkikos' identifies the Orpheus of the Bacchic Mysteries.[10]

The essence of the Christian texts

The story of one of the earlier great god-men deserves special mention, as its likeness to the Jesus Christ story is too similar to be coincidental. The legends surrounding Krishna (Sanskrit for Christ), the celebrated saviour-god of the Hindus, have many direct parallels in Christianity and formed the basic outline for the presbyter's compilations. He became incarnate one thousand years before the Gospel birth of Jesus Christ—the Brahmanical calculations say 6900 years earlier—and the presbyters worked every aspect of his story into the lives of Judas Khrestus and Rabbi Jesus Cunobeline.

Krishna was born of a virgin mother Devaki, his birth being announced by a star, 'spirits and angels danced and sang at his birth'. The Gospel story of the 'wise men who came from the east' (Matt. 1:25) 'with gifts of gold, frankincense and myrrh' (Matt. 2:11) to visit the newborn baby was plagiarized verbatim from the story of the birth of Krishna recorded in the Mahabharata, 'Prophets attended with gifts of gold, frankincense and myrrh'.

Krishna was born in a cave and was adored by shepherds. Although of a lowly status he was of royal descent. Kansa, the ruler of the country in which Krishna was born, tried to destroy him immediately after his birth when he ordered the massacre of all new-born males.

The hiding place to which Krishna was taken for refuge was Mathura, on the Jurma River in India, which parted to let him pass through on dry ground. Mathura was exactly the same place, recorded in the Gospel of the Infancy of Jesus Christ, where Joseph and Mary took baby Jesus to hide from King Herod. This narrative found recorded in buried scrolls (the *Nag Hammadi Scrolls*) provided ancient documentary church evidence of presbyters 'building-in' earlier mythical religious elements to bolster their evolving story of 'a son of God' who was seen alive after his crucifixion.

The mass-murder of baby boys at Bethlehem recorded in the Third Century fabrication of the first two chapters of the Gospel of Matthew (2:1–18), used imagery taken from the Krishna story. The Gospel account was actually a verbatim reproduction of a massacre story that had its literary origin around one thousand years before in the Mahabharata. Plagiarism explained why this Gospel description went unrecorded in the annals of world history. It was a church invention unsupported by all non-church documentation by the numerous authoritative chroniclers of the day. The *Talmud* Rabbis knew nothing of King Herod's wholesale murder of the children and had no belief whatsoever in the Christian Gospel tradition as history. Josephus wrote nothing of child murders despite recording Herod's numerous other crimes without hesitation. The *Talmud* Rabbis hated Herod so well they could not have failed to record such a horror, had he been really guilty of it.

Josephus provided additional insights of this ancient legend that may have pre-dated even the Krishna story. In one of his extensive books, 'Jewish Antiquities', Josephus made a parallel reference to an ancient Egyptian 'sacred scribe' who supposedly lived 1500 years previously. It was said that this scribe predicted 'a dangerous child' would be born 'who would abase the sovereignty of the Egyptians'. The Pharaoh immediately and solely upon 'the sage's advice ordered every male child born to the Israelites be destroyed by being cast into the river'. Abraham, father of the Patriarchs, was also described as 'a dangerous child'[11] as were Zoroaster and Persus.[12]

Krishna was called, 'Lord'. One of his first miracles was the curing of a leper, and a lame woman came with a vessel full of sweet scented oils, made a sign on his forehead and poured ointment on his head. He had a 'beloved disciple' named Arjoon, who was his bosom friend, as John was Judas Khrestus'. He was depicted as a meek person who preached nobly in parables and washed the feet of Brahmans. It was Krishna who first said, 'Give to the poor', indeed 346 striking parallels exist between his and the Gospel Jesus Christ's words and actions, including a 'transfiguration'.

Purity of life and spiritual insight were distinguishing traits 'in the character of this oriental sin-atoning Saviour, and that he was often moved with compassion for the down-trodden and the suffering'. Upon the death of Krishna, the sun was darkened and spirits of the dead were seen all around. Krishna (spelt 'Christ-na' until the 20th Century) met his death by crucifixion upon a tree at the hands of his enemies. A later variation declared he was tied to a cross-shaped tree and pierced with three arrows. Yet another version stated he was pierced in the back with arrows and spread-eagled to the branches of a tree by his murderers.

The British Museum holds transcripts of ancient drawings originally taken from Indian sculptures and monuments by the Englishman Moore (c.1860), who arranged them in his collection, *The Hindoo Pantheon*. One of Moore's depictions represented Krishna on a cross with holes pierced in his feet and a halo of glory over his head while his hands were not shown.[13] Figure 91 showed a hole in one foot, a nail through the other, a round nail through one hand, and the other hand undamaged but ornamented with a dove. Mr Moore said that:

> . . . after having announced his intention to publish his findings to the world he was visited and laboured by members of the church who endeavored to dissuade him from publishing such facts to the world for fear it would have the effect to unsettle the faith of some of the weak brethren in the soul-saving religion of Jesus Christ, by raising doubts in their minds as to the originality of the Gospel story of the crucifixion of Christ.[14]

However Krishna died, the religion of India had its crucified victim long before the advent of Christianity. Thus we have evidence deeply and indelibly carved in the old time-chiseled rocks of India recording that their 'Lord and Saviour, Krishna' atoned for the sins of a guilt-striken world by 'pouring out his blood as a propitiatory offering' while stretched upon a cross.

Krishna then 'went down to hell to preach to the inmates of that dark and dreary prison, with the view of reforming them, and getting them back to heaven, and was willing himself to suffer to abridge the period of their torment'.[15] After three days, Krishna then rose from the dead and ascended into heaven. Hindus believe there will be a second coming of Krishna and when this happens, 'stars will fall from the sky' and 'the earth shall tremble'.

After a journey through India (c.1870), author Robert Cheyne noted: 'All that converting the Hindus to Christianity does for them is to change the object of their worship from Krishna to Christ'.[16]

Why they laughed at Justin Martyr

The established ancient picture of previous 'Saviours' being 'only a type of Christ',[17] was the only explanation orthodox Christian apologists could offer.

Justin Martyr, in his arguments presented in *Dialogue with Trypho* (c.160), acknowledged the parallels, but tried to explain them away saying it was 'the devil, to imitate the truth, who invented the stories of Bacchus, Hercules and Esculapius'.

Trypho's companions 'roared with laughter' at St Justin's trite comments in which he hardly denied the story that Bacchus 'rose again', Hercules 'after his death, ascended into heaven', or that Esculapius 'cured diseases and made people rise from the dead'. Later apologists including bishops Eusebius and Augustine, and the church today, used the same line of blaming the devil for anything that opposed their opinion.[18] This was the general off-hand manner in which the church disposed of such matters. 'Everything in the heathen religions that corresponded with their religion was of the *devil*.'[19]

Again and again pre-Christian beliefs appear in the Gospels. Just as the followers of Mithra would say of broken bread, 'This is the body of Mithra' and of the blessed wine, 'This is the blood of Mithra', so was it with the Adonis and Atys (Attis) cults.

Dionysius (or Bacchus) was nearly always shown as a 'bull' god, often with horns, and generally bull-shaped. He was probably one of the gods associated with Taurus in the Zodiac. But when the Sun moved into the sign of the Ram, Dionysius became more and more like a Goat. So much so, his worshippers would 'rend in pieces a live goat, devour it raw, and believe they were eating the body and blood of the god'.[20]

This custom of tearing in pieces and devouring the bodies of both animals and humans was once a frenzied religious rite, and the true origin of the Christian Eucharist. Catholics are taught to believe Jesus Christ is really present in the appearance of bread and wine. They believe they actually eat the body and drink the blood of Jesus Christ at the ceremony of the Eucharist. Protestants say it is only a symbolic gesture. Both perform the ceremony for exactly the same reason the worshippers of Dionysius did.[21] Roman Emperor Julian (361–363) showed the doctrine of the sacrament or transubstantiation in another light. He asked, 'How can a man be so stupid as to imagine that which he eats to be a god?'

No resurrection verses in first Gospel

The resurrection verses in today's Bibles[22] are now universally acknowledged as flagrant forgeries and are now known to have been added to the earliest story some time later, perhaps as late as the Fourth Century or even into the early decades of the Fifth Century. The entry of these vital verses into the Mark Gospel were as far away from the time of Judas Khrestus and Rabbi Jesus as today is from Christopher Columbus setting off to determine whether or not the earth was flat and his subsequent discovery of America.

It is interesting to observe that some modern Bibles previously carrying the verses have now quietly dropped them in reprints, or make some special footnote in relation to their late entry into the Gospel.

Despite a multitude of long drawn out self-justifications by church apologists, there is still no unanimity of opinion regarding the non-existence of resurrection appearances applied to Jesus Christ in the oldest Christian Gospels of Mark. The verses now appearing in today's Bibles (Mark 16:9–20) are not found in the *Sinai Bible*, the *Alexandria Bible*, the *Vatican Bible*, the *Bezae Bible* and a very ancient Latin manuscript of Mark code-named 'K' by analysts. They are also absent from the old Armenian version of the *New Testament* and in a number of important manuscripts of the Ethiopic version.

More importantly, none of the early presbyters including Irenaeus (115–202), Clement of Alexandria (160–215), Tertullian (160–210), Ammonius Saccas (175–245), Origen (185–251) and Eusebius (260–339) showed any knowledge of these verses. Other later presbyters, subsequently promoted to saints and bishops, confirmed the resurrection description was absent from Greek copies of the Mark Gospel. St Jerome, for example, writing in the Fifth Century and shortly before his death said, 'Almost all of the Greek copies do not have this concluding portion'.[23]

Jerome's statement indicated some versions being translated from the original Aramaic and Hebrew into Greek, (before Latin became the language of theology) and appeared with the false ending attached. Just as remarkable, some existing manuscripts of the Fifth and Sixth Century have the suspect resurrection verses written in asterisks, a mark used by ancient scribes to indicate spurious passages in a literary document. The church would seem to share that doubt, commenting that those verses 'differ so radically from the rest of the Gospel that it hardly seems possible Mark himself composed it'.[24]

Even more suspicious, there were three forged resurrection descriptions, not just one, and each version provided a different and conflicting portrayal of the resurrection event. This conclusion was confirmed by the evidence of a comparison of a series of older Bibles with the modern-day version. In church terminology, they have now become known as the Long Ending (not recorded before the Fourth Century), the Long-Ending Expanded, which included an additional 125 words (early Fifth Century) and the Intermediate Ending, first appearing sometime in the Seventh Century.

The church stated 'The resurrection is the fundamental argument for our Christian belief' yet no supernatural appearance of a resurrected Jesus Christ was ever recorded, nor any reference to an ascension into heaven, in the earliest Christian Gospel. The resurrection and ascension of Jesus Christ is the 'sine qua non' of Christianity, 'without which, nothing'.[25] Even the men who wrote the texts official to the church today agreed, saying, 'if

Christ has not been raised, your faith is in vain' (1 Cor. 5:17).

Documentation supporting the resurrection emanated from a theologically-motivated scribal addition some three hundred years or so after the time Judas Khrestus and Rabbi Jesus lived. That evidence is overwhelming and supports the opinion of many established sources, including the thousands of religious experts who compiled the *Catholic Encyclopedias* and official Christian Reference books, that the 'added' verses to the Mark account of Jesus Christ's resurrection appearances had been co-authored and carried on and expanded into the later publication of the other Gospels. Therefore, all references to resurrection appearances in the later Gospels are of no scriptural or historical value for they are based on copies of forged copies assumed by the church in later centuries to be a fruitful reproduction of the original.

The best and most learned biblical scholars strive to show the late addition of various resurrection narratives in Mark's Gospel were not due to forgery. However, that issue could not be better clarified than in the 1908–1911 Editions of the *Catholic Encyclopedia*, which said of the resurrection verses, 'None of the endings commands itself as original . . . the end of Mark [16:9–20] is not authentic'.[26]

Simply put, the last twelve verses in today's version of the Mark Gospel are not original to the story.[27] The oldest Gospel accounts of Jesus Christ's life ended with Mary Magdalene arriving at the tomb and finding the stone rolled back from the entrance and Jesus gone.

Those fabricated resurrection verses received church blessing at the Council of Trent (1545–1563) when it declared the 'received manuscripts and all their substantial portions to be sacred and canonical'. In 1967, the Editorial Committee that approved the *New Catholic Encyclopedias* openly confessed that the earlier (Trent) decision 'is no longer sustainable in the view of the better knowledge gained concerning the Gospel's (Mark) style and vocabulary'.[28]

The church said the non-existence of the resurrection verses in Mark's Gospel in the oldest existing Bibles[29] might be due to the original author being interrupted, perhaps by death, from finishing his work. This was clearly not so. The author had meant the story to end in this manner for he (or she) had drawn a complex decorative coronis under the end of the last words in the last column to indicate the work was finished. This coronis appeared in various forms in all early Bibles.

A change of wording in the Gospel of Luke also raised doubts. Six words appearing in the current Gospels of Luke, 'and was carried up to heaven' (Luke 24:51), did not appear in any of the oldest and most accepted Gospel of Luke manuscripts available. The later addition (or subtraction, in some cases) of just one sentence or paragraph has proved to have massive consequences on the thinking and beliefs of mankind. When the modern Gospels of Mark and Luke say Jesus Christ resurrected himself from the dead and ascended to heaven, none of the earliest *New Testaments* (nor any historical records) verify the modern Gospel accounts.

This knowledge seriously calls into question the Gospel events following the crucifixion of Jesus Christ. Staunch Christian scholars have had difficulty explaining why, in approximately a six week period during which it was said in modern Gospels Jesus Christ was sighted after the crucifixion, the Gospel accounts violently contradicted one another with regards to the number of places he appeared, eyewitnesses, and even the day and location of his ascension into heaven. Luke's Gospel located all the appearances in Jerusalem and Judea, while Matthew's Gospel referred to a Galilean mountain (Matt. 28:16). John referred to appearances in Jerusalem[30] but added a further story about an appearance of Jesus Christ on the shore of the Sea of Galilee. These contradictions are explained by the fact that they were all presbyter's fabrications. Professor A. H. Sayce said:

> It is difficult to understand why [the *New Testament*] should have had such a hypnotizing effect, for its fictitious nature is its most obvious characteristic.[31]

Roman Emperor Trajanus Decius (249) said he saw developing in the presbyter's stories 'a dangerous creed capable of destroying Rome'. Those and later writings, particularly of Ambrose and Lactantius, mixed 'history with religious fanaticism'[32] and 'crowds were drawn by the activities of larger-than-life preachers . . . and clever Christian preachers soon learnt the techniques of crowd manipulation and audience control'.[33]

CHAPTER NINETEEN

ḣow tḣe twins became God

Why the first Christian council was needed

AROUND THE TIME OF ORIGEN'S DEATH (C.251), THE NUMBER OF PRESBYTER'S writings had increased dramatically and bitter argument raged between opposing factions about their conflicting stories. According to presbyter Albius Theodoret (c.255) there were 'more than two hundred' variant Gospels in use in his time.[1] A considerable amount of presbyter's material of this period is available, particularly the correspondence of Cyprian (c. 258), consisting of eighty-one letters covering many of 'the superstitions of the time'.[2] Further 'embellishments were added' during this period[3] and some presbyters 'listed subjects which looked like additions and are apparently spurious'.[4] As with many things in the governing of the Roman Empire, it was Emperor Diocletian (285–305, originally Diocles) who eventually tried to give order to the presbyter's cult, partly because he saw it as necessary to maintain his power, and partly to provide a religious focus for the Empire as a whole.

From the outset of his rule Emperor Diocletian was convinced that a state religion was necessary to promote unity and loyalty in the empire. Christians could not participate in the worship of Jupiter and other gods or in the imperial cult. Therefore they were regarded as disloyal to the state and dangerous to its unity. In an effort to achieve some form of unity Diocletian then permitted them to worship Jupiter, the supreme god of the Roman pantheon, and restored the old Roman worship of Jupiter

Capitolinius as the official religion of the State. This move did not provide the general revival he had hoped for so Diocletian then issued three edicts of increasing severity against the Christians (303–304). He hoped especially to destroy the presbyters and thus deprive the rabble of 'exhibitions of theatrical declamation'.[5] He demanded that the presbyters hand over their writings to the Roman authorities to be burned, citing they were 'a tasteless imitation of archaic expressions and forms of speech'.[6]

In other respects, Diocletian left an imposing heritage, for he was the most remarkable Imperial organiser since Augustus. One of his reforms that stands in the structure of the Christian church today emanated from the doubling of the number of the provinces, which were increased from fifty to one hundred. Italy was included in his system. It was intended that the governors of these relatively small areas would thus lack the resources necessary to start a rebellion. Another innovation was the grouping of these provinces into thirteen larger units he named after himself and called 'dioceses'.[7]

In 305, Diocletian abdicated after twenty years in office. Gaius Galerius and Aurelius Constantius then became joint emperors. Constantius was a resident of York in Britain and was married to Helena, 'unquestionably a British princess'.[8] After the upheavals in Lundunaborg (c.61) under the tartan-clad Queen Boadicea, the ancient city of York had become a popular resort of the Romans. From York, several Roman Emperors had functioned, probably deeming it a safer haven to rule from than the vicious city of Rome. Several Roman Emperors are buried there.

Princess Helena was the daughter of King Coel (perhaps the legendary Old King Cole), and she was born at Colchester (Coel-chester) in 265 and died circa 336. The remains of King Coel's castle can still be seen at Lexdon, a suburb of Colchester. Of interest was the recent claim that the castle now known as Edinburgh Castle was originally erected by Constanius for Queen Empress Helena, and that a great part of the present walls were part of the walls of the original castle. In the Vatican and British Museums can be seen coins struck with her name, reading 'Flavia Helena Augusta' but she was best known as Empress Helena and so recorded in the annals of history. To all Roman historical records, however, Empress Helena was made to appear as a Roman native, wife of a Roman, and the mother of an illustrious Roman son, Flavius Constantine (272–337), none of which was true. Empress Helena was descendant from Rabbi Jesus Cunobeline's family through his first wife, Princess Cypros, a Nabateean Arab and the daughter of Cypros and Alexas. Cypros, her mother, was King Herod's granddaughter. Her uncle was Joseph of Arimathea[9] who was King Herod's son and the last husband of Mariamne Herod, the 'hidden mother' of 'twin young ones'.[10]

Empress Helena's husband, Emperor Constantius 'the Pale', died suddenly at York in 306 and his troops saluted in their young son Constantine as leader. By hereditary right, he was now Emperor over Britain, Gaul and Spain. It is not generally known that Emperor Constantine was British born and could trace his Ancestries back to the family of Rabbi Jesus Cunobeline. Many in the church have denied the fact but its own records confirmed the issue. Eminent historian, Cardinal Caesar Baronius said:

> The man must be mad who, in the face of universal antiquity, refuses to believe that Constantine and his mother were Britons, born in Britain.[11]

Over twenty European historical authorities also attested to this fact. The descent of Constantine was listed in *The Panegyries of the Emperors* and the genealogy of his lineage given by his descendant, Constantine Palaeologus. Polydore Vergil, in his *History of England* stated:

> Constantine, born in Britain, of a British mother, proclaimed Emperor in Britain, beyond doubt made his natal soil a participator in his glory.

Constantine massed a powerful army in Britain, composed wholly of local British warriors and began to prepare to cross the seas to the continent to engage Emperor Maxentius (Roman Emperor 306–312) in battle. Constantine sailed with his army, landing on the shores in what is today Germany. He then consulted 'the mouthpiece of God' (Irenaeus), the celebrated oracles recorded in the mysterious *Sibylline Books*.

The importance of the Sibylline Books

The *Sibylline Books* were a collection of ancient prophecies written by a woman whose name was Herophile (c. 500BC) and her writings became remarkably important in the later development of Christian literature. She lived in a cave near the ancient town of Cumae, in Campania, Italy and was considered by the populous to be 'a slowly ageing but immortal priestess'.[12] The remains of Cumae and the adjoining caves can still be inspected today. She was one of several women who prophesied under the supposed inspiration of some deity, and delivered their prophecies in a frenzied state. She later became known as the Cumaean Sibyl.[13]

She was considered the greatest seer of Pagan antiquity and her 'heathen oracles'[14] played a most significant part in early Christian times. In such awe was Herophile held by the early presbyters that Justin Martyr recorded he actually made the long overland trip to Cumae to see for himself where she once lived. He related how he saw there a cave made out of a single massive rock from which the oracles were given. Justin referred without reserve to her writings. Clement of Alexandria also quoted freely from the Sibyl's books and even represented St Paul as appealing to her writings.[15] Clement cited the Sibyl as the 'greatest of all prophetesses' and called her 'the prophetess of the Hebrews'. More remarkably he quoted the Pentateuch—the first five books of the Bible—and the *Sibylline Books* in the same sentence.[16] Bishop Irenaeus said she was the 'one who announces the counsels or plans of the gods' and clearly believed her oracles were divinely inspired:

> With lips inspired, she utters words that were mirthless, without ornament, and without perfume, but through the power of the god her voice reaches down a thousand years.[17]

The Sibyl's writings also had a considerable influence on the Third Century Christian apologist Lactantius. Bishop of Hippo, St Augustine, also quoted at length from her oracles in his records called *De Civitate Dei*.[18] The Second Century opponent to the Christian movement, Celsus, was moved to ridicule the early presbyter's frequent use of her psychic predictions in the writings which became Gospels.

Herophile lived some 500 years before the commencement of the Christian era and appeared before the king of ancient Rome, Tarquin the Proud (traditionally 510BC). She claimed she was 'his sibyl'—The Sibyl of Tarquin—and offered to sell him nine volumes of her mysterious writings for 300 gold pieces. Upon his refusal to buy, the prophetess departed from his presence and burned three of her writings in the palace courtyard and then offered the remaining six books for the original price. King Tarquin once again refused, whereupon the Sibyl three days later returned and burned three more of her prophetic writings. Once again, she demanded the original price for the last three books. There was much local gossip about these strange going-ons and the king's curiosity was aroused and he purchased the last three writings at the original asking price. This was an event that proved epoch-making in the history of Rome. The Sibyl then vanished and was never seen again.[19]

The three volumes became highly prized and were carefully kept in a specially sculptured stone chest specially commissioned by the king himself. Priests were appointed to interpret the writings and scribes were assigned to reproduce exact copies. The original collection was jealously guarded in the Temple of Jupiter Capitolinus and was frequently consulted by priests for guidance before prayers were addressed to the God of Fire and the Goddess of Agriculture. In times of peril and disaster the original copies were entrusted to curators who were assisted by two Greek interpreters to read the oracles out loud to the senate.

The Sibyl's works were believed to contain all the directions needed to worship any of the Roman gods and the predictions she made were extensively believed. Her ancient writings were recognised at Rome as one of the most efficacious instruments in Roman religion and the prophecies of the Sibyl eventually were observed and accepted by all Romans. Because they were believed to be 'possessed with the spirit of divination', the *Sibylline Books* became the 'Bible' of the Romans[20] and their misuse was punishable by death. The originals perished in the fire that destroyed the Temple of Capitolinus in 83BC. They were immediately replaced by copies from other temples, unlike the occasion when original copies of the *Old Testament* were burnt and Ezra, a priest and scribe, replaced them by rewriting from memory.[21]

A special priestly college called the Quindecimviri Sacris Faciundis was set up by Julius Caesar (100–44BC) and was officially in charge of the *Sibylline Books*. Its fifteen members (plus the Emperor of the day) exercised great influence on the decisions of government and they continually searched the writings for prophecies that they thought benefited the Roman Empire. In 12BC, the first Roman Emperor and *Pontifex Maximus* (chief priest), Augustus transferred a special pontifex set of the *Sibylline Books* to the Temple of Apollo on the Palatine hill in Rome and there it remained until Stilicho burnt then in 405. Their placement in the Temple of Apollo demonstrated their legality as well as their immeasurable worth. Emperor Augustus, directed the preparation of many identical sets of the Sibyl's oracles and they were supplied to the senate in Egypt and to priests in all Grecized lands.[22]

The Cumaean Sibyl was always the highly regarded clairvoyant of the Roman Catholic church. Even today she can be seen magnificently portrayed by Michelangelo in a prime central position among the great patriarchs of the Bible stories depicted on the ceiling of the Sistine Chapel in the Vatican itself.

Michelangelo's 1510 fresco of the Sibyl of Tarquin on the Sistine Chapel ceiling in Rome. She was the author of the Sibylline Books, and in this presentation, Michelangelo depicted two identical 'assisting genii' looking down upon the open pages of the book held by the Cumaean Sibyl.

© Film Library of Renaissance Art. Italy.

The Quindecimviri Sacris Faciundis monitored all foreign religions or cults that were allowed to function in the Roman Empire after permission had been found by prophecies recorded in the Sibylline Books.[23]

> The use of these oracles was from the outset reserved for the State. As these books recognized the gods worshipped, and the rites observed, they were the principal cause of the introduction of a series of foreign deities and religious rite into the Roman State worship, of the amalgamation of national deities of Greece, and a general modification of the Roman religion after the Greek type.[24]

So important were the *Sibylline Books*, the Roman authorities believed 'decisions of war and peace might be affected greatly by the poems inside, and the words of the Sibyl were taken seriously'.[25]

Following his understanding of the Sibylline prophecies, Constantine was confident that any foe in battle would be destroyed. After 'listening to the oracles', he accepted the advice and advanced forward for a military encounter. At Milvian Bridge (October 312), the site of the famous (even legendary) encounter, the armies of Constantine and Maxentius clashed, and the British, under the shrewd leadership of Constantine, won an overwhelming victory. The rapacious and cruel Maxentius (d. 313) was completely routed, and his seizure of Rome, and the subsequent persecution of its people, ended. Constantine, with his warriors marched victoriously on to Rome, where he received a massive welcome. Amid great rejoicing, he ascended the Imperial throne, assumed the purple, and was officially acclaimed by the Senate and the populace of Rome as its Emperor.

As a result of moves and counter moves in the struggle for power there were five co-emperors ruling the Roman Empire at this time. Constantine demonstrated that as a strategist and tactician he was one of the greatest generals of antiquity. In 313 Constantine and a co-emperor Licinius, who had obtained possession of the whole of the East, met at Milan and tried to reach agreement on a religious policy corresponding essentially to that contained in the earlier edict of Galerius of 311.

The rivalry between Constantine and Licinius led to a large-scale war that ended in the defeat of Licinius in 324. He was subsequently executed on the charge of attempting to reestablish himself in power. The bloodthirsty and ruthless Flavius Constantine then singularly ruled the entire Roman Empire, Britain, Gaul and Spain.

His religious sympathies, as well as those of his mother, were Western, not Roman, and were those of the British Druidic church. The objects of Emperor Constantine's political life were explained in one of his earliest Edicts:

We call God to witness, the Saviour of all men, that in assuming the government, we are influenced by these two considerations: the uniting in one faith, and the restoration of peace to a world rent to pieces by the insanity of religious differences.

One of Emperor Constantine's main fears was that of uncontrollable disorder among the teeming populous. 'Roman expectations of religion's function was to maintain a stable relationship between the gods and the state and Rome's past success was its justification.'[26] The 'peculiar type of oratory'[27] being expounded by the presbyters was a challenge to the stable state of Roman religion. In 313, for example, a great argument developed between bodies of presbyters headed by Donatus, a biscop who gave his name to a schism that later came to be called the Donatist movement. At that time groups of presbyters and biscops violently clashed over the variations in their writings and 'altar was set against altar' in competing for an audience.[28]

The church at war with itself
Eventually a Roman edict of toleration granting the presbyters and the rabble the right to practice their discourses was issued. By this time, groups of presbyters and their sects sprang up like mushrooms, each with different Gospels (Gal. 1:6) and varying lists of apostles (2 Cor. 11:13). The 'toleration' won however, would have no legal basis unless it had the final imprimatur of the priestly college originally established by Julius Caesar. The earlier reforms introduced by Diocletian reached their full development only under Constantine who gave some support to the presbyters but could not bring about a peaceful settlement between the rival factions. Constantine 'never acquired a solid theological knowledge' of the presbyter's orations and 'depended heavily on his advisers in religious questions'.[29]

The confusion of the duel nature
Second, Third and early Fourth Century biscops argued constantly about the dual nature of Jesus Christ, a concept they couldn't understand because they were unaware that their writings now embraced two separate life stories. In official Roman records, Constantine was noted as commenting that among the numerous presbyterian factions, 'strife had grown so serious, vigorous action was necessary to establish a more religious state'. There were decades of ongoing disputes among the presbyters as to whether the god they had developed had one or two natures. They were unable or unwilling to recognize the 'twin' elements in their manuscripts. In 312 Arius, a Libyan presbyter, propounded 'that he is fearful that the biscops shall develop two gods'.[30] However, this wasn't to be. When Constantine conquered the

East in 324 he sent his Spanish religious advisor, Osius of Cordoba, to Alexandria with letters to several biscops exhorting them to make peace among their own.

But the mission failed and Constantine, probably at the suggestion of Osius, then issued a Decree commanding all presbyters and their subordinates 'be mounted on asses, mules and horses belonging to the public and travel to the city of Nicaea' in the Roman Provinence of Bithymia, a country of Asia. The presbyters were instructed by the Emperor to bring with them the manuscripts from which they orated to the rabble, 'wrapped and bound in leather'. Constantine saw in this developing system of belief the opportunity to make a combined State religion and protect it by law. The first general church council was thus convened and the year was 325.[31]

The simple creatures

The desire of the modern-day church to depict the early Christian councils as consisting of a collegiate body of fair-minded senators moving peaceably towards collective decisions is most certainly not reflected in the church's own ancient literature. The early councils were brutal and violent affairs and much can be understood by examining the conduct of them. Dean Milman, the celebrated Christian historian, summarised the general nature of church councils when he said:

> Nowhere is Christianity less attractive, and if we look to the ordinary tone and character of the proceedings, less authoritative, than in the councils of the church . . . The degeneracy is rapid from the Council of Nicaea [325AD] to the first of Ephesus [431AD], where each party came determined to use every means of haste, manoeuvre, court influence, bribery, to crush his adversary; where there was an encouragement of, if not an appeal to the violence of the populace, to anticipate the Decrees of the council, where each had his own tumultuous foreign rabble to back his quarrel, and neither would scruple at any means to obtain ratification of their anathemas through persecution by the civil government.

The first of these gatherings then, the Council of Nicaea, was personally presided over by Emperor Constantine. Historical records depicted him as a rather curious fellow. His nephew Julian (Roman Emperor 361–363) said 'bull-neck' Constantine made himself ridiculous by his strange appearance, wearing weird stiff eastern garments, jewels on his arms, a tiara on his head, perched crazily between tinted bat-wings, and a lion on his chest.

Just previous to this gathering Emperor Constantine had been initiated into the religious order of Sol Invictus, one of the two thriving cults of the time that regarded the Sun as the one and only Supreme God (Mithraism being the other). His entire reign was known as the 'Sun-Emperorship'.

Sun god symbols were prominent throughout the land and were emblazoned on the official coinage. In Rome, Constantine ordered the construction of a huge ornate stone arch still standing today, which he dedicated to the 'Invincible One'.

Emperor Julian's description of Emperor Constantine appeared to have been portrayed by Leonardo de Vinci, c.1475. (Antique Warrior).
© Roma Photos Int.

On 21 June, the day of the Summer Solstice, (and under those cult conditions) a total of 2048 'presbyters, deacons, sub-deacons, acolytes and exorcists' gathered at Nicaea to decide what Christianity really was, what it would be, what writings were to be used and who was to be its god. Participants were mostly Greek, although Africa was represented by Caecilian of Carthage, Spain by Osius of Cordova, Gaul by Nicasius of Die and Pannonia by Dommus of Stridon. When speaking of the men gathered at Nicaea, Sabinius of Hereclea (c. 326), said:

> Excepting Constantine himself, and Eusebius Pamphilius, they were a set of illiterate, simple creatures who understood nothing.

According to surviving records of the Council, Eusebius 'occupied the first seat on the right of the Emperor and delivered the inaugural address on the Emperors' behalf'.[32] It was this same Eusebius who confessed 'that he has related whatever might redound to the glory, and that he has suppressed all that could tend to the disgrace, of that religion'.[33] Emperor Constantine, however, was the most conspicuous figure in this Council. He was, in fact, the ruling spirit and made the ultimate decisions for the presbyters. In his official writings (later entitled *Oration to the Saints*) he spoke of the Garden of Eden as being located on some other planet. This was also the belief of many of the early Christian clergy, amongst them Tertullian, Tatian, Clement of Alexandria, Origen and Jerome.

€mperor Constantine determines the religious state

It was at this curious gathering that the Roman Catholic church had its real beginning, and the ramifications of decisions made at that time are indeed difficult to calculate. It was a remarkable event that provided many details of early clerical thinking and presented a clear picture of the intellectual phenomena that prevailed in the budding church at that time. Eusebius, Athanasius of Alexandria and Philostorgius have given divergent accounts of the special arrangement promulgated by Emperor Constantine that was intended to achieve lasting unity among the biscops. The early church saw the Roman Emperors as 'second only to God, before and above all gods'.[34] Even though he lived around 250 years later, St Augustine called Emperor Antoninus Aurelius, 'Pope'.[35] The power the Emperors wielded was awesome and the decisions they made are still felt today. These extraordinary words of Bishop Tertullian (Third Century) provided an example and reveal the essence of what was eventually determined at the Council of Nicaea:

> There was an ancient Decree that no one should be received for a deity unless he was first approved by the Senate [Roman] . . . but the Senate, without whose consent no deification could take place, rejected it, because the Emperor himself had declined the honour.[36]

Here ancient church evidence established that a new 'god' was to be approved by the Roman Emperor and an earlier attempt (c. 210) to deify either or Judas Khrestus or Rabbi Jesus Cunobeline (or somebody else) had been 'declined'. Therefore, as late as 325, the Christian religion did not have an official god.

That was soon settled. The Council of Nicaea was now in progress and in the ensuing 'discussions' there were some curious scenes recorded, mainly about Arius, a presbyter from Alexandria. He was a man of acknowledged learning and he and his supporters argued violently against the move of deifying Judas Khrestus or Rabbi Jesus. Arius and his followers said they were only men who were 'possessed of free will, so as to be capable of vice or virtue', therefore not gods. This comment angered other presbyters who outvoted Arius and his supporters and moved a motion that the hero of their writings was, in fact, 'a creature and a work'.

One ancient document, that of a presbyter named Eunomis, reported that the red-faced bishop of Myra, Nicholas—who arrived at the council wearing a smelly dog-hair coat and bearing gifts—we sometimes today call him Santa Claus—became so enraged at Arius that he 'punched him on the jaw'. Arius' book 'Thalia', was burnt on the spot to the chant of a repetitive melody by his foot-stomping opponents and Arius was later poisoned. So great was the uproar at that first Christian convention that Emperor Constantine called on members of his 300,000 strong army of guards to restore order.[37] So bitter was the debate that Constantine forcibly dismissed 1730 'credulous, and blundering, passionate and one-sided' presbyters, acolytes and exorcists from the Council proceedings.[38]

The council continued to be interrupted by yells and tumults and the laymen were compelled to remind the presbyters of their clerical 'deportment'. The main cause of dissention centred about establishing the divinity of the composite character central to the presbyter's writings and this topic became the major concern at all church councils until the 16th Century.

The time had now come to make three centuries of presbyters' compilations 'divine'. Following longstanding Roman custom, Emperor Constantine used the remaining body of biscops and the ancient Roman decree to legally deify a new god for the rabble and did so by democratic consent and the blessing of the biscops in attendance. After a long and bitter debate, a vote was finally taken and it was with a majority show of hands that Judas Khrestus and Rabbi Jesus both became God—161 votes to 157. A new god was proclaimed and 'officially' ratified by Emperor Constantine, who declared him to be Homoousious, that is, of the substance of the Father.[39] The ambiguity of this term involved the ensuring Christian councils in centuries of hostility and cost Arius, and many others, their lives. Emperor Constantine effectively joined elements of the two individual life stories of Judas Khrestus and Rabbi Jesus into a singular creation. The doctrine of the Celtic/British church of the West was democratically attached to the presbyter's stories of the East.

Deification was a legal principle

Constantine 'officially' decreed divine honours on the twins whose two separate names had now, by a show of biscops hands, been combined as one entity. This purely political act of deification effectively and legally placed Judas Khrestus and Rabbi Jesus among the Roman gods as one individual composition today called Jesus Christ. It is important to note that the format of the name 'Jesus Christ' was not cemented down until the time of the Reformation (14th–17th Centuries), for in earlier times it had several renditions such as Yeshoua Krst and Yeshu Kristos. An original illustration in the British Museum called the *Harleian Heraldic Manuscript No. 269* (c.1180) evidences the 12th Century spelling as 'Jesew Cryst'. It was possible that Constantine applied 'Yesu' at the Council of Nicaea, for this was a very sacred identity corporated into the Druidic Trinity as the Godhead. Eunomis, a presbyter in attendance at the Council of Nicaea, left a record stating that the name Yesu was actually discussed at the Council.[40] Yesu was the name later applied to Jesus Christ in old Gospels and it seemed the Druidic followers of Rabbi Jesus Cunobeline's Krist knowledge were called the 'Men of Yesu', as St Epiphanius recorded. Yesu Krist was probably the Roman Empire's original epithet for Emperor Constantine's new deity. 'One face, one voice, one habit and two persons' said Shake-speare.[41] The act of deification was a 'broad stroke' political decision that strengthened Emperor Constantine's emperorship. Furthermore, the mythology surrounding the original formation of the city of Rome and the future State by twins Romulus and Remus added critical insight into the nature of Roman belief and must be seen to be beneficial to the thinking of the Roman populous of the time.

The precedent had been set

Early precedents of creating specific new gods for specific reasons had been regularly set in Roman history. On the advice of the *Sibylline Books*, the Romans adopted the cult of Aesculapius during a plague in 293BC.[42] Around nine decades later, the oracles were again referenced:

> In 204BC during the war against Hannibal in Italy, plague was rife in the army, and there were more ill omens than usual. The *Sibylline Books* were consulted, and the usual remedy proposed . . . the introduction of a new cult.[43]

The history of Roman religion exhibits much evidence of non-gods becoming gods and goddesses and many earlier precedents had been set. The daughter of Germanics and Agrippina the Elder, Julia Drusilla (d. 38AD) was deified after her death.[44] The story was often quoted of Emperor Vespasian (70–79) joking on his deathbed, 'Oh dear, I think I am becoming a god'. The Emperor Hadrian (117–138) actually had his handsome young favourite companion, Antinous, deified after he drowned in the Nile in 122. Marcus Aurelius (161–180), one of the greatest emperors in Roman history, had his wife deified after her death, and he himself later became 'a son of a god'.

The 'son of a God' term was used by several emperors to indicate their descent (sometimes through adoption or merely by pious assertion) from a previous emperor, usually an immediate or close predecessor, whose memory was held in particular respect. It was often a political statement, thus Septimius Severus assumed the title 'son of the deified Marcus' in 195 to proclaim and strengthen his legitimacy, though he had never been (nor is likely to have been) adopted by Marcus Aurelius, who died fifteen years before.[45]

> Roman magistrates were frequently adored as provincial deities, with the pomp of altars and temples, of festivals and sacrifices. Deification was a legal principle . . . and received as an institution, not of religion but of policy.[46]

A deification ceremony was performed called 'Apotheosis', and this was the origin of the concept of veneration of saints in the Christian church. Thus, the deified ones were then called 'saviours' and looked upon as gods.[47] Temples, altars and images with attributes of divinity were then erected and public holidays proclaimed on their birthdays. Their surviving male offspring were officially addressed as 'son of a god', the 'god' being the new status of their deified father. Following the original example set by the deification of Caesar, their funerals were dramatized as the scene of their resurrection and immortality.[48] All these godly attributes passed as a legal right to Emperor Constantine's new deity, Jesus Christ.

The everlasting Gospel

Towards the closing of the Council of Nicaea, the *Sibylline Books* were again consulted and another unfulfilled prophecy was found. It predicted that 'an everlasting gospel to preach to them' would be written for those 'that dwell on earth, until they have climbed from the pit of slime'.[49] Constantine saw an unfulfilled Sibylline prophecy that, under Roman religious policy, gave him license to introduce a new Gospel and he officially deemed it so. Many elements of the presbyter's stories carried parallels to the traditional mythical components of the highly-regarded earlier story of Romulus and Remus: the earthly mother and the father a god; the attempt by the reigning king (Amulius) to forestall a threat to his rule, involving danger to the children; a royal blood line through kingly descent; and the birth of twins in curious circumstances.

The Emperor then instructed Bishop Eusebius to compile a uniform collection of new writings 'bound together as one' using the stories from the large collection of presbyter's manuscripts as his reference source. Eusebius was to arrange for the production of 'fifty sumptuous copies . . . to be written on parchment in a legible manner, and in a convenient portable form, by professional scribes thoroughly accomplished in their art'.[50]

'Make them to astonish,' said Emperor Constantine. 'These orders,' said Eusebius, 'were followed by the immediate execution of the work itself, which we sent him in magnificently and elaborately bound volumes of three-fold and four-fold forms.'[51] This was the first mention of finished copies of a Christian *New Testament* in the history of mankind.

Constantine then acclaimed his new god the 'Prince of Peace', a title that had been originally bestowed on Emperor Augustus in the First Century. With his instructions now fulfilled, Emperor Constantine decreed that the new writings be thereafter called the 'words of God' and be attached 'with binding' to copies of the Hebrew *Old Testament*. Emperor Vespasian, in the First Century, had proclaimed the entire Jewish territory the personal property of the Roman Emperors, and his decision was officially ratified by the Senate. In effect, all later Emperors were in control of the Jewish religion, and by combining the *Old Testament* with his new 'everlasting Gospel', Emperor Constantine effectively attempted to amalgamate the earlier Jewish religion with his new cult. By legal inheritance, he was also the messiah.

After Eusebius had finished drawing upon the large array of presbyter's texts,[52] Constantine then ordered them destroyed by fire and 'any man found concealing one should be stricken off from his shoulders' (beheaded). As the record showed, previous complete *New Testament* documentation no longer exists, but some individual segments did survive—the Gospel of Peter, for example—hidden by biscops who held the opinion that the writings were originally compiled by First Century apostles whose names they falsely bore.

Che first 'place of gathering'

Shortly after the close of the Council of Nicaea, Emperor Constantine transferred the use of the Lateran Palace to the biscop of Rome and ordered Marcarius of Jerusalem (d. 333) to design him the 'fairest structure' and build a new church.[53] It was British royalty through Emperor Constantine that authorised the first Christian church at Rome, and he used the original twenty-acre site that was once the home of Rabbi Jesus Cunobeline's family. At this time, the Bath (Casino or garden house) in the grounds of the Palace of the British was enlarged and converted into a 'place of gathering' by command of Emperor Constantine.[54] Constantine then sent Joseph of Tiberias to Jerusalem to construct a small temple over the site of a cave that the presbyters had shown to the rabble as being the actual birthplace of Jesus Christ. A much newer church now stands over the cave and the 'birthplace' is marked with a fourteen-point star. Constantine's instructions are the first recorded instance of buildings being specifically constructed for Christian use, except maybe for a reed church at Edessa believed destroyed by a flood in the Third Century.

To later Christian writers Emperor Constantine became 'the great champion of Christianity and it was given a legal status as the religion of the Roman Empire'.[55] Records show this to be incorrect, for it was 'self interest which led him at first to adopt Christianity'.[56] However, Christianity had been born, and so had Paganism.

The origin of the word 'Pagan'

As a direct result of Emperor Constantine's Council of Nicaea, the word 'Pagan' developed. After finalising the foundation of the Roman State church immediately after the Council, the civil powers of the state began a vigorous campaign to build up the church by compelling people to embrace the new religion of Jesus Christ. Emperor Constantine offered bribes to those who supported the new creed[57] and heaped honors and favors upon the habitués of his court, who most naturally were the first to agree with his wishes. He granted freedom to the slaves, and to those in the ordinary walks of life he gave gifts of white togas and bribed some with twenty pieces of gold.

> The common people were thus purchased at such an easy rate that, in one year, 12,000 were baptized at Rome, besides a proportionable number of women and children.[58]

The church recorded that in eight months many thousands more in Contantinople joined it.[59] Emperor Constantine issued edicts forbidding other belief systems to assemble or hold meetings, and passed laws that any building used by them be destroyed. In this way all who held doctrines and opinions contrary to the new Roman teachings were suppressed. Scholars and philosophers were silenced and banished, and their works burned.[60]

Those who refused to accept the new religion were put to death while others were banished from their homes. Many people fled to the remote rural regions of Pagi to avoid such persecution. They subsequently became known as Pagans and the municipalities and townships they established were called Pagus villages. It was in the largest cities the new church made its earliest gains in numbers because civil powers were strongest and most in evidence.[61] In the far-flung country regions people were not so controlled by the powers of government or church. Because of their isolation they were not as easily forced into accepting Christianity. They resisted to such an extent that the people of Pagi were reviled by the church as objects of scorn.

The negative comments they were subjected to saw them regarded as without religion or heathens. In later Christian writings, the word Pagan was projected backwards and applied to pre-Christian groups who were considered lesser humans because they had not lived in the Khrestian era—that is, non-Christian.

The Royal bloodline

It was probable that Emperor Constantine had another purpose in mind when he deified his long dead twin relatives—to protect a family lineage that had earlier usurped the throne of Britain. The records reveal that the usurper was none other than King Caradoc, for he had foreign blood through the line of his parents Rabbi Jesus Cunobeline and Cypros. This was a predominant Nabatean (Arab) and Indumean (Edomite) ancestry with direct lineage through both parents to the House of Herod the Great. This happened at the time of the slaying of Prince Guiderius in the early days of the Roman invasion of Britain. Guiderius' sudden death created a national emergency requiring the immediate establishment of the Pendragonate, or military dictatorship, on the field of battle. It was at this time that Caradoc assumed the mantle and continued the battle, and his family subsequently retained the crown through Caradoc's son, King Cyllinus.

The true British bloodline inheritance flowed through the lineage of Rabbi Jesus Cunobeline's second wife Princess Mary Magdalene, a pure Royal Celt, making her two boys the true heirs to the Crown of Britain. It was no surprise to find this Celtic Princess defamed in the new church of Emperor Constantine, whose family line remained the primary beneficiaries of the deception. It was probable the defamation of Princess Mary Magdalene started at that time.

Eusebius charged with forging historical records

Immediately after the closing of the Council of Nicaea began the forging of earlier records to establish that Jesus Christ was once an historical personage. The earliest fabrication involved a much discussed passage, the so-called Testimonium Flavianum,[62] in the writings of the most acknowledged historian of the First Century, the great Jewish author Josephus. Particular narratives designed to glorify Jesus Christ were fabricated into Josephus' writings and they have now been exposed as priesthood forgeries. The church confessed the glowing passages about Jesus Christ were later 'interpolations by Christians'.[63] Dr Lardner, one of the ablest defenders of Christianity (c.1760), said the passage 'should be forever discarded from any place among the evidences of Christianity'.[64] Theologians believe it was Bishop Eusebius who forged the passages when he re-wrote a copy of Josephus' works immediately after the Council of Nicaea.[65] As the passage was not found in any edition of Josephus prior to the era of Eusebius, the suspicion fastened upon him as its author, for Eusebius personally argued that falsehood might be used as medicine for the benefit of the church.[66] It was Eusebius who also ordered the destruction of fifteen late-Second Century books originally written by a person called Porphyry, citing that they 'spoke about the Khrestians'.[67]

This was not the only church alteration to the works of Josephus. There was evidence that further 'interpolations were introduced into the text of Josephus long before his (Eusebius) time'.[68] Origen himself admitted adding to the Jewish historian's works.[69] He also affirmed that Josephus 'did not acknowledge Jesus Christ'.[70]

Overview of the outcome of the Council of Nicaea

Out of the first Christian council, a decision was made to use the full moon spring equinox festival, then a heathen festival held annually in honour of the Babylonian goddess Ishtar, as a Christian celebration marking the 'resurrection' of Jesus Christ. The word 'Easter' was derived from 'Ishtar'— the former belief that the sun danced on Ishtar Day now applies to Easter Day. The Sabbath was shifted from Saturday to Sun-day out of respect for the Sun-God Sol Invictus. The presbyters agreed with this merging, denying the once-sacred Law of Moses and the commandment to 'Remember the Sabbath and keep it holy' (Exodus 20:8).

To accommodate the current thriving religion of Sol Invictus and the rising new faith of Christianity, the shrewd Emperor Constantine reasoned the obvious thing to do was make Jesus Christ a personification of the Sun in a manner similar to the god-men of Pagan antiquity—Apollo, Osiris, Orpheus, Bel (Baal) and Bacchus, to name but a few. As both practices taught man's immortality through a divine Saviour, a future judgment and resurrection of the dead, the merging of these eternal principles was entirely feasible.

In an empire seething with religious discontent, this move proved to be a masterstroke and a clever political move by Emperor Constantine that strengthened his standing. Thus, Constantine became Christianity's chief bishop and the commander-in-chief of its army. It was this same Constantine who drowned his wife in boiling water, butchered his young nephew, personally murdered two of his brothers-in-law, killed his son, bled to death several men and women, and smothered an old monk in a well. Existing today is a medal of Constantine depicted as the Supreme Christian pontiff. The church later 'sainted him'.

Constantine ordered the construction of a new city on the site of ancient Byzantium, called it after his own name, and made it capital of the Roman Empire. Constantinople was solemnly consecrated in 330.[71] The transfer of empire from Rome to Byzantium was a great masterstroke in the history of civilization and in a few short years Constantine made it the centre of the world.

The Emperor Constantine remained a homicidal maniac until his death in 337. His decision to merge the presbyter's (now-called) Pagan beliefs with the British Druidic teachings brought many converts. Thus from a period of time in which 'mob rule and tyranny'[72] reigned supreme in the church, a series of presbyter's 'commentaries filled with impositions and fables . . . falsely ascribed to the most holy apostles by fraudulent individuals'[73] became the official church documents of the powerful Roman Empire directly under the control of the State.

From that time on, Jesus Christ was depicted with a halo, the solar symbol, around his head. This may have also derived from the headgear of the Arch Druids of Britain. According to the ancient lunar calendar, the lowest course of the Solar Orb, the December Solstice (Northern Hemisphere), occurred on 25 December and became Jesus Christ' birthday and thus Christ-mass (Christmas) Day. The birthday of the Sun (not Son) was documented as a public holiday and a day of celebration and gift giving on ancient calendars published during the reign of Constantine and existing today. The adoration of the Sun was one of the earliest forms of religious expression and the complex theologies of Christianity have deep-seated roots in this simple early belief. The display of sun-burst patterns gilt-embroidered on the back of the ceremonial garments of the Catholic priesthood, for example, signifies the Christian priest of today is also a time-honoured emissary and representative of the Sun.

Some old documents stated the Council of Nicaea ended in mid-August, 325. Others say the struggle was so fierce it extended into late September. Whenever it ended, the savagery and violence it encompassed failed to be recognized in the title it earnt from the church of the 18th Century, which was the 'Great and Holy Synod'. The earlier church, however, expressed a different opinion. The second council of Nicaea in 785 denounced the first council of Nicaea as 'a synod of fools and madmen'.[74] If one chooses to read the records of the second Nicaean council and note the references to 'affrighted bishops' and 'soldiery' needed to 'quell proceedings', the 'fools and madmen' declaration was surely an example of the pot calling the kettle black.

The new god made legal

It would be incorrect to think of an immediate and total acceptance of Emperor Constantine's new religion. Resistance offered by Roman custom compelled his successors to return to the earlier position.[75] Emperor Julian (361–363) bitterly opposed the Khrestian/Christian movement because they 'had slaughtered most of his family'.[76] In 361 Emperor Julian ordered all biscops and presbyters to centre their discourses only on the Gospels of Matthew and Luke.[77] These writings included the false additions discussed in earlier chapters, and they were the ones Emperor Julian wanted read to the rabble. Emperor Julian was earlier initiated into the Mysteries of Eleusis and Cybelle-Attis and had 'a much more sophisticated knowledge of Christianity'.[78] He knew of its newly created nature.

The war between the biscops continued unabated and every man used his personal followers in violent battles to win the right to be biscop of

Rome and live in the luxurious Lateran Palace. After the election battle between Damasus and Ursinus for the bishopric in 366, Ammonianus recorded 137 dead bodies were found in a church on the site of what is now St Maria Maggiore. The location of that church was the original central hall or basilica of the Palace of the British. Damasus (366–384) was the victor and became the first biscop to adopt the name of 'Papa', this word subsequently becoming 'Pope'. His associates called him 'the man who tickled ladies ears'.[79] The name 'pope' or 'papa' was given indifferently to many biscops of the ensuing times, especially to those who were most renown, eventually attaching itself to only the biscop of Rome in 1073. The title 'Papa' was originally the name of the savior god Attis who was a personification of the Solar Kristos. The writings of Euripedes stated that the name of Attis 'was at one time Papa, at another time Corpse, or God'.[80]

Although Constantine had earlier deified a new god for the rabble, their religion became official to the Roman Empire only in 380, when Emperor Theodosius (d. 395) legally imposed it on all his subjects.[81] By now Theodosius had realized that religious unity was an essential prerequisite for the Roman Empire and tried to achieve it. His official edict was never withdrawn. The various modes of worship that prevailed in the Roman world were all considered by the people as equally true, by the philosopher as equally false, and by the magistrate as equally useful. And thus toleration produced not only mutual indulgence, but also even religious concord. By the end of the Fourth Century, Constantinople, commanding as it did the entrance to the Pontus Euxine (Black Sea), was a city of commercial importance and the biscops dictated the nature of society, working hand in hand with an increasingly centralized government.

The Empire gradually absorbed and adapted to its own ends the multitude of cults derived from all its parts and over the ensuing centuries coupled them together as one, the Roman universal church. Today it is called the Roman Catholic church. Henceforth, much of the literature then written was aimed at propagating a fabricated faith to the world and ensuring Roman Emperors were given places as heads of church and state. The stories portrayed in the 'new' church Gospels were subsequently expanded throughout the entire Roman Empire thanks to the political ambitions of a shrewd Emperor Constantine. The 'message' of Jesus Christ was now on its way, some 300 years after the lifetime of Judas Khrestus and Rabbi Jesus. The 'numerous forgeries under the names of eminent men'[82] were given 'license' and expanded into the minds of people throughout the world by the missionaries of Constantine's new creation, Jesus Christ. It spread like a virus.

Under the appellation of Khrestians/Christians, two distinctions of people were subsequently confounded, the most opposite to each other in their manners and principles, the Essenes, Druids and Ebronites/Ebionites, who had embraced the esoteric faith of Rabbi Jesus Cunobeline, and the Zealots/Nazarenes who had followed the exoteric standards of Judas Khrestus. As the centuries rolled over both individual parties were grouped together as one body now simply called 'early Christians'. Later generations of church-men and academics filled the words 'Christian' and 'Christianity' with complicated theological meanings until being a 'Christian' meant something entirely different than it originally was, and developed a new belief in a complex system of dogmas not originally existing.

The most extraordinary church declaration

The supreme church authority in Rome remained with the Emperors until approximately 553 when they were still in control of Gospel material through Emperor Justinian. He convened and chaired a special council at the instigation of his wife, Theodore, the most notorious prostitute of the time.[83] She severally criticised the teachings of reincarnation in the British church, since those words essentially taught all humans were equal.

This council later became known as the Fifth Ecumenical Council of 553, that was in fact, the second of four councils held in Constantinople, the next being in 680 and the last in 869. The first council of Constantinople was held in 381 and saw Papa Damasus officially ban the Bible and introduce 'curses' into Christian tradition. The express purpose of Emperor Justinian's council was to censor from the Christian Gospels all references with a likeness to 'that foreign superstition', Druidism.[84]

Emperor Justinian obtained a majority vote for new anathemas he issued against the Druidic and Essenic doctrine of the pre-existence of the soul. This historical item proved both obscure and difficult to locate and said:

> Whosoever shall support the mythical doctrine of the pre-existence of the human soul, and the consequent monstrous opinion of its return to earth, let him be anathema.[85]

Three similar anathemas were published as part of the same council and all aimed at pre-existence including references to the Druidic belief of life after death. The council Decrees were later contested in some churches and a schism (division) arose that lasted seventy years.[86] This same council also confirmed the right of later generations to declare dead people heretics.

At that time, the 1000-year-old Sibylline prophecies were again consulted (the last known official consultation) and a reference, 'by sorceries revealing to nations, they struggled out of the pit of slime'[87] was assumed by the Council to have been a clairvoyant prediction applying to Rabbi Jesus for learning 'a magic secret' in Egypt and taking it to the Druids in Britain. Then, in an effort to overawe the Celtic establishment, the Fifth Ecumenical

Council of Constantinople made the most extraordinary decision that can be found recorded in Christian records. Under the direction of its Pontifex Maximus, the Roman Catholic church decreed that Emperor Constantine's deified entity, Jesus Christ, was 'truly the son of God' and Rabbi Jesus' faith was officially declared heretical.[88]

The church records reveal these extraordinary facts and the reader is encouraged to conduct his or her own research to confirm that what is written in this book has an historical foundation.

The End
(Thanks be to God)

The ancient Druidic symbol of the Trinity

Bibliography

Works of reference

For persons seeking further information, a list of books referenced in this study is included. Those in the first section are generally available in public libraries. The second section is material more difficult to access but provides pointers to further material available for serious researchers.

Special note

Due to the demise of some early publishing houses, efforts to trace copyright owners of older works were difficult. Where such works were referenced in this book, copyright is hereby acknowledged and grateful appreciation is extended to those authors and publishers (dead or alive) whose thoughts assisted in the development of this book.

Any omissions, errors or oversights should be brought to the attention of the author for correction and appropriate acknowledgement in future reprints.

About the Bible, Sidney Collett, New Jersey, U.S.A.

Acts of the Apostles—The Problems of Historic Value, World Bible Society, NYC, 1972

Address of Tatian to the Greeks—Masterpieces of Christian Literature, Magill, Harper & Row, 1963

Adepts, The (vols.I–IV), M. P. Hall, Los Angeles, 1949

Alleged Sojourn of Christ in India, The, Max F. Muller, 'Nineteenth Century', Oct. 1894

Allegory and Event, Richard P. Hanson, London 1959

Alterations to the Sinai Bible, Dr. Constantine Tischendorf, Religious Tract Society's 1868 Edition

Analysis of Ancient Mythology, Jacob Bryant, J. Walker, London, 1807

Ancient Christian Writers, trans. J. H. Crehan, Newman Press, c.1900

Ancient Egypt, Gerald Massey 1907

Ancient Library of Qumran, The, F. M. Cross (NY) 1961

Ancient Pagan Symbols, G.P. Putnam's Sons, New York, 1924

Ancient Sacred Symbols, from the Funeral Chamber of Thotmes I, and others. Oriental Antiquities, 1938

Ancient Titles and Subtitles, Prof. P.J. (Kahl) Ritchie (Shro., Shbp.), Newnham Campus 1997

Ancient World, The, H.E.L. Mellersh, 1976

Apollonius of Tyana, G.R.S. Mead 1927

Apollonius of Tyana, H.C. de Delafontaine (undated)

Apostolic Records, Rev. Dr Giles (c.1910)

Arcane Schools, The, John Yarker, William Tate, 1909

Archaeology of the Old Testament, Professor R.K. Harrison, English Universities Press Ltd., London, undated

Aryan Mythology, Rev. G.W. Cox, 1917, London

Asiatic Researches, Sir William Jones (Sanscrit scholar)

Athos: The Mountain of Silence, P. Sherrard, 1960

Atlas of the Roman World, T. Cornell and J. Matthews, 1992

Babylonian Captivity of the Church, The, Martin Luther, reprint 1922

Bacon Is Shakespeare, Sir Edwin Durning-Lawrence, London, Gay and Hancock, 1910

Behind the New Testament, Gilbert Sadler, 1914

Behold a Pale Horse, William Cooper, Light Technology Publishing,1991

Beyond the High Himalayas, W.O. Douglas, Garden City, NY, Doubleday, 1952

Bible and the Tarot, The, Corinne Heline, De Vorss and Co., U.S.A., 1969

Bible As History, The, Werner Keller, Bantam Revised Edition, 1982

Bible Busine$$, Jan McCluskey, Dossier Publ. Australia, 1995

Bible Criticism, (vols.I–II), Prof. Samuel Davidson D.D. LL.D., Chicago Public Library

Bible In Outline, Scripture Union, London, 1986

Bible Interpretation, James J. Megivern, Official Catholic Teachings, Consortium Books, 1978

Bible Myths, T.W. Doane, (1884), Charles P. Somerby, reprinted 1949, Truth Seeker Co.

Bible of today, The, John W. Chadwick, 1878

Bible Unmasked, The, Joseph Lewis, 1940

Birth of Christianity, The, Maurice Goguel, 1933.

Black Bible, The, Saint Anselm of Canterbury, Newman Publ. (date unknown)

Book of Enoch, The, Oxford Clarendon, U.K., 1912, trans. Dr Richard Lawrence

Book of the Penitence of Adam, Library of Paris (undated)

Book of the Popes, The, first draft appeared to have been assembled mid-twelfth Century, Reprinted 1895, London

Brewer's Myth and Legend, ed. J.C. Cooper, Cassell, 1992

British Church, the, Major J Samuels, V.D. R.G.A., undated

Bryant's Analysis of Ancient Mythology, British Library

Butler's Lives of the Saints, Rev. Alban Butler, Burns, Oates and Washbourne, London, 1926.

Cannibalism: The Religious Significance, Eaton University Press, 1943

Canon of the Bible, The, Prof. Samuel Davidson D.D. LL.D., Ms.88, Chicago Public Library, c. 1900

Case Against God, The, Gerald Priestland, Great Britain, 1984

Caution to the Times, Bishop Whately, 1892

Celtic Apostolic Church, The, Official Home Page, Michael J.A. Stewart, 2001

Censoring of Diderot's Encyclopedia and the Re-established Text, The, (NY.1947), D. H. Gordon and N. L. Torrey

Christ and Christna, John M. Robertson, c. 1926

Christ and Culture, H.R. Niebuhr, Discussions of Tertullian, Clement of Alexandria and Augustine, N.Y., 1951

Christ Myth, The, Prof. Arthur Drews, 1910–1912

Christ Question Settled, The, J. M. Pebbles, Boston, 1899

Christian Observer, 1815

Christ's Relevance to the Pygmy Tribes, Brother Lawrence, Viking Publishing, Santa Monica, 1984

Christian Symbolism in the Evangelical Churches, T.A. Stafford, New York-Nashville, 1942

Christian Tradition, The, Jaroslav, Pelikan, University of Chicago Press, 1971

Christianity and Mythology, John M. Robertson, Revised Edition, 1927

Chronicle of the Roman Emperors, Chris Scarre, 1995

Chroniclers of the First Century, trans. R.I. Dent, publ. Lutheran Liberty, 1867

Church History of Brittany, Cressy, c.1944

Church Sex Crimes, Tristan Rankine, Awareness Quest, Australia, 1995

Church Symbolism, F.R. Webber, Cleveland, 1927

Clement of Alexandria, E. Mollano, Oslo, 1936

Clergy and Laity, Odile M. Liebard, Official Catholic Teachings, McGrath, 1978

Commentary on Revelation, Prof. J. Harty, Dublin, 1911

Complete Prophecies of Nostradamus, The, H.C. Roberts trans., Nostradamus Co. 1982

Contra Celsum, H. Chadwick, Cambridge, 1953

Council of Nicaea, The History of, Dean Dudley, first printed 1886, reprinted 1965 by Health Research, California

Critical Handbook, The, E.C. Mitchel D.D., Religious Tract Society, 1880

Cross in Pagan History, The, Baughan, 1922, reprinted by Free Press Society, U.S.A., 1961

Crucifixion of Jesus by an Eyewitness, The, Austin, California, 1919, reprinted by Health Research

Cult of Sol Invictus, The, G.H. Halsberghe, London, 1972

Cult of the Heavenly Twins, Rendel Harris, 1906.

Dead Sea Scriptures, The, T.H. Gaster, N.Y., 1956

Dead Sea Scroll Deception, The, Michael Baigent and Richard Leigh, Corgi Books, 1992

Dead Sea Scrolls, The (Ed.II), J.M. Allegro, Harmondsworth, 1975

Dead Sea Scrolls, The, Documents of the Jewish Christian sect of Ebionites, J.L. Teicher, The Journal of Jewish Studies, vol.II, no.2, 1951

Debate About Christ, The, Don Cupitt, SCM Press, London, 1979

Deceptions and Myths in the Bible, L. Graham, 1966

Decline and Fall of the Roman Empire, E. Gibbons, 1994

Descent of Manuscripts, The, Albert C. Clarke, Professor of Latin, University of Oxford, 1918

Desert Fathers, The, Helen Waddell. N.Y. 1936

Devil's Pulpit, The, Rev. Robert Taylor 1831

Dictionary of Miracles, A, Rev. Cobham Brower, 1884

Did Jesus Ever Live?, L. Gordon Rylands (1927–1935)

Did Our Lord Visit Britain? Rev. C. C. Dobson, M.A., Destiny Publishers, 1944

Disappointment With God, Philip Yancey, Zondervan Publishing House, U.S.A., 1988

Discoveries in the Judean Desert, Oxford Clarendon Press 1992

Discovery of the Essene Gospel of Peace, E.B. Szekely, International Biogenic Society, 1989 Edition

Doctrine of Justification, The, James Buchanan,.DD. LL.D., reprinted 1977 from the 1867 ed. by T&T Clarke, Edinburgh, Baker Book House, Grand Rapids, Michigan

Documents Illustrative of the History of the Church, vol.I, ed. B.J. Kidd, London, 1928

Doomsday 1999AD, Charles Berlitz, New York Publishers, 1981

Early Christian Church, The (vols.I–II), P. Carrington, Cambridge, 1957

Early Church, The, H. Chadwick, Harmonsworth, 1968

Early History of the Israelite People, Thomas L. Thompson, E.J. Brill, 1992, Leiden, Netherlands

Ecce Homo, Joseph Jobe, Macmillan, 1962.

Ecclesiastical Policy of the New Testament, Prof. Samuel Davidson D.D. LL.D., held in the Chicago Public Library, c. 1900

Egyptian Book of the Dead, Gerald Massey, T. Fisher Unwin, 1907

Egyptian Religion, E. Wallis Budge, c. 1930

Empty Tomb, The, Rev. R.L. Mannering, Pastoreal Education, Conn., U.S.A., 1938

Enigma of Jesus, The, Dr P.L. Couchoud, 1939

Esoteric Christianity or the Lesser Mysteries, Mrs.Annie Besant, available in British Library, 1901

Essays on Supernatural Religion, Canon J.B. Lightfoot, c. 1906

Essene Origins of Christianity, The, E.B. Szekely, International Biogenic Society, 1989 Ed.

Essene Writings from Qumran, The, Dupont Sommer, 1953

Essenes and the Vatican, E.B. Szekely, International Biogenic Society, 1989 Ed.

Essenes, The, C. Ginsburg, U.K. (date unknown)

Eusebius of Caesarea, J.B. Lightfoot, World, 1962, N.Y., in *A Dictionary of Christian Biography, Literature, Sects and Doctrines*, London, 1880

Evidences of Christianity From the Early Fathers, The, W. J. Bolton, 1882, (Hulsean Prize Essay)

Extermination of the Cathars, The, Simonde de Sismondi, 1826.

Fabulous Fallacies, Tad Tuleja, 'Use The Stonesong Press' Inc., 1982

Fathers of the Church (vol. VI), trans. Thomas B. Falls, Publ. Christian Heritage, Penns., 1938

Fathers of the Greek Church, The, Hans von Campenhausen, trans. Stanley Godman, (date unknown)

Fifty Years in the Church of Rome, Chas. Chiniquy, first printed 1885, (banned by the church)

First 50 Years, The, Catholic Truth Society, London, 1934

First Apology and the Second Apology, The, Justin Martyr, Oxford University trans., 1933

First Gay Pope, The, Lyn Fletcher, Alyson Publications, 1992

First Seven Ecumenical Councils, The, L. D. Davis, 1987

Five Books of Moses, The, Stanley Hebrew, 1890

Five Gospels, The, The Jesus Seminar, MacMillan Publishing Company, N.Y., 1993

For Christ's Sake, Hugh J. Schonfield, first published in 1975 by MacDonald and Janes

Forgotten Monarchy of Scotland, The, Michael J. A. Stewart, 1999

Founder of Christianity, The, Charles Harold Doad, MacMillan Company, N.Y., 1970

Four Gospels as Historical Records, The, (Anon) possibly by Rev. Sir. G.W. Cox, 1895

Fourth Century Rumours About Christ (vols. I–II), P.M. Cozzia-Leone, Archives de Louvre, Paris, 1857

Fragments of a Faith Forgotten, G.R.S. Mead. Theosophical Publishing Society, 1906

Freemasonry and the Ancient Gods (Second Edition), J.S.M. Ward, London, 1926

Frenzy to Create a God, The, a study of ancient *New Testament* texts, Rev. F.G. Miller, 1895, (revised by Dr A. Frenlon, 1907), U.K.

Genesis: An Essene Interpretation, Edmond Szekely and Purcell Weaver, 1948

Genisis, The First Book of Revelation, David Wood, The Baton Press, 1985

Genuineness and Authenticity of the Gospels, B.A. Hinsdale, Anglo-American Bible Revision, 1872, President of Hiram College

Gibbon's Rome

Glimpses of Masonic History, C.W. Leadbeater, The Theosopical Publishing House, Adyar, India, 1926

Gnostics and Their Remains, The, Bell and Daldy, London, 1887

Gnostic Scriptures, The, Bentley Layton, 1987

God is No More, Werner and Lotte Pelz, Great Britain, 1963

Gods of Eden, The, Dahlin Family Press, California, 1985 reprint

Gods of the Hebrew Bible, J.B. Hannay, 1937

Golden Bough, The, Sir James Frazer, volume by Watts and Co., 1922

Good News of the Kingdoms, The, Norm Segal and Friends, Nambour, Australia, 1995

Gospel of Mary, The, J. Robinson, Nag Hammadi (Scrolls) Library in English, 1960

Gospel of Philip, The, J. Robinson, Nag Hammadi (Scrolls) Library in English, 1960

Gospel of Shame, A, Elinor Burkett and Frank Bruni, Viking 1993

Gospel of the Mystic Christ, The, Duncan Greenless, M.A., 1951

Gospel of the Witches of Italy, C. G. Leland, c.1890

Great News for the World, Alan Haywood, Great Britain 1976

Great People of the Bible, Readers Digest Association, U.S.A. 1972

Guide to the Ancient World, A, Michael Grant, The H.W. Wilson Company, 1986

Guide to the Debate About God, David Jenkins (Bishop of Durham), Great Britain 1966

Handbook of Christian Belief, Lion Publishing, England, 1982

Handbook of Designs and Devices, Dover Publications, New York, 1946

Handbook to the Bible, David and Pat Alexander, Lion Publishing, U.K., 1984

Handy Book of Literary Curiosities, A, William S. Walsh, British Library, date unknown, (maybe 1815)

Harmony of the New Testament, Dr Lightfoot, undated

He Walked Among Us, Josh McDowell and Bill Wilson, Here's Life Publishers Inc., 1988

Henry the Fourth, Edwin Abbott, 1882

Herods of Judea, The, (Oxford), A.H.M. Jones, 1938

Hey God, What About . . .?, James T. Cumming and Hans Moll, Concordia Publishing, Missouri, U.S.A. 1977

Hidden Life in Freemasonry, The, C.W. Leadbeater (33°), The Theosophical Publishing House, Adyar, India, 1926

Hidden Symbols of the Rosicrucians, The, Harold Bayley, first published in 1903, reprint in 1988 by Sure Fire Press, Edmonds, W.A.

Historical Jesus, The, Gaalyah Cornfield, MacMillan Publishing Co. Inc., 1982

History in the Encyclopedia. (NY, 1947), D. H. Gordon, N. L. Torrey

History of Christian Names, Miss Charlotte Yonge, date unknown

History of Magic, Joseph Ennemoser, Henry G Bohn, London 1854

History of Protestantism, The, Rev, J.A. Wylie. (Author of *The Papacy*), Cassell and Company Ltd, London, Paris and New York., vols.I–III, undated

History of Purple as a Status Symbol in Antiquity, M. Reinhold, Brussels, 1970

History of Roman Religion, A, F. Altheim, Dutton 1938

History of the Bible, Bronson C. Keeler, C.P. Farrell, 1881, reprint 1965 by Health Research (highly recommended)

History of the Bible in English, F.F. Bruce, New York, 1961

History of the Christian Religion (to the year 200AD), Judge C.B. Waite, 6th Ed., 1908, (an excellent work)

History of the Church from Christ to Constantine, Eusebius trans. G.A. Williamson, Harmondsworth, 1981

History of the Council of Trent, A, Thomas Nelson and Sons, 1949, vols.I–II, Hubert Jedin, trans. D.E.Graf

History of the Popes, B. Maclean, 1907, Ferrier, London

History of the Turin Shroud, Mgr. Umberto Benigni, Rome, c. 1911

History of Torture, The, Daniel P. Mannix Dell, N.Y., 1964

Holy Blood, and the Holy Grail, The, Michael Baigent, Richard Leigh and Henry Lincoln, Corgi Books 1990

Homosexuality in the Church, Confidential Diocesan Report to the Bishops, U.K., 1994

Horse of God, The, by M.G.E.H. Neyman: Belgique, books on CD-Rom

How the Great Religions Began, J. Gaer, New York, 1954.

How to Read the Bible, Gordon D. Fee and Douglas Stuart, The Zondervan Corp., 1982

How to Read the New Testament, Les Éditions du Cerf, 1980

How We Got Our Old Testament, Terry Hall, Moody Monthly, 1969

I Believe, David Watson, Hodder and Stroughton, London, 1982

Iconographie de l'Evangile, some quotes in Millet, undated

In God's Name, An Investigation Into the Murder of Pope John Paul I, David Yallop, Corgi Books, London, 1984

In My Father's House, Carrie Ten Boom, Fleming H. Revell, Company, New Jersey, 1976

India and the Apostle Thomas, Medlycott, London, 1905

Indulgences: Their Origin, Nature and Development, Quaracchi, 1897

Initiations and Initiates in Tibet, A. David-Neel, London, 1931

Inscriptions of Sinai, The, ed. Jaroslav Cerry, Egyptian Exploration Society, London, 1955

Inside the Vatican, G. Bull, London, 1982

Institutes of Christian History, Johann Mosheim, 1755

Introduction to the New Testament (revised), A.H. McNeile, Oxford, at the Clarendon Press 1953

Introduction to the Philosophy of Religion, Peter Anthony Bertocci (in *Masterpieces of Christian Literature,* Harper and Row, 1963)

Introduction to the Talmud and Midrash, Herman L. Strack, Harper Torchbooks, Harper and Row, N.Y. 1931, First Ed.

Introduction, New Testament Theology, SCM Press Pty Ltd, London, 1977

Iolo Manuscripts, The, (a collection of ancient traditions)

Isis Unveiled, H.P. Blavatsky, Theosophical University Press, Calif., 1976

It Says So In The Bible, Sheldon Edwards Centenary Press, Conn., 1972

James the Brother of Jesus, Faber and Faber Limited. Robert Eisenman, 1997

James the Just in the Habakkuk Pesher, R.H. Eisenman, Leiden, Netherlands, 1986

Jesus and Christian Origins, F.F. Bruce, Hodden Christian, London, 1984

Jesus and Judaism, E.P. Sanders, London, 1985

Jesus and the Word, R. Bultman, Second Edition, trans. Louise Pettibone Smith and Ermine Huntress, N.Y. 1934

Jesus Christ in the Talmud, Cambridge, 1893

Jesus Christ: The Amazing Truth, James F. Cullinan, Finbarr, U.K., 1986

Jesus—God, Man or Myth, Herbert Cutner, The Truth Seeker Company, N.Y., 1950

Jesus in the Koran, Parrinder, 1947

Jesus the Jew, G.Vermes, London 1977, (also by the same author, *The Dead Sea Scrolls in English*, Penguin Books)

Jesus the Magician, Morton Smith, San Francisco, 1978.

Jesus the Mystery, D.C. Jefferies, Pan Pacific Publications, Australia, 1991

Jesus the Myth, Prof. M.N. Lowe, Free Thinking Press, Chicago, USA, 1984

Jesus: The Evidence, I. Wilson, London, 1984

Joseph of Arimathea, Skeats, 1933

Keeper of the Keys, The Pope in History, Sir Nicolas Cheetham, MacDonald and Co. (Publishers) Ltd., London, 1982

Kenny's Masonic Cyclopedia and Handbook of Masonic Archaeology, History and Biography, George Kenny, London, 1878

King Jesus (Ed.IV), R. Graves, London, 1960

Kingdom of Christ, The, John Cotton, in *Masterpieces of Christian Literature*, Magill, 1963

Krishna and Orpheus, E. Schure, London, 1909.

Lead Us Not Into Temptation: Catholic Priests and the Sexual Abuse of Children, Jason Berry, Doubleday, NY, 1992

Legends of the Madonna, Mrs. Jameson, available at the British Library

Lesbian Deaconesses, L.M. Farrell, Timeson Publishing, London, 1982

Let There by Light, William Tyndale and the Making of the English Bible, British Museum Publication 1994

Life of Caligula, Suetonius, Histories 1867

Life of Claudius, Suetonius, Histories, 1867

Life of Christ, Rev. Dr Geikie, c. 1940

Life of Constantine, A, (7th Ed.), Dean Dudley, Attorney at Law, 1925, Ill., USA

Life of Jesus Critically Examined, D.F. Straus, first edition 1835

Life of Pythagoras, Iamblichus, trans. T. Taylor, London, 1818

Lives of Saints, The, Rev. Alban Butler. London, Burns Oates & Washbourne Ltd., London, 1926

London Morning Post, March 27, 1931

Look at the Bible, A: Fact or Fiction, L.E. Rees, Durban, N.Y., 1986

Lives of the Saints, Rev. S. Barring-Gould

Lost Book of the Graal, The, An examination of the Graal Legend, M.Versaille, undated

Lost Books of the Bible, The, Bell Publishing Company, N.Y., reprinted from 1926

edition originally published by World Publishing Co. Cleveland, U.S.A.

Lost Language of Symbolism, Harold Bayley, J. P. Lippincott Co., Philadelphia, 1913

Lost Scrolls of the Essene Brotherhood, The, E.B. Szekely, International Biogenic Society, 1989 Edition

Lost Ship of Noah, The, Charles Berlitz, Ballantine Books, U.S.A., 1987

Lost Wisdom of the Ancient Masters, Professor Hilton Hotema, reprint by Health Research

Lost Years of Jesus Revealed, The, Rev. Dr Charles F. Potter, Ballentine Books 1962

Lost Years of Jesus, The, Elizabeth C. Prophet, Summit Publishers, U.S.A.

Maccabees, Zadokites, Christians and Qumran, R.H. Eisenman

Magical Mystical Sites, Elizabeth Pepper and John Wilcock. Sphere Books Ltd, London, 1976

Magi—The Quest for a Secret Tradition, Adrian G. Gilbert, Bloomsbury, London, 1996.

Mahabharata, The Hindu Epic, trans. Minisus, London, 1910

Man in the Shroud, The, Peter M. Rinaldi, SPB, Great Britain, 1972

Manner and Customs of Bible Times, Ralph Gowler, Moody Press, Chicago, 1987

Martyrdom of Francis Bacon, Alfred Dodd, c.1940

Mary in the Babylonian Talmud (Baby. Tal.), G.R.S. Mead, (BA, MRAS) London & Benares, 1903

Masonry and Theology, E.D. Bufmyer, Health Research Reprint, original date unknown

Masterpieces of Christian Literature, Magill Harper Row, N.Y., 1963

Mehgheehlla Scroll, The, D.B. de Waltoff, 1882

Men Who Hid the Dead Sea Scrolls, The, A. Douglas Tushingham, National Geographic Magazine, December 1958

Mentality of the Clergy, The, Psychologist Quarterly, by Richard L. Hugo, Calif., 1969, U.C.L.A.

Messianic Legacy, The, Michael Baigent, Richard Leigh and Henry Lincoln, Henry Holt and Company, N.Y., 1987

Misread Record, The, Isaac Newton Vail, reprint under *The Deluge and its Cause*, undated

Monks of Athos, The, 1936, R.M. Dawkings

Monks of War, The, D. Seward, St Alban's, 1974

Monumentum Ancrya, The, E.G. Hardy, 1923

More Light on the Dead Sea Scrolls, Burrows, Millar, Viking, N.Y., 1958

More Than an Ark on Ararat, James B. Irwin, Nashville, 1978

Mount Sinai Manuscript of the Bible, The, published by the Trustees of the British Museum, 1934

Much Abused Letter, A, George Tyrell in *Masterpieces of Christian Literature*, Harper Row, N.Y., 1963

Mystery Clouds, The, Donald Coverdell, The Children's Bread, Orlando, U.S.A.

Mystery of Francis Bacon, The, William T. Smedley, John Howell, San Francisco, 1910

Mystery of the Oracles, The, Philipp Vandenberg, Macmillan Publ.,1979

Mystical Life of Jesus, The, H. Spencer Lewis, AMORC, California, 1937

Myth of Christ, The, Dr Jonathon A. Jenkins Jrn, Conn., U.S.A., 1952

Myth of Eternal Return, The, Mircea Eliade, trans. William Trask, N.Y. Pantheon, 1954

Mythology of all Races, Archeological Institute of America, 1925–1932, Marshal Johns Co.

Natural History, Pliny the Elder, 1934 reprint, Hepworth and Sons, UK

New Encyclopedia of Freemasonry, A, (vols.I–II), A.E. Waite, London 1921

New Testament Apocrypha (vols.I–II), E. Hennecke, ed. W. Schneemelcher, trans. R. McL. Wilson, London 1963–65

New Testament Composition, Dr B.S. Shaw, Sphere and Associates, London, 1968 (first printing 1927)

New Testament Quotations from the Old Testament, Richard France, Loin Publishing, U.K.

New Testament Theology, Leon Morris, Zondervan Publishing House, Michigan 1986

New Testament World, John and Kathleen Court, Cambridge University Press, Cambridge, 1990

Nexus New Times, Nexus Magazine Pty Ltd, Australia, ed. Duncan M. Roads

Nostradamus and the Millenium, John Hogue, Bloomsbury Publishing, U.K.

Not the Whole Truth, J.C. Heenan, Hodder, London, 1971

Old Christian Literature, Van Manen of Leyden, contributor to *Encyclopedia Biblica,* c.1860

On the Canon of the New Testament, Brooke Foss Westcott, D.D., Ms.489, Chicago Public Library

On the History of the Dominican Order (to 1500), W.A. Hinnesbusch, OP, 1966

On the Track of the Mad Saints, Psychologist Quarterly, by Richard L. Hugo, Calif. 1969 (U.C.L.A.)

Origen, Explicit References in the Works of Origen to Variant Readings in the New Testament, Freiburg, 1963, B.M. Metzger, pp.78–95

Origins of Christianity, The, Thomas Wittaker, 1933

Our Bible and the Ancient Manuscripts, Sir F.G. Kenyon, c.1934

Pagan Christs, J.M. Robertson, U.S.A., 1983

Passover Plot, The, Hugh Schonfield, MacDonald, Futura, 1977

Pastoreal Theology, Prof. J.Beck, 1910.

Peake's Commentary on the Bible, Thomas Nelson and Sons Ltd, London, N.Y., 1962

Peodophile Priests, Rape Crisis Centre Report, Victoria, Australia, 1994

Phoenician Origin of Britons, Scots and Anglo-Saxons, The, L. A. Waddell, 1924, also reprint 1983 by The Christian Bookclub, Hawthorne, Calif., 90250

Primitive Christianity, Professor Rudolf Bultman, The Fontana Library, 1956

Primitive Culture, Sir E.B. Tylor, 1871

Printer's Marks, W. Roberts, G.W. Bell and Sons, London, 1892

Probability of God, The, Hugh Montefiore, SCM Press, London, 1985

Prophet of Nazareth, The, Evan Powell Merideth, 1864

Prophet, The, Dr Alberto Rivera, Chick Publications, P. Chino, California, 1969

Psalms, The, American Bible Society,1970

Reincarnation in the New Testament, James M. Pryse, facsimile reproduction from Health Research, first printed 1900

Religion and the Decline of Magic, K. Thomas, Harmondsworth, 1980

Religion in Ancient History, S.G.F. Brandon, Great Britain, 1973

Reports of the Babylonian Expedition, Cuneiform Texts, University of Philadelphia, Dept. of Archaeology, 1914

Responses to 101 Questions on the Dead Sea Scrolls, Joseph A. Fitzmyer, Paulist Press, N.Y., 1992

Revelations in 'Revelation', George Weiman, Kregal Publishers, U.S.A., 1952

Riddle of the Scrolls, The, H.E. Del Medico, Bourke Publ. Co. Ltd., London, 1958

Riddle of the Sphinx, J. Munsell Chase, 1915

Rise of English Culture, The, Edwin Johnson, date unknown

Rock of Truth, The, Arthur Findlay, Psychic Press, London, 1933

Roman Emperors, The, Michael Grant, 1985, George Weidenfeld & Nicolson Limited

Roman Invasion of Britain, The, Graham Webster, 1980

Roman Myths, Jane F. Gardner, 1993, The Trustees of the British Museum

Rome Has Spoken. A Guide to Forgotten Papal Statements, Maureen Fiedler and Linda Rabben, Crossroad Publishing Co., 1998

Royal Dynasty of Ancient Britain, Historia Britannia, pre-1860

Rule of St Benedict, Saint Benedict of Nursia, reprint 1995

Sacred Symbols in Art, G.P. Putnam's Sons, 1912

San Francesco d' Assisi, Rome, 1928, a bibliography

Sayings of the Christian Priests, Rev.J. Desmond, Russell Square, London, 1936, WD

Scribes and Correctors of the Codex Sinaiticus (1938), H.J.M. Milne, T.C. Skeat, British Museum, London

Scrolls From the Dead Sea, The, Edmund Wilson, Fontana Books, 1955

Search in Secret Egypt, A, Paul Brunton, Rider and Company, (undated)

Second Messiah, The, Christopher Knight and Robert Lomas, Arrow, 1997

Second Treatise of the Great Seth, J. Robertson, Nag Hammadi Library in English

Secret Doctrines of Jesus, The, H. Spencer Lewis, AMORC, California, 1937

Secret Gospel of Mark, The, Morton Smith, Harper and Row, 1973

Secret Life of Jesus, The, Robert Macklin, Pan Books (Australia) Pty Ltd, 1990

Secret Path, The, Paul Brunton, 1935

Secret Sects of Syria and the Lebanon, Bernard H. Springett, 1922

Secret Teachings of All Ages, Manly P. Hall, The Philosophical Research Society Inc., L.A., Calif., 1901

Secrets in the Vatican Vaults, Du Ryer, Netherlands, 1989

Secrets of Mount Sinai, James Bentley, Orbis Publishing, 1985

Secrets of the Black Madonna, Dr B.J. Dean, Publ. Centre for Pastoreal Studies, Israel, 1969

Secrets of the Dead Sea Scrolls, Hugh Schonfield, London, 1956

Secrets of the Torah, Henry Burr, Complete Book of Biblical Secrets, House Publishing, Boston 1972

Self-Portraits, Ludwig Goldscheider. 1943

Sermon on the Mount, An Essene Interpretation, Edmond Szekely, 1948

Servetus and Calvin, R. Willis M.D., London, 1877

Short History of the Bible, A, Bronson C. Keeler, Farrell, 1881 (highly recommended)

Sistine Chapel, The, Harry N. Abrams Inc, 1947

Society in Imperial Rome, Michael Massey, Cambridge University Press, 1982,

Some Difficulties of Belief, Rev. T. Teignmouth Shore, MA, Mayfair, London, undated

Some Dogmas of Religion, John Mc Taggart and Ellis McTaggart, Kraus Reprint, N.Y., 1969

Some New Testament Problems, Rev. Arthur Wright M.A., Longman's Press, 1964

Sorcery and Magic, T. Wright, London, 1851

Spear of Destiny, The, Trevor Ravenscroft, Sphere Books Limited 1990

Stowe's Bible Astrology, Lyman E. Stowe, 1907

Strange Facts About the Bible, Garrison Webb, New York 1976

Study of Early Christianity, A, Joseph B. Tyson, MacMillan 1973

Supernatural Religion, W.R. Cassels, Watts and Co. 1905

Tacitus and Bracciolini, W.J. Ross 1818

Talmud, The, British Library

Telling Lies for God, Ian Plimer, Random House 1994

Temple Scroll, The, Y. Yadin, London 1985

Ten Lost Books of Moses, The, Daggett Publishing Co., Chicago, Ill., USA, 1934.

Theology of the New Testament, Rudolf Bultman, trans. Kendrick Grobel, Charles Scribner's Sons

Tiberius the Tyrant, Tarver, London, 1902

Totem and Taboo, Sigmund Freud

Translation Problems, The Bible, Prof. Lennox, English Language and Literature, Catholic University of America, 1911

True Language of Rennes-le-Chateau, The, by M.G.E.H. Neyman: Belgique, books on CD-Rom

Twelve Caesars, The, Suetonius, trans. R. Graves, 1958

Twenty Thousand Religions, Institute of World Religions (ISWR), N.Y.C., 1986

Two Babylons, The, Rev. Alexander Hislop, late 19th Century

Uncertain History of Christian Beginnings, The, Mr Jack Patterson, B.A., B. Arch., Auckland, New Zealand, 1996

Understanding the Dead Sea Scrolls, Hershel Shanks, Random House, N.Y. 1992

Unknown Books of the Essenes, The, E.B. Szekely, International Biogenic Society 1989

Unknown Life of Christ, The, Nicolas Notovitch, Published by Health Research Calif. 1959

Vatican Bible Reviewed, Library of the Society of Ancient Literature, Leningrad 1967

Verdict of the Shroud, K.E. Stevenson and G.R. Habermas, Robert Hale Ltd., G.B. 1982

Was Jesus Married?, William E. Phipps, Harper and Row, N.Y. 1970

What Colour Was Jesus?, Prof. L.A. Fuller-Langley, Religious Education Publishing House, Greenwich, U.S.A. 1972

What the Bible Really Says, Manfred Barthel, Econ Verlag GMBH, 1980

When Were our Gospels Written?, Dr Constantine Tischendorf, Religious Tract Society's Edition, London 1869

Whence the Gospel According to John, W.H. Brownlee in James H. Charlesworth (Ed.), John and Qumran, London 1972

Where Did Jesus Die? J. D. Shams, Qadian (Punjab), India, 1959.

Which Religion if the True One?, Fazlur Golliner, Islam Development Press, Jerusalem 1979

Who Wrote the Bible?, Walter Clynsdale, Rinchart and Co., 1938

Winding Sheet of Christ, The, W. Frean, Majellan Press, Victoria, Australia 1964

With Mystics and Magicians in Tibet, A. David-Neel, London, 1931

Women Around Jesus, The, Elizabeth Moltmann, Wendel, Germany, 1982

World Religions, From Ancient History to the Present, University Paper, Connecticut, U.S.A., 1983

Worship of Priapus, R. Payne Knight, reprint

Wrestling with Christ, Luigi Santucci, Italy 1969

Writings of Thomas Paine, The, Putnam's Sons. NY. 1896

Young's Analytical Concordance to the Bible, Robert Young LL.D., Thomas Nelson Inc. Publishers 1982 (also Young's Literal Translation of the Holy Bible, 3rd Edition)

Zeus, The Early Christian God of Worship, E.S.M. Harris (Jnr.), Philadelphia, 1915

List of historical or hard-to-find documents

The following list of rare archival manuscripts and difficult-to-find ancient books were referenced and some material extracted and recorded for the benefit and instruction of readers. Many of these works are priceless historical documents, and difficult to date. Much of the material was compiled by the church using complicated technical theological jargon that presumed an acquaintance with already published reference books and other religious literature.

About the Acts of Thomas, A paper, Professor John S. J. Lingard, 1952

About the 'Books of Hystaspes' (Quoted by Justin Martyr), Chicago Public Library

About Sozomen, author unknown, Brit. Lib, date unknown

Acta Archelai—The Dialogue Between Manes and Archelaus (issued by one Hegemonius), trans. 1806

Acta Concilii Niceni, Colon, 1618.

Acts of Justin (Martyr)

Acta of Pilate (or the so-called *Gospel of Nicodemus*)

Adverse Autolius, Rare and undated, pre-Sixth Century

Adverse Scapala, Ms.1790

Against Heresies (Adv. Haer.), Irenaeus, (originally called by its author *The Detection and Overthrow of False Gnosis,* retitled at the Council of Trent)

Against Marcion (Adv. Marc.), Tertullian, Ms.1727

Against Peleg

Against the Ebronites, St Epiphanius (Contra Ebronites)

Against the Gentiles, Tertullian (Adv. Gentiles)

Against the Jews, Tertullian

Agricola, *Histories*, 1867

Alford's *Regia Fides*

Ammian, O'Neil's trans. 1898

Anacalypis, Godfrey Higgins

Analects of Confucious, The

Ancient Egyptian Dictionary, R. Johnson and E. Rumbel (in Cairo Library)

Ancient Faiths in Ancient Names, (vols.I–II), Thomas Inman M.D., 1868, (very rare)

Ancient Pagan and Modern Christian Symbolism, T. Inman, New York

Annales ecclesiastici (vols I–XII), Cardinal Caesar Baronius, Vatican Librarian and church historian. 1598–1607.

Annals of St Paul, H.H.Milman. 1791–1868, church historian

Annals of Tacitus, Furneaux, Oxford, 1907

Ante Nicene Library, The, A collection of all the works of the early churchmen prior to the Council of Nicaea, ed. Rev. Professor Roberts, D.D, and Principal James Donaldson, L.L.D, St Andrews. vols.I–XXIV (c.1900), includes additional volume containing recently discovered manuscripts

Apocryphal Codex of the New Testament (Codex Ap. NT.)

Apocryphal Gospels, The (6th Ed.), Cowper, London, 1897

Apocryphal New Testament, The, Montague R. James, Oxford, 1924

Apollonius of Tyana, Benares, 1901

Apology of Aristides, Aristides

Apology of Athenagoras, Athenagoras

Apology of Plato

Apology, Tertullian—originally called *The Apology of Tertullian*

Apostolic Constitutions (Const. Apost.)

Apostolic Constitutions, The, Osaf Translations

Apostolic Fathers, The, trans. Kirsopp Lake, Harvard University Press

Apostolical Canons—85 Ecclesiastical Laws, Dionysius the Less

Arethas Codex, The Chief Works of Clement of Alexandria: *Protrepticus* (or *An Exhortation of the Greeks*) and *Paedagogus* (or *On Christian Life and Manners*)

Arguments of the Emperor Julian, The, (Later retitled: Against the Christians). Thomas Taylor (translator) London. 1818

Assyrian Deeds and Documents, Rev. C.H.W. Johns, M.A. Cambridge, 1901

Astrology Theologised, London, 1886

Athanasius, Festal Epistle, Library of the Fathers, Oxford, 1854

August de Constans Evang

Augustus, Opera, c.400AD

Authentic and Acknowledged Standards of the Church of Rome, The, J. Hannah D.D.,1844

Babylonian Sanhedrin (Baby. Sanhedrin)

Babylonian Shabbath (Baby. Shabbath)

Baconiana, T. Tenison, 1679

Bacon and the Rosicrucians, W. F. C. Wigston, 1902

Bazaar of Heraclides, Nestorius, trans. by G.R. Driver and L. Hodgson, Oxford

Bea-Methodius (Bermechobus), the supposed writings of St Methodius of Olympus
    (d.311).

Bell's Pantheon, c. 1900

Berossus, History of Babylonia, 1892

Beveridge's Pandecta Canonum—includes the 60 Canons of the Synod of Laodicea
    which are still extant in their original Greek

Bible Criticism (vols. I–II), Professor Samuel Davidson D.D. LC.D

Bible, Inadequate Translation, N. Taylor-Edwards, 1868

Biblitheca sanctorum, Rome 1965

Bilateral Cipher of Sir Francis Bacon, London, 1900

Bingham's Antiquities of the Christian Church, Straker's ed. 1840, London

Book of Constitutions of the Freemasons, The, Rev. James Anderson. 'Being the first
    announcement to the world of the Brotherhood', 1723

Book of Enoch (or *1 Enoch*), Dr Richard Lawrence L.L. D. Also the Ethiopic text of
    1 Enoch, R.H. Charles D.L. D.D. (Oxford at the Clarendon Press 1912)

Book of the Cock, The, The Story of Jesus and a Slain Cock

Book of the Masters, W.M. Adams 1898

Book of Taliesin, Gildas, 516–570

British Chronicles, a collection published by Fowler and Rowe, c. 1854

British Church, The, Maj. J. Samuels, V.D., R. G. A. (pre-1931)

Buddhist Catechism, The, Henry S. Olcott. 1915

Calmet's Fragments, Abraham, 1896

Catechetical Lectures, The, Cyril, Bishop of Jerusalem

Catechism of the Council of Trent, vols. I–VIII 1829, Dublin

Catiline, Clodius and Tiberius, Beesly, 1878

Cave's Primitive Christianity, 1790

Censorship of Hebrew Books, W. Popper, New York 1899

Centuriators of Magdeburg, A Lutheran polemical history of the church, c.1557

Christ in Art, Mrs Jameson, available at the British Library

Christ-Child Symbol of Wisdom, Siculus, 1513

Christian Astrology, William Lilly, 1648

Christian Topography, Cosmas Indicopleustes (Christian monk, c.535)

Chronicles of:

Geoffrey of Monmouth 1100–1155
John Hardynge
Matthew of Paris
Robert of Gloucester
William of Malmesbury
The Anglo-Saxon Chronicle

Chronologie, author unknown but possibly Levine, 1925

Church History, Neander, 1825

Church History, Socrates Scholasticus (380–450) Jenning's trans. 1911

Ciceronians es, non Christianus

Cipher Signatures, Francis Bacon's, Frank Woodward, 1923

City of God, Augustine, from 1609 translation

Claudia and Pudens, Archdeacon Williams, c.1940

Clement of Alexandria—writings contained in the Ante-Nicene Fathers, N.Y., 1926

Codex Amiatinus—Abbot Ceolfrith's edition of 690

Codex of Hillel—600 Manuscripts, first published in England in 1780

Commentaries on the Law of Moses, Jonathon D. Michaelis, 4 Vols. 1814.

Commentary on Ephesians, St Jerome

Comte De St Germain, The, I. Cooper Oakley,. 1912

Confessions of Augustine, Augustine

Constantine's Letter, in regard to having fifty copies of the scriptures written and bound

Constitutions of Constantine

Contra Celsum (Against Celsus)

Cottonian Manuscript, Gildas, undated

Court of the Gentiles, The, Oxford 1671

Creed of Nicene, The Formulary, (first printing 1807)

Critical Essays, Rev. T.E. Espin, London 1864

Critical History of Primitive History, Gfroger, 1835

Crosses in Tradition, W.W. Seymour, N.Y. 1898

De Anima, Ms.1730, Tertullian, c.205

De Chorographia, Pomponius Mela, d.c.37 AD

De Civitate Dei, Augustine, Bishop of Hippo

De Corona, Ochler, About Tertullian

De Divinatione daemonum, undated

De Fide Orthodoxa (De. Fid. Orthod, John of Damasus) c.800AD

De Pallio, Ms.1730

De Principle, Ms.1729

De Pudicion (*De Pudic.*), Tertullian

De Resurrection, Ms.1730

De Viris Illustribus, D. Vallarsi, Vols. I–XI, Verona, 1734–42

Decree of the Fifth Council of Constantinople, 553, Church Records

Delphian Oracle, The Visit of Apollonius of Tyana, author unknown—date maybe 1750

Demonology, The evangel of, Eusebius

Demonstratio Evangelic, Eusebius

Despectae, Tertullian

Development of the Catholic Church, Ernest Renan, French Academy, 1880

Dialogue with Trypho the Jew—in 'the works now extant of St Justin the Martyr'—trans. E.B. Pusey, Oxford 1861

Dialogues, Theodoret

Didache, or the Teaching of the Twelve Apostles, author unknown

Digest, undated

Dio Cassius, Histories, 1867

Diondi, very rare, undated

Disputatio Cum Herbano Judea, attributed to Gregontius, Bishop of Taphar in Arabia, second half of Fifth Century AD

Disputoilis super Dignitatem Anglis it Gallioe in Councilio Constantiano, c.1517, Theodore Martin

Divine Institutes, The, Lucius Caecilius Firmianus Lactantius

Divine Names, The, Dionysius, trans. C.E. Rolt, Publ. Christian Knowledge

Doctrine of Christ, The (De Doct. Christ), Ms.1742

Dorotheus, Synod. De Apostol., Synopis ad Sim. Zelot

Dove of Venus, A Dissertation, I.S. Scheible, 1862

Early Christian Classics, 2 vols. 1916. J.A. Robinson

Early Theological Writings, G.W.F. Hegal

Ecclesiastical History (Eccl. Hist.), Eusebius of Caesarea

Ecclesiastical History, Sozomen

Ecclesiastical Policy of the New Testament, The, Professor Samuel Davidson D.D. L.C.D.

Eclectric Review, Melancthon, 1497–1560

Edict of Callistus I, Bishop of Rome 217–222

Edict of Callistus I, Commentaries, J. Cosin, Bishop of Durham, 1594–1672.

Edicts of Justinian, Dictionnaire de Théologie, 1920

Eleusinian and Bacchic Mysteries, The, Thomas Taylor. New York, 1875

Elliott's Delineation of Romanism, Weslyan Conference Office, 1844

Elxai Fragments, author unknown, 1876

Enchiridion of Faith, Hope and Love, Augustine

English Hexapla, six English translations of the *New Testament*, London 1841

Epic of Creation, The

Epistola, Melancthon, 1497–1560

Epistle Vir., (Ep. Vir.), Jerome (Hedibium)

Epistle of Aurelius, (Epist. Ad Aurelium)

Epistle of Barnabas, author unknown

Epistle of Jerome (Jerome Epist.), Hedibium

Epistle to Diognetus, author unknown

Epitome of the Divine Institutes III (Ep. Div. Inst.)

Extant Fragments of the Works of Dionysius, Dionysius the Great

Extermination of the Cathars, The, J.C.L. Simonde de Sismondi, 1826 original, published by Wightman and Cramp, S. Wilkin, Waugh and Innes' and M. Ogle.

Extortations (Exhort), Clement of Alexandria

Extracts from a letter from Francis Bacon to King James, c.1610

Facts and Speculation on the Origin and History of the Christian Church, Jacob Bryant, London 1793

Fabiola, Cardinal Wiseman, c.1935

Fides Regia Britannica, Cardinal Alford

First Epistle of Clement to the Corinthians

First Part of King Henry the Fourth, The, Basil Montague, 1834

Five Theological Orations, Gregory of Nazianzius

Fountain of Wisdom, The, John of Damascus

Fragments of a Faith Forgotten, G.R.S. Mead, London 1900

Francis Bacon's Cipher Signatures, Frank Woodward, undated

Francis of Assisi, Prof. P.J. Lennox, Catholic University of America, 1911.

Freculphus, apud God, c.1820

Freemason's Pocket Companion, 1771

Genealogies of the Saints of Britain (Achau)

Genesis of Christianity, Plummer, Edinburgh, 1876.

Glascock, Dr Henry (Notes from the Desk of), McLaughlin Foundation, Los Angeles

Glossographia Anglicana Nova, 1707

Gnostics, King, date unknown

Gospel of James, (Protevangelion) trans. by Alcock, 1750

Gospel of the Gnostics

Gospel of Thomas, from the Greek translation

Gospels and the Gospel, The, G.R.S. Mead, London 1902

Great Catechism, The, Gregory of Nyssa

Habet Ergo Diabolus Christos Suds, Julius Firmicus, c.323, (*The Devil has his Christs*)

Haeret., Theoderet, c.255

Handbook of Christian Symbolism, W. and G. Audsley 1865

Harnack, E.T, undated

Hauber's Bibliotheca Magica

Heresies (Epip, 'Haer'), Epiphanius

Heresies (Hippo, Haer), Hippolytus

Herods, The, Dean Farrar

Hidden Ceremonies of a Liberal Catholic, C.D.A.. Edwin, London. 1878

Hidden Symbols, Oliver, 1898

High Priest of Israel, The, W.C.Rhind, London 1868

Hillel Letters, The, seven in total

History of Dominic, Castiglio, Venice 1529

History of Dominic, The, Drane. London, 1891

History of Joseph the Carpenter, (Epiphanius, iv)

History of Latin Christianity, H.H. Milman D.D. 1871

History of Magic, Joseph Ennemoser, Henry G. Bohn, London, 1854

History of the Alphabet, The, Isaac Taylor, 1900

History of the Christian Church, Philip Schaff, D.D., Ms.283, Chicago Public Library

History of the Christian Church, H. H. Milman, 1871

History of the Commonwealth of Israel, Dr Isaac Wise, 1880 (approx.)

History of the Latin Language (intro), Oxford 1841

History of the Reign of King Henry VII, Francis Bacon

Homilies of Clement, The

Homilies on the Statues, John Chrysostom

Hours With The Mystics, Robert Alfred Taylor, B.A. 1856

Hymn to Wisdom, De Angelo, translation of 1807 (found in the Gospel of John)

Hymns of Ephraem the Syrian, The, Ephraem the Syrian (sometimes called *Homily*)

Hypatia, Pagan Origins of Christianity, 1792

Hyptoyposeis, quoted in *Ecclesiastical History* (Eusebius) seven books

Iambi Ad Seleucum

Iamblichus on the Mysteries of the Egyptians, Chaldeand and the Assyrians, trans. from the Greek by Thomas Taylor, 1845

Ichthus, Smith and Cheetham's *Dictionary of Christian Antiquities*, London 1875

Incarnation of the Word of God, Athanasius

Institutes of Christian History, Johann Mosheim, Ecclesiastical historian, 1755

Intellectual Development, Draper

Introduction to the New Testament (vols.I–III), Professor Samuel Davidson D.D. LL.D

Irenaeus, A. Stieren, Leipzig, vols.I–II. 1848

Irenaeus of Lyons, trans. John Keble, London 1872

Irenaeus, writings contained in the ante-Nicene Fathers, N.Y. 1926

Jasher (Yasher), The Book of God, first English language printing 1751 (twice mentioned in *the Old Testament*), oldest known version in the world is held in the secret archives of the Vatican under the title *The Essene Book of Genesis* (E. B. Szekely).

Jebamoth, The

Jerome, Prof. Isaac Muir, A Summary of his Three Writings, 1889

Jesus of History and the Jesus of Tradition Identified, G. Solomon, London, 1880

Jewish and Heathen Testimonies, Dr Lardner, c.1760

Jewish Theological Seminary at Breslau, also another copy in the Orient, Dept. Of the British Museum, Add. 26964

Justin Martyr, writings contained in the ante-Nicene Fathers, N.Y., 1926

Justinian's Novella, Immanuel Deutsch, date unknown, maybe 1896

Key of Truth, The, a manual of the Pauline Church of Armenia, Oxford, 1898. F. C. Conybeare, available in the British Library

Keys of St Peter, The, or *The House of Rochab*, Ernest de Bunsen (Bunson), London, 1867

Koran, the Holy, trans. A. Yusuf Ali, Publ. By Amana Corp., Maryland, U.S.A.

Krata Repoa or *Initiation into the Ancient Mysteries of the Priests of Egypt*, C.F.Koppen and J.W.B.Von Hymmen, Berlin,1782

Last Will and Testament of Jesus Christ,V. Baisle 1761

Laws of the High Priest, The

Laws of the Temple Service, The

Letters and Inscriptions of Hammurabi, The, L.W.King, London, 1900

Letter of Melker, Priest of the Synagoge at Bethlehem

Letter to Heliodorus, originally written in 374 by Jerome

Letter to the Bishops of Egypt and Libya

Liber Pontificalis, Duchesne, undated c. 1900

Life of Antony

Life of Augustine, Ferdinand Rosso, 1888

Life of Cardinal Caesar Baronius of the Roman Oratory, The, A. Kerr, New York, 1898

Life of Constantine, attributed to Eusebius, Bishop of Caesarea

Life of Jehoshua, The, untitled, but possibly by Ferdinand Rosso. 1888

Life of Mary Magdalene, The, Archbishop Maar, vols.I–VI, undated but c. 1900

Lingard's History of England

Little Genesis, under Mastiphal, quoted by Cedrenus

Lives of the Popes, Mann, c.1905

Longer Rules and the Shorter Rules, The, Basil of Caesarea, from *The Ascetic Works of Saint Basil*, trans. W.K.L. Clarke, Christian Knowledge

Lost and Hostile Gospels, S. Barring-Gould

Lost Book of the Nativity of John, The, Hugh J. Schonfield, Edinburgh, 1929

Lost Letters of Jerome, The, 1801

M. V. Anastos, 1946

Marcellus Britannus, Tungrorum episcopus postea Trevirorum Archiepiscopus, Mersoeus, De Archiepiscopis Trvirensium.

Martyrdom of Jesus Christ, The, S. Owen, 1891

Martyrs of the Colosseum, O'Reilly, undated

Masonic documents from the Lodge of the 'Grand Orient' of France (N4 98), 1882

Masonry Dissected, Samuel Pritchard, 1730

Matthew's Gospel in Review, McClintock and Strong Encyclopedia

Meditations, Marcus Aurelius

Metrophanes Critopulus, he claimed the *New Testament* should contain 'thirty three books in all, equal to the number of the years of Jesus' life'

Mirror of Pallas, The, David Mallet, 1740

Miscellaneous Papers and Legal Instruments Under the Hand and Seal of King James I, London 1796. (Papers from the English-Record Office)

Monumental Christianity, Reverend J.P. Lundy, 1876

Moses and Aaron, Dr Thomas Godwyn, 1625—Godwyn devotes the 12th Chapter to the Essenes

Mosheim's Ecclesiastical History (ed. 1832)

Mosheim, Ms.248 Chicago Public Library

The Name of the Furies, The, Eumenides

Narrative of Joseph of Arimathea, The

Nazareth, the City, Dr Stanton, Gemma, London, c.1905

Neimyer, Collectio Confessionum, 730

New Edition of the Babylonian Talmud, English translation, Michael I. Rodkinson, Cincinnati, 1897

New Jerusalem Symbolised, A. Ramsay, N.Y., 1801

Nicodemus of the Christos (Kristos), O'Brien-Cooper, 1907

Norwich Constitutions

Notes on a Curious Certificate, Pernety, 1882

Octavius IX, Minucius Felex

Old Christian Texts, A Collection, M. Collins, London, 1890

Oldest Laws in the World, The, (The Hammurabi Code) Chilperic Edwards, 1906. London

On Chastity, Ms.1730

On Modesty, Tertullian

On Monogamy, Tertullian, c. 205

On Synods, Hilary of Poitiers, 358

On the Christian Conflict, Bishop Augustine, (F.W. Ghillany trans.)

On the Errors of the Trinity, Michael Servetus

On the Pentateuch, Colenso

On the Trinity, Hilary of Poiters

Optatus of Minevis, early Fourth Century

Oracles of Callistus I, translated by Victor Germaine, 1822

Oral Law and its Heredity, London & Benares, 1903

Oratione, Tertullian, c.205

Origen Against Celsus, translated by James Bellamy, London, 1660

Origen, De. Princip. Commentary on Rome

Origines Celticae, Dr Guest, c.1909

Origin of Freemasonry, Thomas Paine. 1896

Origin of Religious Belief, Barring-Gould

Origin of Religious Belief, Draper

Paedagogus, Clement of Alexandria.

Panarion (Pana.), Epiphanius of Salamis

Panegyric on the Emperor Trajan, Pliny the Younger

Panegyric to the Emperor Theodosius (Pacatus)

Passing of Peregrinus, The, Lucian, circa 312

Philiad

Philo Judas, His Works, London 1854

Philosophy, Hippolytus

Pontius Pilatus, G.A. Mueller, Germany. 1888

Precepts of Ptah-hotep, The: The Oldest Book in the World, Phillipe Virey, c. 1900

Prescriptions of Tertullian

Prologues: of Marcus; of the Psalms (Prol.)

Promeaus, Homilies of

Queen Mabel, 1813

Records of Rome, The, 1868, British Library

Records of the Past, Professor A.H. Sayce, vols.I-II, c.1898

Records of the Sanhedrin, The

Records of the Synod of Arles (Fragmented)

Regio Fides, Griffiths—Next to Cardinal Baronius, he was considered one of the most learned of the Roman Catholic historians

Reinstating the New Testament Reincarnation Verses, Beaumont, Angelus 1911

Report of Caiaphus to the Sanhedrin

Res Gestae, E.G. Hardy, 1923

Resuscitatio or *Bringing into Publick Light, Several Pieces hitherto Sleeping*, Dr William Rawley, 1657

Revelationum, Lib.1, cap.X, Rome, 1628 reprint, St Bridget of Sweden

Revised New Testament, Preface, Fifth Rule of 25 May, 1879

Roman Antiquities, Dionysius of Halicarnassus (five of eleven books survive)

Roman Britains, Conybeare, pre-1898

Roman Martyrology, (available in the British Library)

Rose-Cross Mysteries, Max Heindel, 1921

Saint Dominic, Lacordaire. Paris, 1840

Secret of the 'Presence', The, undated, very rare

Secrets of the Christian Fathers, J.W. Sergerus, 1685

Secret Shake-spear, The, Alfred Dodd. Rider and Co., 47 Princes Gate, London, 1941

Servetus and Calvin, R. Willis M.D., London 1887

Seven Books of History Against the Pagans, Paulus Orosius, trans. I.W. Raymond, Columbia University Press

Seven Epistles of Ignatius, The, Ignatius, Bishop of Antioch

Shepherd of Hermas, English language printing originally from the Sinaiticus

Sibylline Oracles, Extant are Nos. 1, 2, 3, 4, 5, 6, 7, 8, 11, 12, 13, 14

Sibyllini Libra

Sod, Son of Man, date unknown

St Paul, Migne, undated but pre-1900

St Paul in Britain, R.W. Morgan, 1860

Star Lore of the Bible, W.W. Westcott, London, 1912

Story of the Church of England, The, G. H. F. Nye

Stromata (or *Miscellanies*), Clement of Alexandria, held in the Florence manuscript

Sungods in Mythology, Dr J. L.C. Lugo, Vienna, c.1870

Suppliants, The, trans. by D. Williams, undated

Survey of London, 1598, continued by Munday 1618, 1633 and by Strype 1720, 1755

Synopsis ad Aristobulum, undated.

Syntagma, rare, author or editor: Taylor

Talmuds of Palestine and Babylonia, The, 1868. trans. Prof. Chevalier

Temples of the Orient, London, 1902

Theology of Sumna

The Day They Wrote the Bible, John Cosin, Bishop of Durhan. 1594–1672

Theophilus to Autolycus, Theophilus of Antioch

Three Early Doctrinal Modifications of the Text of the Gospels, The Hibbert Journal, London, 1902

To His Wife, Tertullian, c.210

Traditions, Apostolic, by Hippolytus

Translations in Progress, Moise Schwab (the Jerusalem *Talmud*)

Translations of Christian Literature, (1920), J.A. Robinson

Tree in Religion and Myth, The, Mrs. J.H. Philpot, 1897

Triads of the Isle of Britain

Valleus' Notes, (Valleus Paterculus) (Acta Pilati)

Victims of the Marmertine, The, Rev. A. J. O'Reilly, D.D., undated but pre-1929

Virgil's Fourth Eclogue

Vitellius, Suetonius, *Histories*, 1867

Volume Archko, archeological writings of the Sanhedrin and *Talmud*s of the Jews

Weimarer Ausgabe, Weimar, 1883. The standard critical edition of Luther's works (100 vols).

What is the Talmud?, The Quarterly Review, London 1867

Wisdom of the Ancients, Francis Bacon, 1609

Wisest Fool in Christendom, The, W. McElwee, Declaratio Pro Iure Regio, 1615

Works of Flavius Josephus, The, Oxford 1839 (see note 'About Josephus, Flavius')

World's Sixteen Crucified Saviours, Mr Kersley Graves, publisher unknown, c.1850

Writings of Saint John of Damascus, The, trans. F.H. Chase, Fathers of the Church

Writings of Saint Justin Martyr, The, trans. T.B. Falls, Christian Heritage (includes Justin Martyr's *Apologies*)

Zadokite Work, The, (from the Cairo Genizah), Solomon Schechter

The Library of the Fathers

The series of early English translations of selected writings of the now-called Christian fathers. The first volume to appear was *The Confessions of Augustine*, 1838, (published under the name of the Oxford Movement 1833–45). Includes a later attachment called *Sayings of the Fathers*.

The books of Dr Constantine Tischendorf

Available in the British Library, London

Alterations to the Sinai Bible; Are Our Gospels Genuine or Not?; Codex Sinaiticus; The Authenticity of Our Gospels; The Origin of the Four Gospels; The Various Versions of the Bible; When Were Our Gospels Written?

Encyclopedias and dictionaries consulted

Annals Ecclesiastici, J. D. Mansi and D. Georgius, 38 vols., Lucca, 1738–59.

Blair's Chronological Tables, undated but c.1890

Catholic Encyclopedia, The (*Catholic Encyclopedia*), 15 volumes plus index, 1907–1914

Catholic Encylopedia, The, Robert C. Broderick, Thomas Nelson, 1976

Classical Dictionary, William Smith, Harper and Brothers, New York, 1877

Code of Canon Law, The, The Canon Law Society of America, 1985

Companion Encyclopedia of Theology, Routledge, 1995

Decrees of the Ecumenical Councils (2 Vols.) Sheed and Ward

Dictionary of Biblical Tradition, A, David Lyle Jeffrey, William B. Eerdman's Publishing Co., Grand Rapids, Michigan

Dictionary of Christian Antiquities, ed. Smith and Cheetham, London, 1875

Dictionary of Christian Biography, Literature, Sects and Doctrines, A, London, 1880

Dictionary of Classical Mythology, Religion, Literature and Art, Oskar Seyffert, Random House, 1995,

Dictionary of Greek and Roman Antiquities

Dictionary of Islam, London 1895

Dictionary of Proper Names and Places in the Bible, O. Odelain and R. Seguinean. 1981

Dictionary of Sects, Blunt, 1934

Dictionary of the Bible, original edition by James Hastings DD, revised by F.C. Grant and H.H. Rowley, 1963

Dictionary of Universal Knowledge for the People, A, Lippincott and Co., 1877

Dictionnaire de Théologie, 1920

Encyclopedia Biblica (one volume edition of 1914)

Encyclopedia Britannica, particularly volumes VIII, IX, X and XI

Encyclopedia Dictionary of the Bible, McGraw, New York, 1963

Encyclopedia Judaica (16 volumes), Ed. Cecil Roth, Jerusalem, 1974

Encyclopedia Judaica Jerusalem, 1971

Encyclopedia of Catholic Doctrine, 1997

Encyclopedia of Catholicism, 1989

Encyclopedia of Early Christianity, Everett Ferguson (ed.), St James Press, Chicago and London, 1974

Encyclopedia of Freemasonry, Albert Mackey MD, McClure Publishing, 1917

Encyclopedia of Religion and Ethics, ed. By James Hastings, T. & T. Clark, Edinburgh, 1914

Encyclopedia of Occultism, An, Lewis Spence, 1920

Encyclopedia of the Early Church, English trans., 1992

Encyclopedia of the Roman Empire, Matthew Bunson, Facts on File, N.Y., 1994.

Expository Dictionary of Biblical Words, An, W.E. Vine, M.A., Merrill, F. Unger and William White Jnr., Thomas Nelson, 1984

Funk and Wagnalls New Encyclopedia, 1988, (also 1913 *New Standard Dictionary*)

Harper's Bible Dictionary, Paul J. Achtemeier, Harper and Row, 1985

Historical Dictionary of the Orthodox Church, Prokurat, Golitizin, Peterson, Scarecrow Press Inc., 1996

Illustrated Encyclopedia of Mysticism and The Mystery Religions, An, J. Ferguson, Thames and Hudson, London, 1976

Jewish Encyclopedia, N.Y. 1903

Lakeland Bible Dictionary, Zondervan Publ. House, 1966

Latin Dictionary, A, Oxford, 1933

London Encyclopedia

Modern Catholic Encyclopedia, The, The Liturgical Press, 1994

New American Cyclopedia, The, (c. 1890)

New Bible Dictionary, Inter-Varsity, Leicester, England, 1986

New Catholic Encyclopedia, (*New Catholic Encyclopedia*), 1976

New Dictionary of Theology, Inter-Varsity, Leicester, England, 1988

New Encyclopedia Britannica, 1987

New Jewish Encyclopedia, The

New Larousse Encyclopedia of Mythology, 1984

Our Sunday Visitor's Catholic Encyclopedia, 1986

Oxford Classical Dictionary, The, 1949

Oxford Dictionary of Popes, The, Oxford University Press

Oxford Dictionary of the Christian Church, Cross, 1974, 1997

Papal Pronouncements, (vols. I–II) The Pierian Press, 1990

Popular and Critical Bible Encyclopedia, Samuel Fallows, Chicago, 1919

Smaller Classical Dictionary, A, *Smith's Smaller Classical Dictionary*, ed. E. H. Blakeney, J. M. Dent and Sons Ltd. 1937

Tanner's Notitia Monastica, 1744

Theology Dictionary of the New Testament, W.M.B. Eerdman's Publ. Co., U.S.A., 1981

Universal Encyclopedia, undated

Universal Jewish Encyclopedia, The, Universal Jewish Encyclopedia Inc., New York

Vines Expository Dictionary of New Testament Words, W.E. Vine MA, 1996

Wade's British Chronology

Bibles used as comparative references

Alexandrian Bible, translation by Tischendorf

American Standard Version by the American Revision Committee, 1901

Anonymous Bible, The, 1762, 'In this Bible a serious attempt was made to correct the text of the King James Version'—preface by F.S. Paris

Bear Bible, The, First Protestant Spanish Bible

Bezae Bible

Bible in Verse, The, vols.I–IV, 1778

Bishop's Bible, The, 1608 Ed.

Christian's Divine Bible, corrected by Henry Southwell, London,1773

Fool Bible, The, printed during the reign of Charles I. The text of Psalm 14:1 reads: 'The fool has said in his heart there is a god'. The printer was fined £3000 and all copies suppressed.

Forgotten Sins Bible 1638. See Luke 7:47

Good News Bible, The, Today's Version (English), 1976

Holy Bible, The, Oxford, 1896

Interlinear Translation of the Greek Scriptures, The, 1969

Jerusalem Bible, The, 1966

Judas Bible, 1611. Misprints of Judas for Jesus at Matthew 26:36, reviewed by J. Bergman

King James Bible (K.J.B.), versions used: 1611, revised 1881–1885 and 1901, again revised 1946–1952; Second Edition, 1971

Latin Vulgate, trans. R. Challoner, Donay, 1609, 1749 First Revision, 1750 Second Revision, 1752 Third Revision, 1764 Fourth Revision, 1772 Fifth Revision

Mount Sinai Manuscript of the Bible, 1934, British Museum Ms.43725, English trans.

New American Bible, The, St Joseph Edition, 1970

New English Bible, The, (three versions)

New International Version, The, 1973

New Testament According to the Eastern Text, George M. Lamsa

Printers Bible, 1702

Profit Bible, an Oxford edition, 1711

Revised Standard Version, Catholic Edition, 1966

Syrian Bible

The Common Translation Corrected, Oxford, 1718–1724

Universal Bible, 1766

Variorum Teacher's Edition, The, Eyre & Spottiswoode

Vatican Bible

Acknowledgement

Very special thanks to Mrs. Lucy Ogilvie of London, who kindly offered access to her vast private collection of ancient Bibles (763 at the last count) and other rare old religious texts.

About Josephus (Flavius)

Josephus was an independent chronicler of events of the First Century, and was regarded as the foremost historian of his time. He was born into a priestly family in 37 and his actual Jewish name was Joseph ben Matthias and became Titus Flavius Josephus when he took Roman citizenship later in life. Probably his most famous writing was *Jewish Antiquities*. It was a massive work, about the same size as the

Bible. He also wrote *Autobiography*, *Against Apion* and *Jewish Wars*. The works of Josephus were compiled by Ekaba, a Jewish Rabbi, at the close of the Second Century, as were most of the historians who lived during the First Century. Josephus' works were published in book-form by Havercamp, in Amsterdam in 1729. Havercamp was guided by what Rabbi Ekaba compiled of Josephus' works but it is believed there were many more writings attributed to Josephus.

Research assistance

Sincere thanks are extended to the courteous staff members of various research centres, libraries, societies, institutions and publishers of books and periodicals who generously offered assistance and granted copyright and reproduction rights for the re-use of material produced or held, by their organisations. Special acknowledgment to:

Advanced Theological Studies of Jerusalem

Awareness Quest Research (Rare Books), Australia

Bible Society, The (International), Stuttgart (Bible Copyrights)

Biblical Research Association, Ohio, U.S.A.

British Library Reading Room, London, U.K.

Brother Phillipp and the monks of St Leonards (Australia)

Bureau of Research and Survey, New York, U.S.A.

Christian Research Trust, London, U.K.

Church Surveys, Boston University, U.S.A.

Institute of Holy Land Studies, Jerusalem

Maguire's Foundation of Biblical Research (Australia)

Mother Superior (Janine the Blessed), and her two nuns

Nicholas and Gabriella Donchokoulous of Melbourne, Australia for patiently translating the sixty Canons of the Synod of Laodicea

Pontifical Biblical Institute of Jerusalem

Professor Karl von Ritchie

The House of Silver, 1986

Rare Manuscripts Division, British Library, London, UK

Religious Research Centre, Atlanta, Georgia

Shed 20, and the Group of Five (Australia)

Statistical Unit of Westminster, London, U.K.

The Celtic Library

The John Telfer Institute of Knowledge, N.Z.

The New Zealand Theosophical Society

An expression of appreciation is also extended to Phillip Arthur, Tristan (Tristar), Toni, Michelle, Leslie Victor, Steve and Julie, Greg and Wendy, Damian and Leonie, Helen Mary, the Ritchie family, Peter and Carol, Virginia, Deborah, Amanda and Nigel, James the Tall and 'Young Mick'.

254

Endnotes

Preface
1. Nostradamus, *Quatrain* X.65, *The Complete Prophecies of Nostradamus*, H.C. Roberts trans. 1982.

Chapter One
1. *The Phoenician Origin of Britons, Scots and Anglo-Saxons*, L.A. Waddell, 1924, p.393.
2. *Henry the Fourth.* Also W. McElwee, *Declaratio Pro Iure Regio*, 1615, Sully, King James I 1566–1625.
3. *James I*, Charles Williams, c.1640.
4. *Proceedings in Parliament*, 17 March 1621.
5. *Bacon and the Rosicrucians*, W.F.C. Wigston.
6. *The Martyrdom of Francis Bacon*, Alfred Dodd, p.141, undated but c.1940.
7. *Resuscitatio, or Bringing into Publick Light, Several Pieces Hitherto Sleeping*, Dr William Rawley, 1657.
8. *The Mystery of Francis Bacon*, William T. Smedley, c.1910, p.128.
9. *Encyclopedia Britannica*, Ed.IX, vol.X, p.814. Also Papias, *Ecclesiastical History*.
10. *The Rise of English Culture*, Edwin Johnson, Preface.
11. *The Secret Shake-speare*, Alfred Dodd, 1941.
12. *Bacon and the Rosicrucians*, W.F.C. Wigston. Also see *The Mirror of Pallas*, David Mallet, 1740.
13. *Francis Bacon's Cipher Signatures*, Frank Woodward, undated.
14. *The Secret Shake-speare,* also *The Martyrdom of Francis Bacon,* Dodd.

Chapter Two
1. *Jesus the Magician*, Professor Morton Smith, 1978, Dea. Lea. 1973–1974.
2. Ibid.
3. *Contra Celsus,* Against Celsus, Origen, 1:28.
4. See notes on both passages by Lommatzech, in his *Origen Contra Celsus*, Berlin, 1845.
5. *Heresies*, Epip., *Haer*, Epiphanius, lxxvii, 7.
6. *Jebamoth*, 49A.
7. *Commentaries on the Law of Moses*, Jonathon D. Michaelis, Vols.I–IV, 1814.
8. *Babylonian Shabbath*, 104 b, repeated in almost identical words in the *Babylonian Sanhedrin*, 67 a.
9. *Translations in Progress*, Moise Schwab, The Jerusalem *Talmud*.
10. *Mary in the Babylonian Talmud,* G.R.S. Mead, London & Benares, 1903.
11. St Jerome 347–420.
12. *The Name of the Furies,* Eumenides.
13. *Babylonian Sanhedrin (b. Sanh.)* 106 a.
14. *Babylonian Shabbath* 104 b.

15 *Commentary to Matthew,*
Hieronymus, bk.ii, ch.xii, 13.
16 *James the Brother of Jesus,* Robert
Eisenman, p.471.
17 See *Syrian Bible,* for example.
18 *Catholic Encyclopedia,* vol.XV, 1
October 1912, pp.459–472.
19 *Encyclopedia Judaica Jerusalem,* 1971,
p.443.
20 Ibid, p.601.
21 Ibid., pp.740–744.
22 *The Herods,* Dean Farrar. Also *Joseph
of Arimathea,* Skeats.
23 *Catholic Encyclopedia,* vol.V1, 1910,
p.291–292.
24 *Antiquities,* Josephus, 16:355.
25 *The Herods of Judea,* Oxford,
A.H.M. Jones, 1938.
26 *Catholic Encyclopedia,* vol.VI, 1910,
p.292.
27 The *New Testament,* however,
sometimes called him 'king': Matt.
14:9, Mark 6:14.
28 *Bible Myths,* T.W. Doane, 1882,
p.431.
29 *Catholic Encyclopedia,* vol.V, 1909,
p.546. Also Josephus, *Jewish Wars,* II,
p.120.
30 *The Records of Rome,* 1868, British
Library, ILS 7317, 'Silvani', plural.
31 Born in 42BC, Emperor during the
years 14–37AD..
32 *The Life of Augustus,* Suetonius,
trans. Philemon Holland, Tudor
Series, 1893.
33 *Res Gestae,* E. G. Hardy, 1923.
34 *Shorter Oxford Dictionary,* p.1503.
35 *The Reign of Tiberius,* F. B. Marsh,
1931.
36 *Brewer's Myth and Legend,* Editor J
C.Cooper, Cassell, 1992, p.213.
37 *Catiline, Clodius and Tiberius,* Beesly,
1878.
38 *Smaller Classical Dictionary,* 1910
Ed., 'Tiberius'.
39 *The Twelve Caesars,* Suetonius,
ch.3:5, p.112.
40 Ibid., ch.2:70, p.89.
41 Ibid., ch.2:18, p.60.
42 Ibid., ch.2:88, p.98.

43 Suetonius, op.cit., ch.3:18, p.119.
44 Ibid., ch.3:17, p.119.
45 Ibid., ch.3:9, p.114.
46 *Smaller Classical Dictionary,*
'Tiberius'. Also *The Records of Rome,*
1868, British Library.
47 *Encyclopedia Britannica,* 'Palatine'.
48 *Encyclopedia Judaica Jerusalem,* 1971,
p.601.

Chapter Three
1 *Chronicles of Geoffrey of Monmouth,*
4,11.
2 *The Phoenician Origin of Britons,
Scots and Anglo-Saxons,* L. A.
Waddell, 1924, p.390.
3 *British Chronicles.*
4 *Encyclopedia of the Roman Empire,* M.
Bunson, 1994, 'Augustus'.
5 *Jewish Wars,* Josephus.
6 11:16, 20:24 and 21:2.
7 Song of Solomon 7:14.
8 *Encyclopedia of Early Christianity,*
Everett Ferguson, 1990, pp.899–
900.
9 *Homily on the Life of a Pilgrim,*
Ephraem the Syrian, CPG 1, 1152–
1155. TLG 1214.
10 *Chronologie,* ii, 172.
11 *About the Acts of Thomas—A Paper,*
Professor John S.J. Lingard, 1952,
cap.31, p.148.
12 138:7f, 138:19f.
13 Prologue, Gospel of Thomas. Also
Introduction to the Acts of Thomas.
14 *Catholic Encyclopedia,* vol.XIV, 1912,
p.658.
15 *The Gnostic Scriptures,* Bentley
Layton, 1987, p.370.
16 Acts of Thomas, 108:1.
17 Syrian Version of the Acts of
Thomas, 110:56.
18 Schaff, *History of the Christian
Church.*
19 *Cult of the Heavenly Twins,* Rendel
Harris, 1906.
20 *Natural History,* Pliny (Caius Plinius
Secundus), bk.VI.
21 *Annals,* Tacitus, 11,84.
22 Alexander VI, 1492–1503.

23 *Leo X*, Giovanni de Medici, 1513–1521.
24 *Oxford Dictionary of Popes*, p.258.
25 British Museum, Ms.279 V.
26 *Catholic Encyclopedia* vol.IX, 1910, p.163. Also T. W. Doane's *Bible Myths*, p.438.
27 The name 'Rennes'(-le-Chateau) is of more recent origin. The Romans called it 'Rhedae'.
28 *The Holy Blood, and the Holy Grail*, Michael Baigent, Richard Leigh and Henry Lincoln, Corgi Books, 1990.
29 *The True Language of Rennes-le-Chateau*, M.G.E.H. Neyman, Belgique, Books on CD-Rom.
30 *The Horse of God*, by M.G.E.H. Neyman, Belgique, Books on CD-Rom.
31 Baigent, Leigh and Lincoln, op. cit.
32 John 20:24.
33 Mark 6:3, Matt.13:55.

Chapter Four

1 Chairman, Department of Religious Studies and Professor, Middle East Religions, California State University, Long Beach, U.S.A.
2 Paul often boasted of being 'a Pharisee of the Pharisees', Acts 23:6.
3 *The Dead Sea Scrolls, Documents of the Jewish Christian sect of Ebionites*, The Journal of Jewish Studies, vol.II, no.2, 1951, J.L. Teicher.
4 'Epiphanius of Salamis', *Dictionary of Christian Biography*, Smith and Wade, undated.
5 'Maccabean' was another name for the Hasmoneans, Josephus, *Antiquities*, 12:263.
6 *Encyclopedia of Freemasonry*, Albert G. Macey, 1917, p.258.
7 Bell, Gall., vi. 13.
8 Oxford, 1671.
9 William Tate, 1909, p.27.
10 *Bible Myths*, T. W. Doane, 1882, pp.424–425.

11 *Anacalypsis*, Godfrey Higgins, vol.I, p.747, vol.II, p.34.
12 *Ecclesiastical History*, Eusebius., lib. 2, ch.xvii.
13 Higgins, loc. cit.
14 Damasus Document, *Dead Sea Scrolls.*
15 *Encyclopedia of Freemasonry*, Albert G. Macey, 1917, p.258.
16 Luke 1:36, In some old Gospels, Elizabeth's name was written, Enishbai.
17 The *Torah*, the first five books of the *Old Testament*. See *Commentaries on the Law of Moses*, Jonathon D. Michaelis, vols.I–IV, 1814.
18 *The Court of the Gentiles*, Oxford, 1671.
19 Particularly Heb.7:22, Heb. 8:6–13, 2 Cor. 3:6.
20 1888, p.128.
21 *The Lost Book of the Nativity of John*, Hugh J. Schonfield. Edinburgh, 1929. Preface, p.x.
22 vol.I, p.620.
23 *Harmony of the New Testament*, Dr Lightfoot, vol.I, p.333.
24 Origen, vol.ii, p.150.
25 *Facts and Speculation on the Origin and History of the Christian Church*, Jacob Bryant, London, 1793.
26 *Heresies, (Epiph. Haer.), liii, I.
27 Ibid., xxix, 3.
28 1 Kings 19:16. Also 1 Kings 1–53.
29 *Lakeland Bible Dictionary.*
30 Professor Hilton Hotema, Historian and author.
31 Mark 14:3–5, Matt. 26:7.
32 Luke 4:41, *Sinai Bible.*
33 Philos., vii, 34.
34 p.xlix.
35 *Catholic Encyclopedia,* vol.V, 1909, p.547.
36 For examples see *The Key of Truth, a manual of the Pauline Church of Armenia*, Oxford, 1898, F.C. Conybeare, British Library.
37 The reference to Jesus being in the Temple Luke 2:42 with the priests

when he was twelve years old was a forgery: *Catholic Encyclopedia* vol.IX, 1 October 1910, p.425.

38 *New American Cyclopedia*, vol.I, p.620.

39 4:11 and 4:33–34.

40 *Encyclopedia Judaica Jerusalem*, vol.8, p.388.

41 See Matt. 14:1, Luke 3:1,19, Mark 6:4.

42 *The Smaller Classical Dictionary*, p.260.

43 Matt. 2:1; Luke 2:15–18.

44 *Oxford Dictionary of the Christian Church*, Cross, 1974, p.132.

45 See also Numbers 24:17.

46 Plato in *Apology, Anacalypis*, ii, p.189.

47 Mark 14:22–24; Matt. 26:28; 1 Cor. 11:25.

Chapter Five

1 Deut., 21:20–21.

2 *Encyclopedia of the Roman Empire*, Matthew Bunson, 1994, pp.182–183.

3 *Ant. Jud*, xiii, p.xv

4 Matt. 12:24; Mark 3:21–22; Luke 19:45; John 8:48 and 10:20; 1 Cor. 14–23

5 Mark 4:38–39, *Sinai Bible*.

6 Mark 11:12–20.

7 Ibid.

8 John 19:25–27.

9 *The First Gay Pope*, Lyn Fletcher, Alyson Publications, 1992. Lists religious gay and lesbian 'firsts'.

10 Winsdor, 12572. Also Louvre, 1597.

11 *Monumental Christianity*, 1876, p.385.

12 *Origin of Religious Belief*, Barring-Gould, vol.1, p.391.

13 *Development of the Catholic Church*, 1880.

Chapter Six

1 *Life of Christ*, p.79.

2 *The Bible of Today*, John W. Chadwick, 1878.

3 Josephus in *Antiquities*, bk.xviii, ch.i, I and *Wars of the Jews*, bk.ii, ch.viii, I.

4 *A Guide to the Ancient World*, Michael Grant, 1986, p.261.

5 *Antiquities*, Josephus, xviii, 23.

6 *Ecclesiastical History*, Eusebius, Lib.III, ch.xxiii.

7 Ibid., Lib.7, ch.xxx.

8 *Apology I*, Eusebius, ch.xxvi.

9 Acts 5:37. Also Mosheim's *Ecclesiastical History*, 1825, cent.XVI, sect.iii, ch.I, 8vo.

10 *Catholic Encyclopedia*, vol.VIII, 1910, p.375.

11 *Lakeland Bible Dictionary*.

12 *The Martyrdom of Jesus Christ*, p.42.

13 *Catholic Encyclopedia* op. cit., p.539.

14 Ibid., vol.X, 1911, pp.674–678.

15 Ibid., vol.V, 1909, pp.163–164.

16 Ibid.

17 *The Keys of St Peter*, Bunson, 1867. Also *Bingham's Antiquities of the Christian Church*, Straker's Edition, 1840, See also 'rock', *New Catholic Encyclopedia*, vol.X, p.191

18 *Against Heresies, (Adv. Haer.)*, iii, 3, 2, c.202.

19 *The Lost 'Book of the Nativity of John'*, Hugh J. Schonfield, 1929, p.35.

20 22:57, 22:59, 23:6.

21 *Catholic Encyclopedia*.

22 See *Catholic Encyclopedia*s.

23 *Catholic Encyclopedia* vol.VIII, 1910, p.539.

24 *New Catholic Encyclopedia*, vol.VI, 1967, p.737.

25 *Jewish Wars*, Josephus, IV, 7.

26 Ref. X:17.

27 *The Dead Sea Scroll Deception*, Michael Baigent, Richard Leigh, Corgi Books, 1992.

28 *Jewish War*, Josephus, 7:29.

29 Luke 6:15, Acts 1:13.

30 Dorotheus, Synod. De Apostol., Synopsis ad Sim. Zelot.

Chapter Seven

1 *Encyclopedia Judaica Jerusalem*, 1971, p.1118. Judas Khrestus' grandson Eleazar, was also crucified after Jerusalem was taken in 70, *The*

Decline and Fall of the Roman Empire, Edward Gibbons, 1994, p.531.

2 *The Dictionary of Classical Mythology, Religion, Literature, and Art,* Oskar Seyffert, 1995, p.611.

3 *The Records of Rome,* 1868, British Library.

4 Matt. 26:36, *Syrian Bible.*

5 *The Canon of the Bible,* Professor Samuel Davidson, Chicago Public Library, Ms.88. Also the *Judas Bible,* J. Bergman, Archbold, Ohio.

6 *Life of Caligula,* Suetonius, XXII.

7 Flavius Josephus.

8 The first Delatore mentioned by name was Romano Hispo, circa 15AD, Tacitus.

9 Roman Emperor 79–81.

10 *Encyclopedia of the Roman Empire,* Matthew Brunson, 1994, p.164.

11 Luke 10:1, 10:17, *Sinai Bible.*

12 Babylonian Sanhedrin (b. Sanh.), 43 a.

13 Acta Pilate, 1:1–2, 3: 98.

14 Institutes of Christian History, Johann Mosheim, Ecclesiastical historian, 1755.

15 Acta of Pilate IX.

16 *History of Purple as a Status Symbol in Antiquity,* M. Reinhold, Brussels, 1970.

17 Luke 23:50, see also the prophecy of the Cumaean Sibyl in Virgil's *Fourth Eclogue* that predicted the coming of 'the new Kingdom of God'.

18 *Joseph of Arimathea,* Rev. Smithett Lewis, M.A.

19 *Encyclopedia Judaica Jerusalem,* 1971, p.848.

20 *Catholic Encyclopedia* vol.XVI, 1912. p.718.

21 Acta Pilate, xiii, XXIX.

22 *Pontius Pilatus,* G.A. Mueller, Germany. 1888.

23 Mariamne and Herodias Herod's brother, d.44.

24 *Dio Cassius,* bk.xlix, p.405.

25 See also *The Martyrdom of Jesus Christ,* p.106.

26 *New Catholic Encyclopedia,* 1967. vol.VII, p.631.

27 *Catholic Encyclopedia,* vol.II, 1907, p.582.

28 *Ecclesiastical History,* Eusebius, iv, 7.

29 *1.24: 3–7.*

30 Named Gestas, meaning violent, and Dysmas, a Galilean innkeeper, *Acta of Pilate.*

31 *Catholic Encyclopedia,* vol.XIV, 1912, p.658.

32 *Jewish Encyclopedia,* T.J.Yev, 16:3, 15c.

33 Luke 23:52; John 19:38; Mark 15:42.

34 *Against Heresies,* 1.24. 3–7.

35 Gospel of Peter, 1: 9–10.

36 An apocryphal book was, originally, one too sacred and secret to be in everyone's hands. Many of them were believed to 'contain ancient and truthful elements' (*The Apocryphal New Testament,* Montague R. James, Oxford, 1924) but have degenerated into meaning spurious or false. There is, then, some confusion here, because they were once official church writings and used in the early centuries of Christianity. They were written by the church and showed what was acceptable to the unlearned Christians of the first ages. When they were eventually sorted out, those going into the *New Testament* were labeled 'canonical' and those excluded were named 'apocryphal'. The distinction was purely arbitrary.

37 Gen. 25:27–34.

38 Acts of Thomas, 110:15.

39 *King Jesus,* ed.IV, R.Graves, London, 1960.

40 Acts of Thomas.

41 *The Apocryphal New Testament,* Montague R. James, Oxford, 1926.

42 Acts of Thomas 1:2.

43 *The First Act,* 3.

44 *Catholic Encyclopedia* vol.XIV, 1912, p.658.

45 Ibid.
46 *Acts of Thomas*, 'In the Country of India', *112:75*.
47 See *India and the Apostle Thomas*, Medlycott. London 1905.
48 *Homily In Hebrew* 26.
49 *Dio Cassius* 77.12.
50 *Facts and Speculation on the Origin and History of the Christian Church*, Jacob Bryant, London 1793.

Chapter Eight
1 p.197.
2 Oxford University Press, Third Edition, 1997, p.333.
3 *Ecclesiastical History,* Eusebius, 3:22.
4 *Annales ecclesiastici*, Cardinal Caesar Baronius 1538–1607, vols.I–XII, printed in Rome 1598–1607.
5 *The History of Torture*, Daniel P. Mannix, Dell, N.Y., 1964.
6 *Institutes of Christian History*, Johann Mosheim, ecclesiastical historian, 1755. Also *The Birth of Christianity*, Maurice Goguel, 1933.
7 *I Apology*, Justin Martyr, 26:7.
8 *Annales ecclesiastici*, Cardinal Caesar Baronius, Vatican librarian 1597 and church historian, Vols.I–XII, Rome, 1598–1607.
9 *Meditations,* Marcus Aurelius.
10 *Panegyric To The Emperor Theodosius*, Pacatus.
11 His 'exact date is unknown, but late Second Century', *Catholic Encyclopedia*.
12 *Haer.*, 26:45.
13 *Epistle*, Jerome, 22.
14 *City of God*, Augustine, 1609 trans., quoted by Mosheim, 1694–1755.
15 *Confessions*, St Augustine, 6:2, c.401.
16 *Cannibalism, The Religious Significance*, Eaton University Press, 1943.
17 *Catholic Encyclopedia* vol.VIII, 1910, p.374–375.
18 Ibid.
19 Ibid.
20 *Ammian*, xxii. 5, O'Neill's trans., 1898.

21 *Jewish and Heathen Testimonies*, vol.ii. pp.102–103.
22 See also *The Decline and Fall of the Roman Empire*, Edward Gibbons, 1994, p.531.
23 *Epiphanius*, editor Petar, vol.1, p.117.
24 Gibbons, loc. cit.
25 *Oxford Dictionary of the Christian Church*, Oxford University Press, Ed.III, 1997, p.333.

Chapter Nine
1 *Sayings of the Fathers*, 1, 12.
2 *Anacalypis*, Godfrey Higgins, vol.I, p.747; vol.II, p.34.
3 *Book of Taliesin*.
4 *The History of the Kings of Britain*, Geoffrey of Monmouth, Penguin Classics, p.119.
5 *An Encyclopedia of Occultism*, Lewis Spence, 1920, 'Celts'.
6 Higgins, loc.cit.
7 *The Uncertain History of Christian Beginnings*, Jack G. Patterson, 1996, Auckland, N.Z, p.157.
8 *Antiquities*, Josephus.
9 *Catholic Encyclopedia*, vol.V, 1909, p.546–547.
10 *Bible Myths*, T.W. Doane 1884, p.431.
11 *Monumental Christianity* 1876, p.385.
12 *The Essenes*, C. Ginsburg, U.K., date unknown.
13 5:30. Also Luke 8:45–46, *Sinai Bible*.
14 *Talmud*. See also Rev. C. C. Dobson, *Did Our Lord Visit Britain?*, Destiny Publishers, 1944.
15 Mark 15:40.
16 1 Cor. 9:5, *Sinai Bible*.
17 *Encyclopedia Brittanica*, Ed.IX, vol.X, 'Gospels'.
18 Mark 6:3; Matt. 13:55.
19 Mark 3:18; Matt. 10:3; Mark 15:40.
20 *The Roman Invasion of Britain*, Graham Webster, 1980. p.212.
21 *Catholic Encyclopedia*, vol.IX. Oct. 1, 1910. Gospel of Mark, also *Catholic*

Encyclopedia, vol.XII, Oct.1, 1911.

22 *History of the Kings of Britain*, Geoffrey of Monmouth, 1100–1155.

23 *Encyclopedia of Occultism*, p.97.

24 1 Cor. 9:5, *Sinai Bible*.

25 *The Secret Gospel of Mark*.

26 Deut. 21:10–14.

27 1 Cor. 9:5, *Sinai Bible*.

28 1 Cor 9:4–5; Luke 4:38, *Latin Vulgate*, trans. R. Challoner, Donay, 1609, 1749, first revision.

29 1 Cor. 7:8, *Variorum Teacher's Bible*.

30 1 Cor. 9:5, *Sinai Bible*.

31 *Encyclopedia of Freemasonry*, Albert Mackey, McClure Publishing, 1917.

32 Ibid.

33 *The Phoenician Origin of Britons, Scots and Anglo-Saxons, L. A. Waddell, 1924, p.390.*

34 *Catholic Encyclopedia,* vol.VI. 1909, p.395.

35 Paris, 1767, *Fonds Notre-Dame,* 101.

36 *The Life of Mary Magdalene*, Archbishop Maar, vols.I–VI.

37 *Catholic Encyclopedia* vol.IX. 1910, p.97.

38 *Dictionnaire Étymologique des noms de Lieux en France*.

39 Freculphus, *apud God.*, p.10.

40 *Demonstratio Evangelica*.

41 *Catholic Encyclopedia* vol.11, 1967, p.105

42 *Annales ecclesiastici*, vol.1, p.327, quoting the Act of Magdalene, vols.I–XII, Rome, 1598–1607.

43 *St Paul in Britain*, R. W. Morgan, 1860.

44 *Catholic Encyclopedia* vol.IX. 1910, p.98.

45 Mark 3:18, 15:40, Matt. 10:3.

46 Morgan, op. cit., p.62.

47 *Disputoilis super Dignitatem Anglis it Gallioe in Councilio Constantiano*, c.1517, Theodore Martin of Lovan.

48 Conybeare, *Roman Britains*, pp.48–50.

49 *Harlyn Bay Discoveries*, R.A. Bullen, undated.

50 *Universal Encyclopedia.*

51 Matt.13:55; Mark 6:3.

52 Harleian, British Museum Ms.3859f, 193b. Also Jesus College Ms.20.

53 *Annales ecclesiastici*, Cardinal Baronius, 1538–1607.

54 Ibid.

55 *Domesday Survey Folio*, p.249b.

56 Morgan, op.cit.

57 *The Anglo-Saxon Chronicle*.

58 Freculphus, *apud God.*, p.10.

59 Suetonius, *Vita Claudius.*

60 *Cottonian Manuscript*, Gildas. Also Morgan, op.cit.,pp.62–65.

61 Geoffrey of Monmouth, *The Kings of Britain*. Also *Royal Dynasty of Ancient Britain*, (Historia Brit.).

62 Morgan, op.cit.

63 Ibid.

64 *The Martyrs of the Colosseum*, O'Reilly, date unknown.

Chapter Ten

1 Suetonius, *Vitellius*, xl viii. Also *Dio Cassius*, LX, 19–23.

2 *Phoenician Origins of Britons and Scots*, p.392.

3 Ibid.

4 Tacitus. Also *Agricola*, xi.

5 Tacitus.

6 *Annals*, 14:30.

7 Ibid., lib. ii. c.24.

8 Mab. 11, 309.

Chapter Eleven

1 *Annals*, bk. XII, Cp. 36.

2 *St Paul in Britain*, R. W. Morgan, Orig. 1860. p.99, extracted from Tacitus.

3 Ibid.

4 Tacitus, *Annals*, 12:37.

5 Ibid., 12:36.

6 Soon to be Roman Emperor, 54–68.

7 *Annals*, 12:37.

8 in some translations 'The British Palace'.

9 Philippians, 4:22.

Chapter Twelve

1 Celtic for 'Princess', by collation, she was born in 36.
2 *The Twelve Caesars*, Suetonius, trans. R. Graves, 1958, p.109.
3 *St Paul in Britain*, R.W. Morgan, Orig. 1860, pp.103–107.
4 Romans 16:14.
5 *The Roman Martyrology*.
6 Prassede, died 2 September 150, one month after Timotheus.
7 *Against Marcion, (Adv. Marc.)*, Tertullian, v, Ms.1727, p.368.
8 *Anacalypis*, Godfrey Higgins, vol.1, p.747, vol.2, p.34.
9 The references used in this section were drawn from *The Holy Bible*, Oxford University Press, British and Foreign Bible Society, 1896.
10 *Catholic Encyclopedia*, vol.VII, p.645.
11 1 and 2 Timothy, plus Titus.
12 *The Oxford Dictionary of the Christian Church*, 1974, Ed.II, 'Pastoral Epistles'.
13 Acts. 24:5, *King James Bible*.
14 *Prescriptions*.
15 *Epiph.*, Ed. Petar, vol.1, p.117.
16 *Jewish and Heathen Testimonies*, vol.ii. pp.102–103.
17 See also *The Decline and Fall of the Roman Empire*, Edward Gibbons, 1994, p.531.
18 *St Paul in Britain*, Edwin Wilmshurst, Chichester, 1910.
19 *The Victims of the Marmertine*, Rev. A. J. O'Reilly, undated but pre-1929.
20 Acts. 24:5, *King James Bible*.
21 *Claudia and Pudens*, Archdeacon Williams. Also *Fabiola*, Cardinal Wiseman and *Development of the Catholic Church*, Ernest Renan of the French Academy, 1880.
22 *Triads of the Isle of Britain*.
23 *London Morning Post*, 27 March 1931.
24 *Revised New Testament*, Preface, Fifth Rule of 25 May 1879.
25 In the *Talmud*, Jesus was sometimes called Autu H-ais, meaning 'that man'.
26 Romans 16:1.
27 Ibid., 16:22.
28 p.1148.
29 Romans 16:9.
30 Ibid., 16:1.
31 Ibid., 16:23.
32 Ibid., 16:13.
33 Wilmshurst, op. cit.
34 Alford's *Regio Fides*. Alford's proper name was Griffiths. He assumed the name of Alford on entering the Society of Jesuits. Next to Cardinal Baronius, he was considered one of the most learned of the Roman Catholic historians.
35 Wilmshurst, op.cit., p.10.
36 *The Oxford Dictionary of the Christian Church*, 1974, Ed.II, 'Pastoral Epistles'.
37 *The Holy Bible*, Oxford, printed University Press 1896, p.1206.
38 *Irenaei Opera*, 3:1.
39 Gal 1:4, *Sinai Bible*.
40 Luke 6:15, Acts 1:13.
41 *The British Church*, Maj. J. Samuels.
42 Morgan, op. cit.
43 Coelbren, p.25.
44 *The Kings of Britain,* Geoffrey of Monmouth.

Chapter Thirteen

1 *Magia Jesu Christi*.
2 Fabrius, *Cod. Apoc. N.T.*, I, 243. Also Tischendorf, *Evang. AP.,* p.214.
3 Ten books, quoted by Origen, dated to circa mid–Third Century.
4 *Hidden Symbols*, Oliver, 1898.
5 *Dialogue*, p.69.
6 *Encyclopedia of Freemasonry*, Albert G. Macey, 1917, p.258.
7 *Apology*, Justin, xxxvi, 2.
8 *Ecclesiastical History,* Eusebius.
9 *Gnostics*, King, p.145.
10 *Against Heresies*, Bk.V, 13.
11 Mark 6:3; Matt. 13:55.
12 *History of Magic*, Joseph Ennemoser, Henry G Bohn, London, 1854.
13 *Clementine Homilies*.
14 *Encyclopedia of Religion and Ethics*, Ed. James Hastings, T. & T. Clark,

Edinburgh, 1914.

15 Augustine, in his commentary on the *Gospel of John*, vol.I, p.240.

16 2 Samuel 5:4; 1 Kings 11:42.

17 *The Secret Path*, Paul Brunton, 1935, Also *On the Round Towers of Ireland*, O'Brien.

18 Matt. 27: 62–63.

19 For example Luke 23:33.

20 *Encyclopedia of Freemasonry*, Albert Mackey, McClure Publishing, 1917.

21 Josh. 4:19–20.

22 2 Kings 2:1; 4:38.

23 Matt. 26:3; Acts.4, 5, 6, 12, 22, 30.

24 Mark. 14:55.

25 *Babylonian Sanhedrin*, 103a.

26 *Old Christian Texts*, M. Collins, London, 1890.

27 *The Adepts*, vols.I–IV, M. P. Hall, Los Angeles, 1949 reprint.

28 *Adv. Judeaus*, C.IX, last paragraph.

29 *Babylonian Sanhedrin*, 106b.

30 *Sanhedrin*, 67a.

31 1 Chron. 1:11.

32 *Ragnar Lodbrog Saga*.

33 *Chronicles*.

34 *Survey of London*, 1598; cont. by Munday 1618, 1633 and by Strype 1720, 1755.

35 *Acts of the Apostles*, 5:40.

36 *New Catholic Encyclopedia*, vol.IV, p.475.

37 *Crosses in Tradition*, W.W. Seymour, N.Y., 1898.

38 *Origin of Religious Belief*, Draper, p.252.

39 *Mrs. Jameson*, vol.2, p.317.

40 *Talmud*.

41 *Babylonian Sandhedrin*, 106 a.

Chapter Fourteen

1 *The Forgotten Monarchy of Scotland*, Michael J.A. Stewart.

2 Suetonius, *The Twelve Caesars*.

Chapter Fifteen

1 Act I, sc.ii.

2 This fresco is on display in the Church of St Stephen, Bologna.

3 p.28.

4 See *Baconiana*, T. Tenison, 1679, ch.11, p.29.

Chapter Sixteen

1 *Church History*, Socrates Scholasticus 380–450 Jenning's trans., 1911.

2 Bureau of Research and Survey, New York, U.S.A.

3 Austin Publishing Co., California.

4 1 Thessalonians 5:27, Colossians 4:16.

5 *Catholic Encyclopedia*, vol.11, 1907, pp.581–582.

6 Contributor to the Encyclopedia Britannica. *The Canon of the Bible*, 156.

7 *Panegyric on the Emperor Trajan*, Pliny the Younger, Roman Senator, c.112.

8 *Catholic Encyclopedia*, vol.II, 1907, pp.581–582.

9 *Prologue* in Ps.15.

10 *History of the Christian Church*, Philip Schaff, Chicago Public Library.

11 *Catholic Encyclopedia* vol.XI, 1 June 1911, p.652.

12 *The Detection and Overthrow of False Gnosis*, Irenaeus.

13 *Catholic Encyclopedia* 1907, vol.I, p.106.

14 *Catholic Encyclopedia*, vol.II, 1907, pp.581–582.

15 Ibid., p.583.

16 *New Catholic Encyclopedia*. vol.XII, 1967, p.577.

17 *Gibbon's Rome*, ii, 272.

18 *Catholic Encyclopedia* 1908, vol.IV. p.583.

19 *Eccl. Hist*, Eusebius, vol.I, pp.381–382.

20 Dr Donaldson wrote the classic *History of Christian Literature*.

21 Ps.111:9, *Sinai Bible*.

22 *Servetus and Calvin*, R. Willis, London, 1877, p.308.

23 260–339, author of *Ecclesiastical History*.

24 354–430, author of *City of God*.

25 *The Monks of Athos*, 1936, R.M. Dawkings.

26 *Contra Celsum* (Against Celsus), Origen, ii, 27.

27 Ibid., bk.I, lxvii and bk.III, ch.xliv.

28 Ibid., bk.I, chs. Ix; x.

29 *Adv. Rufin*, Apol., 1,18.

30 *De Viris Illustribus*, 135, D.Vallarsi, vols.I–XI, Verona, 1734–42.

31 *Epistle*, 48:13, Migne, Pl XXII, p.502.

32 *Jerome*, v, 445. Also *Sod, the Son of the Man*, p.46.

33 Origen, op. cit., ii, 27.

34 *Confessions* (Conf.), 2:9, Augustine, c.401AD.

35 Ibid., 5:21, trans. Prof. Jackson, 1917.

36 *Encyclopedia of Early Christianity*, Ed. Everett Ferguson, p.121.

37 *Ecclesiastical History*, Mosheim, bk.II.

38 *Sungods in Mythology*, J. L.C. Lugo, Vienna, c.1870.

39 Taylor's *Syntagma*, p.52.

40 *Secrets of the Christian Fathers*, J.W. Sergerus, 1685.

41 *Oxford Dictionary of the Christian Church*, Cross, 1997 ed., p.128.

42 *The Desert Fathers*, Helen Waddell, N.Y., 1936.

43 *Jerome*, Prof. Isaac Muir, (A Summary of his Three Writings), 1889.

44 *De Viris Illustribus*, 135, D.Vallarsi trans., Verona, 1734–42.

45 *Butler's Lives of the Saints*, Rev. Alban Butler, 1926.

46 *Genesis of Christianity*, Plummer, Edinburgh, 1876

47 *Catholic Encyclopedia*, vol.XV, 1912, p.515. Also *Biblitheca sanctorum*, Rome 1965, VI, 1132–7.

48 *Ecclesiastical History*, Eusebius.

49 *Oxford Dictionary of the Christian Church*, Cross, 1997, p.360.

50 *Epistle Ed.*, Corinth, XXV.

51 *De Resurrect*, Ms.1730, vol.2.

52 *Contra Celsus*.

53 *De Principle* 1, 7, Ms.1729.

54 *The Catechetical Letters*, xviii, 8.

55 Ibid., vi, 20, Ms.1589, p.70.

56 *Epistle. of Barnabas*, Ch. X.

57 Ibid.

58 *Apology of Justin Martyr*, ii, 5.

59 Ibid., 1:18.

60 *Adverse Autolius*, ii, 23, rare and undated—pre-Sixth Century.

61 *De Pallio*, 3, Ms 1730.

62 *Ad. Scap.* 3, Ms.1790.

63 Ibid., Ms.1730.

64 *Oratione*, Tertullian, 39.

65 *De Anima*, 57, Ms 1730.

66 *Apology of Tertullian*, xxiii.

67 *Stromata*, vi, 3.

68 Ibid., ii, 6.

69 Ibid., vi, 6.

70 *Paedag.*, iii, 5, Ms 1724.

71 *Stromata*, iii, Ms 1724.

72 *History of the Bible*, Bronson C. Keeler, C.P. Farrell, 1881.

73 *De. Divinatione daemonum*, cap.iii, 7.

74 Matt. 8:16; Luke 10:17–20; Mark 9:22.

75 1 Cor. 1:26.

76 Eccles 1:15.

77 *Adv. Marcion*.

78 *The Arguments of the Emperor Julian*, T. Taylor trans., London, 1818.

79 *The First Seven Ecumenical Councils*, 325–787, L.D. Davis.1987, p.40.

80 Acts. 19:32–41. Also Elliott's *Delineation of Romanism*, 1884, p.442.

81 *De Anima*, 51, p.524.

82 *Christian Observer*, 1815, vol.XV.

83 *Catholic Encyclopedia*, 1908, vol.IV, p.584.

84 *The Passing of Peregrinus*, Lucian, c.312.

85 *Digest*, XLVIII, XXIX, 30.

86 *De Anima*, 51.

87 *Oxford Dictionary of the Christian Church*, Cross, 1997 ed., p.1592.

88 *Old Christian Literature*, Van Manen of Leyden, contributor to *Encyclopedia Biblica*, c.1860.

89 *Church History*, Socrates Scholasticus 380–450, Prof. Jenning's trans., 1911.

90 1:22–24, *Sinai Bible*.
91 Acts 17:5.
92 *Panegyric on the Emperor Trajan*, Pliny the Younger.
93 An 'apologist' is 'one who defends by argument', *Oxford Classical Dictionary*.
94 *Christian Topography*, Cosmas Indicopleustes, c.610.
95 *M. V. Anastos*, 1946.
96 *De Civitat*, Dei, xxii, 8.
97 iii, 24.
98 *Intellectual Development*, Draper, ii, 159.
99 *Apology*, 1:54.
100 *Stromata*, ii, 6.
101 Ibid., vi, 5.
102 Ibid., ii, 4.
103 Ibid., iv, 26.
104 *On Chastity*, vii, Ms.1730, vol.3.
105 *On Monogamy*, vi.
106 *On Modesty*, vi.
107 Demon, *Evang.*, vi, 19.
108 *Adv. Marcion*, iv, 7–36, Leiman's trans.
109 *The Lives of Saints*, Rev. Alban Butler, London, 1926.
110 *Encyclopedia of the Roman Empire*, Matthew Brunson, 1994, p.226.
111 *Catholic Encyclopedia* vol. VIII, 1910, p.736.
112 *History of the Christian Religion*, to 200AD, C.B. Waite, ed. VI, 1908.
113 *Catholic Encyclopedia*, 1908, vol. IV, p.583.
114 *Despectae*, Tertullian, ch. xxx.
115 Thirty-one of Tertullian's writings exist today.
116 *City of God*, X, 18.
117 *On the Christian Conflict*, Augustine, c.426.

Chapter Seventeen

1 *Church History*, Socrates Scholasticus 380–450, Jenning's trans. 1911.
2 *Codex Sinaiticus*, Dr. C. Tischendorf, Alfonso Rosetti's trans. 1921.
3 *Catholic Encyclopedia*, vol. IX, 1 October 1910, pp.674–682.
4 *Catholic Encyclopedia*, vol. III, 1 June 1910, pp.438–443.
5 *Dialogue*, Oxford trans. 1861, vol. II, p.42.
6 Ed. Cecil Roth, Jerusalem, 1974.
7 *Encyclopedia Britannica*, ed. IX, vol. XI, p.59.
8 *Adv. Marc.*, Tertullian, v, Ms.1727, p.368.
9 *Marcellus Britannus*, Tungrorum episcopus postea Trevirorum Archiepiscopus, Mersoeus, De Archiepiscopis Trvirensium.
10 2 Tim. 4: 21.
11 *Church History*, Socrates Scholasticus 380–450 Jenning's trans. 1911.
12 *Epiph. Haer.*, vol. xlii,, p.1.
13 *Catech.*, 4:4.
14 *St Paul in Britain*, Rev. W. Morgan, 1860. Also *Sulpicius Severus*, ii, 31. Severus used the word 'heretic', not Druid.
15 Hieronymus, *Commen. to Matthew*, bk. ii, ch. xiii. Jerome added that it was written in the Chaldaic language but with Hebrew letters.
16 *Catholic Encyclopedia*, vol. VI, 1 September 1909, p.410.
17 Matt. 3:1ff.
18 *Catholic Encyclopedia*, vol. IX, 1 October 1910, 'Marcion', pp.645–649.
19 *Adv. Haer.*, Tertullian, iv, 2, Ms 1727, p.180.
20 *Catholic Encyclopedia* vol. IX, Oct.1, 1910, p.645–649.
21 Luke 9:51–18:14, approx. 8500 words.
22 *Catholic Encyclopedia*, vol. IX, Oct. 1, 1910, p.425.
23 Ibid., vol. VI, 1 September 1909, p.410.
24 *Ecclesiastical History*, Eusebius. Also *New Catholic Encyclopedia*, p.1080.
25 Encyclopedia Britannica, ed. IX, vol.10, p.783ff..
26 *The Edict of Callistus*, Victor Germaine's trans., 1822.
27 Eusebius, op. cit.
28 New Catholic Encyclopedia, 1967, p.1087.

29 Volume VIII, p.441.

30 Modern scholarship has rejected the attribution of the Epistle of Barnabas to the person of Barnabas in the *New Testament*.

31 *Catholic Encyclopedia*, vol.VI, 1 September 1909, pp.135–137.

32 Ibid., vol.VI, p.656.

33 Ibid., vol.VI, pp.135–137.

34 *Encyclopedia Britannica*, ed.IX, vol.V, pp.7–8.

35 Origen, 185–251. Also Eusebius, *Ecclesiastical History.*

36 *Catholic Encyclopedia*, vol.IX, 1 October 1910, 'Marcion', pp.645–649.

37 *Sulpicius Severus*, ii, 31. Also Eusebius I, iv, c.6 *and The History of the Decline and Fall of the Roman Empire*, Edward Gibbons, 1994, p.454..

38 *Catholic Encyclopedia* op. cit., pp.674–682.

39 *Fabiola*, Cardinal Wiseman, undated.

Chapter Eighteen

1 *Caution to the Times*, Bishop Whately, 1892.

2 *Institutes of Christian History*, Johann Mosheim, ecclesiastical historian, 1755.

3 *Synopsis ad Aristobulum.*

4 *Catholic Encyclopedia*, vol.XV, 1 October 1912, pp.459–472.

5 *Dictionary of Christian Antiquities*, Eds. Smith and Cheetham.

6 *City of God*, Augustine.

7 *History of Latin Christianity*, H.H. Milman, 1871, church historian.

8 *The History of the Decline and the Fall of the Roman Empire*, Edward Gibbon, 1994 ed. p.986.

9 *History of the Christian Church*, Philip Schaff, D.D., Ms.283 Chicago Public Library.

10 Kaiser Friedrich Museum of Berlin.

11 *Calmet's Fragments*, Abraham.

12 *Bell's Pantheon*, vol.I. p.9.

13 Fig. 98.

14 *The World's Sixteen Crucified Saviors*, Kersey Graves. 1900. p.96.

15 *Mahabharata.*

16 *Asiatic Researches.*

17 *Catholic Encyclopedia* vol.VIII, 1910. pp.374–385, Pagan Sources.

18 *Ecclesiastical History* and *City of God.*

19 *Habet Ergo Diabolus Christos Suds*, Julius Firmicus, c.323AD, The Devil Has His Christs.

20 *The Golden Bough*, Sir James Frazer.

21 *Cannibalism: The Religious Significance*, Eaton University Press, 1943.

22 Mark 16:9–20.

23 Jerome, *Epist.*, CXX.3, Hedibium.

24 *New Catholic Encyclopedia*, 1967, p.240.

25 *Catholic Encyclopedia*, vol.XII, 1 October 1911, p.792. Also 1908 Edition, 'Resurrection'.

26 Ibid., vol.IX, 1 October 1910, pp.674–682. Also vol.XII, 1 October 1911, p.792, 1908 ed., 'Resurrection'.

27 *New Catholic Encyclopedia*, vol.XII, 1967, p.409.

28 p.240.

29 Sinai, Vatican, Alexandria, Syria and ancient individual Mark manuscripts.

30 John 20:11; 26:29.

31 *Records of the Past*, vols.I–II, 1898.

32 *Encyclopedia of the Roman Empire*, Matthew Brunson, 1994, p.241.

33 History of Latin Christianity, H.H. Milman, 1871.

Chapter Nineteen

1 *Haeret.*, Fab., 1:20.

2 *Catholic Encyclopedia*, vol.IV, 1908, p.583.

3 *Catholic Encyclopedia*, vol.XII, p.658.

4 *Catholic Encyclopedia*, vol.V. p.635, also vol.X, p.443.

5 p.546.

6 *The Dictionary of Classical Mythology, Religion, Literature and Art*, Oskar Seyffert, 1995, p.546.

7 *The Roman Emperors*, Michael

Grant, 1985. George Weidenfeld and Nicolson Limited. p.204.

8 *Epistola*, Melancthon, 1497–1560, p.189.

9 *Talmud.* Also Rev. C. C. Dobson, *Did Our Lord Visit Britain?*, Destiny Publishers, 1944.

10 Acts of Thomas.

11 *Annales ecclesiastici*, vols.I–XII, 1598–1607.

12 *Society in Imperial Rome*, M. Massey, 1982, p.103.

13 The Sibyls were variously numbered from one by Plato to twelve by later writers.

14 *Catholic Encyclopedia*, vol.XIII, 1912, p.720.

15 *Stromata*, VI.

16 *Exhort*, IV.

17 *Irenaeus of Lyons,* trans. John Keble, London, 1872.

18 xviii: 23.

19 Livy. Also *The Records of Rome*, 1868, available in the British Library.

20 *Dictionary of Greek and Roman Antiquities,* 'Sibyllini Libra'.

21 2 Edras 14:21.

22 *Funk and Wagnell's New Standard Dictionary*, 'Sibylline Books', 1913.

23 *Encyclopedia of the Roman Empire*, Matthew Brunson, 1994, p.354.

24 Seyffert, op. cit., p.584.

25 Brunson, op. cit., pp.387–388.

26 *Roman Myths*, Jane F. Gardner, 1993. British Museum.

27 Seyffert, op. cit., pp.544–546.

28 *Optatus of Minevis*, 1:15,19, Early Fourth Century.

29 *New Catholic Encyclopedia*, vol.XII, 1967, p.576.

30 *The Ancient World*, H.E.L. Mellersh, 1976, p.377.

31 *New Catholic Encyclopedia*, vol.I, 1967, p.792.

32 *Catholic Encyclopedia*, vol.V, 1 May 1909, p.619.

33 Ibid., p.620.

34 *Tertullian, Apology*, 21–22, See also, Harnack ET, vol.I, p.298.

35 Augustus, *Opera*, tom.ii, Epist. Ad Aurelium, Epist xli, lxxvii, col.87, c.1679.

36 *Apolegiticum* V, XXI.

37 *Acta Concilii Niceni*, Colon 1618.

38 D.D. Davidson.

39 *Acta Concilii Niceni*, op. cit.

40 Ibid.

41 *Twelfth Night*.

42 *The Mystery of the Oracles*, Philipp Vandenberg, 1979, p.234.

43 *Roman Myths*, Jane F. Gardner, British Museum, 1993, p.56.

44 *Encyclopedia of the Roman Empire*, M. Bunson, 1994, p.140.

45 *Chronicle of the Roman Emperors. Chris Scarre, 1995, pp.28–35.*

46 *The Decline and Fall of the Roman Empire*, Edward Gibbon, 1994 ed., p.94–95.

47 *The Bible for Learners*, vol.III, p.3.

48 Brunson, op. cit., p.204.

49 *Sibylline Book,* II, 14:6.

50 *Life of Constantine*, IV, 36,37, attributed to Eusebius.

51 Ibid.

52 *Haeret.*, Fab. 1:20.

53 See Life, iii, 30–33, Constantine's Instructions to Marcarius.

54 *Fabiola*, Cardinal Wiseman, undated.

55 Brunson, op. cit., p.86.

56 *Smaller Classical Dictionary*, 1910, p.161.

57 Socrates Scholasticus, 380–450.

58 *Gibbon's Rome*, vol.II, p.274.

59 *Institutes of Christian History*, J. Mosheim, 1755.

60 *Genesis of Christianity*, Plummer, Edinburgh, 1876.

61 *Institutes of Christian History*, Johann Mosheim, ecclesiastical historian, 1755.

62 *Antiquities*, xviii, ch.3.

63 *Encyclopedia of Early Christianity*, Cross, p.549.

64 *Life of Lardner*, Dr Kippis, p.23.

65 *On the Canon of the New Testament,* Dr B. Westcott.

66 *Ecclesiastical History*, Eusebius, vol.I.

pp.381–382.

67 *Bible Myths*, T.W. Doane, 1882 p.438.

68 *Catholic Encyclopedia* vol.v. May 1, 1909 p.620.

69 *Against Celsus*, Origen, 1.c.

70 *Against Celsus*, ch.xxxv, bk.1. Also *Lardner*, vol.vi, ch.iii.

71 *Smaller Classical Dictionary*, 1910, p.161.

72 *Cyril of Jerusalem, 386.*

73 *Ecclesiastical History*, bk.I, pt.ii, ch.ii, Ms.248, vol.I, p.93, Mosheim.

74 *History of the Christian Church*, H.H. Milman, 1871.

75 *Diondi*, Diritto rom. Crist. 3:pp.151–187.

76 *The Arguments of the Emperor Julian*, later titled *Against the Christians*, Thomas Taylor trans. London, 1818.

77 *Encyclopedia of the Roman Empire*, Matthew Bunson, 1994, p.21.

78 *Encyclopedia of Early Christianity*, E. Ferguson, 1990. p.511.

79 *Lives of the Popes*, Mann, c.1905.

80 *The Suppliants*, p.72.

81 *New Catholic Encyclopedia*, vol.XII, 1967, pp.563–578.

82 *Ecclesiastical History*, bk.I, cent.II, pt.ii, ch.iii.

83 *The Records of Rome*, 1868, British Library.

84 *Edicts of Justinian*, in *Dictionnaire de Théologie*, 1920. Also *Three Early Doctrinal Modifications of the Text of the Gospels*, The Hibbert Journal, London, 1902.

85 *Decree of the Fifth Council of Constantinople*, 553.

86 *Encyclopedia Britannica*, ed.IX, vol.X, p.783ff.

87 *Sibylline Book* II, 14:1–6.

88 *Decree of the Fifth Council of Constantinople*, 553. Also *Edicts of Justinian Dictionnaire de Théologie*, 1920, *The Celtic Apostolic Church*, Michael J. A. Stewart.

Index